FAST TRACK ENGLISH

Part One

Lower Intermediate

Robert Parr
Günther Albrecht
Keith Jones

Die Fernsehsendungen zu FAST TRACK ENGLISH, PART ONE wurden von den Pilgrim Productions 2000 (Canterbury, England) im Auftrag des Westdeutschen Rundfunks (Redaktion: Peter Teckentrup) für das Telekolleg produziert.
Drehbücher: Gillian Jones; Language Consultant: Keith Jones; Kamera: George Pellett; Regie: Brian Earley, David Pick.
Zu diesem Buch gibt es den Vokabeltrainer „Fast Track English" (CD-ROM).

Autoren: Robert Parr, Günther Albrecht, Keith Jones

7. Auflage 2008

Bildnachweis: The Hemlyn. Road Atlas of Great Britain (S. 210); Ursula Hilbert/Ursula Paulick, München (S. 23, 120, 184); Elaine Milner, Sevenoaks (S. 56, 200, 217); National Trust Handbook (S. 40); PUNCH, Ausgabe vom 3.6.1988 (S. 70); Daniel Schwarz, Köln (S. 178). Alle anderen Fotos: Videoprints aus den Fernsehsendungen.
Umschlaggestaltung: Franziska Schob-Bergmeir, München (unter Verwendung eines Fotos der Bavaria Bildagentur, Gauting)
Lektorat und Innenlayout (Buch): Gabriele Rieth
Gesamtherstellung: Druckerei Bremberger, München
ISBN 978-3-9812051-5-2

VORWORT

FAST TRACK ENGLISH, PART ONE bietet Ihnen die Möglichkeit, Ihre Englischkenntnisse aufzufrischen und zu vertiefen. Die Fernsehsendungen, zu denen dieses Begleitbuch entstand, wurden mit *native speakers* an Originalschauplätzen gedreht, vornehmlich in der englischen Grafschaft Kent.

Die Sendungen sind nach der Modul-Technik aufgebaut. Das heißt, jede der insgesamt 13 *units* ist einem bestimmten Thema gewidmet – z.B. Reisen (OUT AND ABOUT, 2), Familie (A FAMILY HOME, 3), Sport (SPORT IN WINTER, 7) – das dann in fünf Abschnitten unter einem jeweils anderen Blickwinkel präsentiert wird.

Die Module A und B zeigen Alltagssituationen, meist in Form von kurzen Dialogen oder *statements*, zunächst – was Wortschatz und Thematik betrifft – eher allgemein (*Everyday English*) und dann spezifischer (*Specialised English*). Im Modul C (*A Personal View*) berichten Einzelpersonen, die zu dem jeweiligen Thema eine besondere Beziehung haben, aus ihrem beruflichen oder privaten Erfahrungsbereich. So lernen Sie z.B. Liz Roberts kennen, die in einem *tourist information centre* arbeitet, Tony Pulis, der sein Leben dem Fußball gewidmet hat, oder John und Jean, die *landlords* eines typisch englischen *bed and breakfast*. Für Entspannung sorgt Meterman in Modul D, der mit skurrilem Witz und englischem Humor seinen Beitrag zum Thema liefert. Und zum Ausklang Modul E, *Use Your Eyes*, im wahrsten Sinne des Wortes etwas zum Anschauen – kurze Tips und Informationen zur Vorbereitung auf einen Besuch in Großbritannien.

Die Sendungen sind rein englischsprachig. Individuelle Akzente und Sprechtempo der *native speakers* wurden bewusst nicht beeinflusst. So ist es ganz natürlich, wenn Sie nicht alles auf Anhieb verstehen. Lassen Sie sich davon auf keinen Fall entmutigen. Ziel dieses Kurses ist es u.a. auch, Ihre kommunikativen Fertigkeiten zu trainieren, und dazu gehört in erster Linie das sogenannte *gist listening*, d.h. die Fähigkeit, das Wesentliche, den Kern einer Aussage zu erfassen. Haben Sie etwas Geduld und Sie werden feststellen, wie gut Sie sich mit der Zeit einhören und wieviel an Wortschatz und Wendungen Sie zugleich aufnehmen.

Das Begleitbuch orientiert sich am Modul-Aufbau der Sendungen. Die Abschnitte A und B geben die Dialoge und *statements* im Wortlaut, in Ausschnitten oder in Zusammenfassungen wieder. Da es sich bei FAST TRACK ENGLISH nicht um einen Anfänger-, sondern um einen Auffrischungskurs handelt, wird natürlich ein gewisser Grundwortschatz vorausgesetzt. So haben wir die *wordlist* zu den einzelnen Texten auf Wörter und Wendungen (im Text selbst durch Kursivdruck hervorgehoben) beschränkt, die zumeist dem sogenannten Aufbauwortschatz zuzuordnen sind. Und dabei wurden selbstverständlich nicht alle Bedeutungen eines Wortes, sondern nur die jeweils kontextbezogene angegeben. In diesem Zusammenhang möchten wir Sie auch ausdrücklich darauf hinweisen, dass nicht zu knapp gehaltene Wörterbücher (zweisprachig und einsprachig) zum „Handwerkszeug“ des Fremdsprachenlernens gehören.

Da Sie die Module A und B in besonderer Weise auf die Prüfung vorbereiten sollen, ist es wichtig, dass Sie die Texte nicht nur lesen, sondern auch mit ihnen arbeiten, d.h. die unter der Überschrift *"Understanding the text"* bzw. *"And what about you?"* gestellten Fragen beantworten. Und da zur Beherrschung einer Sprache immer auch ein solides grammatikalisches Fundament gehört, wurden in die Module A und B *Helping Hands* (HH) eingebaut, die wichtige Strukturen und Besonderheiten des Englischen auf Deutsch erklären. In den meisten Fällen orientieren sich die *Helping Hands* an den Sendungen. Für eine optimale Prüfungsvorbereitung wurden im Buch jedoch Erweiterungen vorgenommen. Aber auch hier gilt, wie zuvor beim Wortschatz erwähnt, dass Grundkenntnisse vorausgesetzt werden und zudem nicht jedes Thema bereits mit allen Besonderheiten behandelt werden kann und soll. Der abwechslungsreiche Übungsteil gibt Ihnen Gelegenheit, das (Wieder-)Gelernte zu trainieren und aktiv anzuwenden.

Die im Inhaltsverzeichnis als *communicative functions* bezeichneten Sprechabsichten ziehen sich im Prinzip wie ein roter Faden durch die Module A bis D. Besonders intensiv werden sie jedoch in A und B thematisiert und zwar sowohl in den Texten, als auch in den *Helping Hands* bzw. den Übungen.

Modul C ist eine ausgesprochene Hörverständnisübung, mit der Sie Ihr *gist listening* testen können. Dazu wäre es natürlich günstig, wenn Sie sich das betreffende Modul der Sendung (wie übrigens auch die anderen Teile der Sendung) mehrmals ansehen bzw. anhören könnten. Wer aber die Aussagen von Liz Roberts, Tony Pulis und all den anderen lieber noch einmal schwarz auf weiß nachlesen möchte, kann dies im Abschnitt *"Module C Tapescripts"* tun. Auch hier gibt es nach jedem Text wieder eine *wordlist*, eine Serviceleistung, um Ihnen zu häufiges Nachschlagen im Wörterbuch zu ersparen. Im Modul D haben wir Metermans humorvolle Auseinandersetzung mit dem jeweiligen Thema noch einmal mit eher spielerischen Übungen nachvollzogen. Modul E rundet das Ganze, analog zur Sendung, mit primär optischen Elementen ab.

Im Abschnitt *"Key to Exercises"* finden Sie zu jeder Übung eine Lösung bzw. einen Lösungsvorschlag, z.T. mit Zeilenangaben, die auf die in Frage kommenden Textstellen in den Modulen A und B bzw. den *tapescripts* zu C verweisen. In diesem Zusammenhang noch ein letzter Tip: Machen Sie es anders als wir, notieren Sie nicht nur Satzfragmente bzw. Nummern oder Buchstaben, sondern schreiben Sie immer ganze Sätze. Sie werden erstaunt sein, wie viele Wendungen und Strukturen Sie sich durch häufiges Schreiben ganz unbewusst einprägen.

Wir wünschen Ihnen viel Spaß und vor allem Erfolg mit FAST TRACK ENGLISH

Robert Parr, Günther Albrecht und Keith Jones

CONTENTS

GETTING STARTED UNIT 1

1A

A year in England

In this *module* we get to know three young people who are staying in England to learn English.

“Hello, I’m Jana. I come from Slovakia. I’m living with an English family and I’m working as an au pair. I help the mother with the children and the housework.”

“Hello, my name is Manuela. I come from *France*. I’m staying with an English family. This is Pam and she helped me with the *accommodation*. She’s my friend. And she’s very helpful with my English.”

Jean-Charles outside the Plough

“My name is Jean-Charles. I’m *French*. I come from Annecy. I’m staying in England because it is the best way to learn the language. This is really important for me because I want to travel all around the world and of course English is the international language. I work at the ‘*Plough*’. I’m a *waiter*.”

module	Modul, Baustein, Einheit	accommodation	Unterkunft, Unterbringung, Quartier
France	Frankreich		
French	Franzose, Französin; französisch	plough	Pflug (*hier: Name eines Restaurants*)
(the French)	(die Franzosen)	waiter	Ober

Understanding the text. True or false? Tick the correct box.

	True	False
1. Jana and Manuela are living with English families.		
2. Jean-Charles and Manuela come from the same country.		
3. Jana and Jean-Charles do the same sort of work.		
4. Jean-Charles probably earns more money than Jana does.		

Find the English for these German words and expressions.

5. jemanden kennenlernen
6. Hausarbeit
7. die beste Methode, die Sprache zu lernen

Jana helps with the housework

Manuela has lunch in the pub

And what about you? Answer in full sentences.

8. Which of the three people do you think will learn the most English in the year they are away? Give a reason.
9. Which of the three do you think will earn the most money?
10. Which of the three has the most interesting job? Why?

H The present continuous
Die Verlaufsform der Gegenwart

Are you **doing** anything at the moment, Pam?	Machst du gerade etwas, Pam?
Yes, I **am reading**.	Ja, ich lese.
Is Jana **living** in England?	Lebt Jana in England?
Yes, she**'s working** there as an au pair.	Ja, sie arbeitet dort als Au-pair.

- Die **Verlaufsform der Gegenwart** beschreibt eine **zum Zeitpunkt des Sprechens ablaufende Handlung**. Auch für **zeitlich begrenzte Situationen und Ereignisse** wird diese Form benutzt.
- Die Verlaufsform wird mit einer **Form von *to be* + -ing Form des Verbs** gebildet, z.B. *He is talking*.
- Im gesprochenen Englisch werden gerne **zusammengezogene Formen** *(contracted forms)* verwendet *(She's working = She is working; We're eating = We are eating)*.
- Die **Frageform** wird durch das **Umstellen** von **Subjekt** (Satzgegenstand) und der jeweiligen Form von ***to be*** gebildet *(Are you listening?)*.
- Zur Bildung der **Verneinung** verwendet man ***not*** *(They are not coming. They aren't coming.)*.

Exercises

I. Complete the sentences by using the words in brackets. Use contracted forms of the verbs. ●●

Example:
I'm sorry. He's not at home. He (work)
I'm sorry. He's not at home. He's working.

1. Hurry up! Our train (come)!
2. Could you be quiet, please. I (try) to read.
3. We can go out now. It (not, rain) anymore.

4. The film begins soon. We (leave) now.
5. Jana is not tired. She (not, go) home yet.
6. Look! It's Manuela and Pam, isn't it? They (cross) the road.

II. Form questions using the words in brackets. ●●

Example:
Why (you, wear) shorts today?
Why are you wearing shorts today?

1. Why (you, feel) so tired this morning?
2. (David, stay) with his brother this week?
3. (the other students, enjoy) this exercise?
4. (Stephen, look for) a new job?
5. Why (Karl, work) in the USA at the moment?
6. We're doing English this year. What (you, study)?

III. Use the prompts (Stichwörter) *below to form complete sentences. Use contracted forms of the verb. You will also need to add some words.* ●●

Example:
Jana / Slovakia
live / with an English family
work / as an au pair / a year
at the moment / shop / for the family

This is Jana. She's from Slovakia. She's living with an English family. She's working as an au pair for a year. At the moment she's shopping for the family.

1. Manuela / France
   stay / with / friend Pam
   work / at a home for elderly residents
   today / shop / at the local market
   buy / some fruit and vegetables
2. Erich / Germany
   student
   live / on a university campus
   stay / in England / learn the language
3. I / Lazlo / Hungary
   live / in a friend's flat
   work / as a waiter in a restaurant
   at the moment / set up / the tables

4. Tadziu / Poland
   stay / at a guesthouse near Victoria Station
   tourist
   today / visit / the British Museum
5. Sven and Mara / Sweden
   stay / at a campsite / Wales
   have / a two-week holiday / Britain
   today / travel / to Scotland
6. My name / Guido / Switzerland
   ride around Britain / on / motorbike / ten days
   stay / at bed and breakfasts

IV. Manuela and Pam have gone to Brighton for the weekend. While she is there, Manuela writes a postcard to her English friend, Sally. Complete it by using the following verbs in the continuous form. (Be careful. There are ten verbs in the box, but you only need eight!) ●●

begin • buy • do • drink • earn • have • learn • shop • watch • write

Dear Sally,

The English south coast is lovely. Pam and I ... a great time. We ... a lot of sightseeing and I ... a lot about England. By the way, the weather is fine: sunny but quite cold.

I ... this card in a little café in Brighton. I ... tea and ... the people outside. Pam ... at the moment. She ... the stamps for our postcards.

See you next week.

Love

Manuela

V. Use words from text 1A (see page 9) to complete these sentences. The first letter is given. ●●

1. A dictionary is very h... when you are studying a language.
2. It is i... to understand that English is not an easy language to learn.
3. If you stay in another country for a year it is nice to have your own a... .
4. Working abroad is a good w... to learn the language quickly.
5. You can speak English in England and in many other countries all over the w... .
6. English is an i... language.

VI. Countries and nationalities. Complete the table below. Use a dictionary if you wish.

	The country is:	The people are:
1.	England	the English
2.	France	...
3.	...	the Germans
4.	...	the Portuguese
5.	...	the Scottish
6.	Wales	...
7.	...	the Dutch
8.	...	the Spanish
9.	Italy	...
10.	...	the Greeks

VII. Don't mix them up. Which words are missing?

Great Britain is three countries: England, ... and ... . Together with Northern Ireland these four countries form the ... .

VIII. Write a short paragraph about yourself in English. Use the questions and words in brackets to help you.

What is your name?	(My name is ... .)
Where are you from?	(I'm from ... .)
Where do you live?	(I live ... .)
What's your job?	(I work ... .)

Add any other information you would like.

1B

An English lesson in England ●●

Deborah is an English teacher at an *adult education centre*. Lots of her students have studied English before in their home countries, maybe at school. When they come to England, however, they find it very difficult because English people speak very quickly. Deborah knows how important it is that students learn how to *ask for* repetition and for people to speak more slowly.
Deborah gives her class some useful *expressions* such as “Could you repeat that, please?”, “Could you say that again, please?” and “Could you speak more slowly, please?”.
Deborah is not *surprised* that her students do not always understand an English word or phrase. There are millions of words in the English language. Deborah teaches her class some useful phrases so that they can *ask about* the meaning of words: “I don’t understand ‘breakfast’.” “What does ‘breakfast’ mean?”, “How do you say ‘Frühstück’ in English?”.
Deborah’s students come from many different countries so the English class is an *opportunity* for them to make friends. Questions like, “Excuse me. Can I *join* you?”, “Is it all right if I join you?” and “Do you *mind* if I join you?” are very useful when you first arrive in a *strange* country.

adult education centre	Bildungszentrum für Erwachsene (*entspricht in etwa einer Volkshochschule*)	ask about	fragen nach
		opportunity	Möglichkeit, Gelegenheit
ask for	bitten um	join	sich anschließen
expression	Ausdruck	mind	etwas ausmachen, dagegen haben
surprise	überraschen		
(a surprise)	(eine Überraschung)	strange	fremd

Understanding the text.
Choose a suitable ending (a–c) for the statements (1–3) below.

1. An adult education centre is a place where ...
   a) children do their homework.
   b) grown-ups learn new things.
   c) old people live.
2. Learners of English often find it difficult in England because many English people speak ...
   a) too unclearly.
   b) too fast.
   c) with a foreign accent.

Deborah teaches her class some useful phrases

3. The correct translation of „Was heißt 'Pause' auf Englisch?" is ...
   a) "What means 'Pause' in English?"
   b) "What does 'Pause' mean in English?"
   c) "What is in English 'Pause'?"

Which expression comes closest to the meaning of the underlined word(s)?

4. Deborah is not <u>surprised</u> that the students don't understand everything.
   a) shocked b) worried c) astonished d) angry
5. The English class is <u>an opportunity</u> for them to make friends.
   a) good luck b) an event c) an occasion d) a chance
6. England is <u>a strange</u> country for them.
   a) an alien b) an odd c) an exotic d) a foreign
7. The students have studied English in their home countries, <u>maybe</u> at school.
   a) as well as b) perhaps c) or d) never
8. "<u>Excuse me</u>. Can I join you?"
   a) Hello. b) Please. c) Oh dear. d) Really.

And what about you?

9. Where did you learn English?
10. How often do you need English in your job?

H The present simple (I)
Die einfache Form der Gegenwart (I)

Deborah **teaches** English.	Deborah unterrichtet Englisch.
Does she **speak** any foreign languages?	Spricht sie irgendwelche Fremdsprachen?
She **doesn't work** with children.	Sie arbeitet nicht mit Kindern.

- Die **einfache Form der Gegenwart** bezeichnet eine **allgemein gültige Tatsache** oder **Gewohnheit**.
- In der **dritten Person Einzahl** *(he, she, it)* erhält das Verb die **Endung -s** *(He speaks English.)* oder **-es** *(He watches football.)*.
- Mit dem **Hilfsverb *do*** bzw. ***does, don't*** bzw. ***doesn't*** werden **Fragen** *(Do you come from Germany?)* und **Verneinungen** *(They don't eat meat.)* gebildet.
- Zu den wichtigsten **Ausnahmen** gehört das Verb ***to be***:
  Hier werden **Fragen** durch das **Umstellen** von **Subjekt** und **Verb** gebildet *(Is Jana from Slovakia or from France?)*, **Verneinungen** durch ***not*** *(The students aren't from England.)*.

Exercises

I. Ask questions to get the information which is missing.
The question words are given in brackets. ●●

Example:
Deborah lives in .?. , not far from Sevenoaks. (Where?)
Where does Deborah live?

1. Deborah gets up at .?. every morning. (When?)
2. She goes to the adult education centre by .?. . (How?)
3. She teaches English every .?. and on some evenings. (How often?)
4. She likes teaching because .?. . (Why?)
5. She speaks .?., .?. and a bit of .?. . (Which?)
6. In the afternoon she does some .?. . (What?)

II. Make these sentences about Jana negative. (Be careful. In two sentences you don't need a form of "do".) ●●

Example:
I have many English friends.
I don't have many English friends.

1. I go to bed late.
2. I can get up late.
3. I have a lot of free time.
4. The children always do what I say.
5. School is easy.
6. Deborah, my teacher, corrects my English all the time.

III. Interview Simon, another English teacher at the adult education centre. Use the prompts to form questions. ●●

1. What time / you / get up in the morning?
2. you / go to work by car?
3. When / lessons / begin at the centre?
4. you / work in the evening?
5. you / earn enough money?
6. you / like your job?

IV. Find Simon's answers to the questions in exercise III. (Be careful. There are more answers than questions!) ●●

a. Yes, twice a week – on Mondays and Wednesdays.
b. It's not a lot but it's enough.
c. Quite early. I always go jogging before breakfast.
d. I don't like the winter when it gets dark early.
e. The train is often late.
f. Yes, very much. I don't want to do anything else.
g. No, by bike. I live only a mile away.
h. We stay at school for lunch.
i. At eight-thirty, and nine o'clock on Saturdays.

H Two forms of the present tense

Zwei Gegenwartsformen

She **is coming** now.	Sie kommt jetzt.
She **comes** from Scotland.	Sie kommt (stammt) aus Schottland.

Die Module 1A und 1B haben gezeigt, dass es im Englischen sowohl eine **Verlaufsform** als auch eine **einfache Form der Gegenwart** gibt.
Vor allem die im Deutschen nicht vorhandene Verlaufsform des Verbs bereitet Lernenden Schwierigkeiten. Wörter wie ***now, just, at the moment*** sind oft ein **Signal** für den Gebrauch der **Verlaufsform**. In diesen Fällen geht es, wie oben im ersten Beispielsatz, um eine **zum Zeitpunkt des Sprechens** ablaufende Handlung.
Aber auch bei einer für den Sprecher **zeitlich begrenzten Handlung** wird die **Verlaufsform** verwendet *(She's staying in England for a year.).*

V. Present simple or present continuous?
Put the verbs in brackets into the correct form.

1. Hello. My name's John. I ... (come) from Texas.
2. Why ... (you, go) now? The party has only just started!
3. Emma is in Italy for a week. She ... (live) with her sister.
4. Where ... (you, live)? In London?
5. ... (you, go) to school on Saturdays as well?
6. Please wait for us. We ... (come) now.

VI. An English visitor.
What questions do you ask him? The words in brackets will help you.

Fragen Sie ihn,

1. wo er herkommt;	(Where ... from?)
2. wie lange er in Deutschland bleibt;	(How long ... ?)
3. wie gut sein Deutsch ist;	(How ... German?)
4. was er beruflich macht;	(What ... do?)
5. was er in seiner Freizeit macht;	(What ... freetime?)
6. wie ihm Deutschland gefällt.	(Do you ...?)

1C

Vos van Ginneken – a student of English in England

Vos with her son, Deurn, and the family dog, Pooh

Listen to the interview with Vos van Ginneken carefully and answer the questions below.

I. Choose one of the alternatives (a – c) to complete the three sentences.

1. Vos lives in ...
   a) the USA. b) England. c) Germany.
2. Vos comes from ...
   a) England. b) Holland. c) France.
3. In the interview Vos talks about ...
   a) her job. b) her parents. c) the English language.

II. Now try and answer these questions.
The lines show you how long the words are.

1. Which country does Vos come from? _ _ _ _ _ _ _
2. How old was Vos when her family moved to America? _ _ _ _ _ _ _ _
3. How many words of English did Vos speak when she arrived in America? _ _ _

4. Which type of English does Vos find easier to understand – British English or American English? _ _ _ _ _ _ _ _ _   _ _ _ _ _ _ _ _
5. In Britain people say "autumn". What word do Americans use? _ _ _ _
6. What country does Vos's husband come from? _ _ _ _ _ _ _ _
7. How many children does the couple have? _ _ _
8. What is the family dog's name? _ _ _ _
9. Which language do the van Ginneken's speak at home? _ _ _ _ _
10. Which man does Vos speak to in the garage? _ _ _ _ _ _ _ _

III. Complete the sentences by using a word (or a word from the same family as that word) in the interview. The first letter has been given.

1. If a person can speak two languages very well we say that he or she is b... .
2. The way you say a word, especially in a foreign language, is your p... .
3. There is a d... between the way the British and the Americans say the word "tomato".
4. A person who was born in, and grew up in, the East End of London is called a C... .
5. It can be very c... when someone speaks English to you very quickly.
6. One problem for learners of English is the e... vocabulary the language has.

1D

Meterman the language teacher

I. The six lines of Meterman's song have been mixed up. Can you put them into the correct order?

"Meterman is my name
Everyone knows me
Have a cup of tea"
I know everyone
Read your meter and
Reading meters is my game

II. These six sentences (a – e) are the first sentences from the paragraphs in the text below. Which sentence goes where in the text?

a. At that moment Meterman remembers the problem with the bell.
b. Finally Meterman looks into the camera again.
c. Meterman looks into the camera and speaks to the viewers.
d. Obviously Meterman is very impressed.
e. She is a German student learning English.
f. Suddenly Meterman notices the language learning materials.

---

1. "Oh hello. It's you. My name's Meterman. And today I've come to read the meter at Mr and Mrs Brown's house." He presses the doorbell but the bell doesn't *work*. He looks through the window. In the lounge he sees a young woman with her back towards him.

---

2. "Hello, hello, hello," shouts Meterman. "Would you mind? Hello. Hello. Meterman. Can you open the door?" Eventually the woman hears him and lets him in. She understands meters and helps him by reading out the numbers.

---

3. "You can read meters?" he says. "Excuse me. I'm Meterman. You can't read meters, can you? You can read meters! You could become a Metermaid and work with me." The student reacts with horror. "No thank you. No!"

---

4. "I think we'd better *fix* the doorbell. We'll have this fixed *in no time at all.* That's one of our little sayings – in no time at all."

---

5. "What's all this? This is no way to learn English. Books. Dictionaries. Cassettes. You don't need those. I learnt English once and I was only three. And look at me. Meterman! No. If you want to learn English you come right along with me in my *van* and meet real English people. Give me those." He *gathers* the woman's books and cassettes. She protests: "Hey, come back. My books." "This is where these books should be," says Meterman and *drops* them *in* a *wastepaper basket*.

---

6. "You come with Meterman," he says. "And we'll meet lots of English people and I'll show you England by the back door."

work	funktionieren, gehen	van	Last-, Lieferwagen
fix	reparieren, instand setzen	gather	einsammeln
in no time	im Nu,	drop in	(hinein)werfen
at all	im Handumdrehen	wastepaper basket	Papierkorb

III. Match the idioms (1–5) with their meanings (a–e).

1. to be ahead of the game
2. to play games
3. the game is up
4. a game plan
5. to play a waiting game

a. You're not being serious enough about the problem.
b. You need to look at new technologies to keep ahead.
c. We can't carry on. The police have found out.
d. Let's wait and see how things develop.
e. This is what we need to do to meet our objectives.

1E

Adult education

Match the course descriptions to the correct course titles. There are seven pairs.

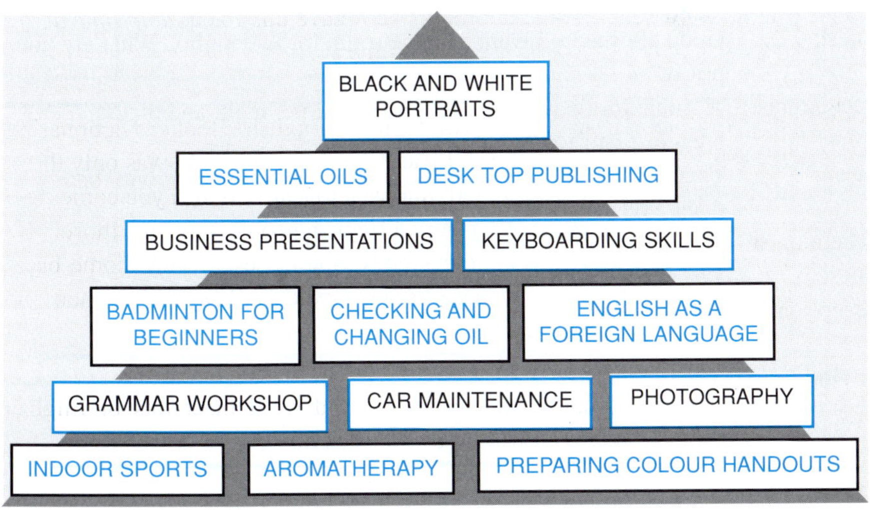

OUT AND ABOUT UNIT 2

2A

Staying in Britain

What are some of the things tourists do when they are in Britain?

Changing money

Clerk: Hello. How can I help you?
Tourist: I would like to change these *travellers' cheques* into English money, please.
Clerk: Do you have a passport?
Tourist: Yes, I do.
Clerk: Thank you. One hundred pounds?
Tourist: Yes, please.
Clerk: You just need to *sign* your cheques *at the top* for me, please.
Tourist: There you are.
Clerk: Thank you. How would you like the money?
Tourist: I would like some tens and twenties, please. And five pounds in one-pound *coins*.

Finding a hotel

Receptionist: Good afternoon, sir. How can I help you?
Guest: Good afternoon. I want a single room for two nights. What are your prices?
Receptionist: A single for two nights, sir. That's £52 per night and that *includes* breakfast and *VAT*.
Guest: That will be all right. I'll have a single for two nights with bath, thank you.
Receptionist: Would you like to see the room, sir?
Guest: Yes, please.
Receptionist: Follow me.

Buying tickets for the theatre

1 Woman: Hello.
Clerk: Hello.
1 Woman: Can I have two tickets for *Amadeus* tonight, please?
Clerk: OK. I have two seats in *Row* E at ten pounds each.

1 Woman: Ten pounds. What do you think?
2 Woman: No, that's too *expensive*.
Clerk: *I can do* two in Row B and they're eight pounds each.
1 Woman: Eight pounds?
2 Woman: Yes, that's all right.

Asking about a room for the night

Paying for theatre tickets

change money	Geld wechseln	VAT (value added tax)	Mehrwertsteuer
clerk	Angestellte, r		
travellers' cheques	Reiseschecks	*Amadeus*	*Theaterstück nach Mnouchkine über das Leben Mozarts*
sign	unterschreiben		
at the top	am oberen Rand, oben		
coins	Münzen	row	(Sitz-)Reihe
receptionist	Empfangsdame bzw. Herr am Empfang	expensive	teuer
		I can do	*hier*: ich habe
include	beinhalten, umfassen		

Understanding the text.
Identify the correct sentence (a–c) to complete the statements (1–3).

1. The woman in the bank wants to change ...
   a) travellers' cheques into English money.
   b) one hundred German Marks into English money.
   c) one hundred pounds into tens and twenties.
2. The man at the hotel wants ...
   a) two rooms for one night.
   b) a single room for two nights with shower.
   c) a single room for two nights with bath.
3. The two ladies at the theatre would like ...
   a) to buy two seats in Row E at ten pounds each.
   b) to have two tickets in Row B for eight pounds each.
   c) to buy no tickets at all because they are too expensive.

Which word best completes the sentence?

4. The woman at the bank ... her cheques .
   a) signifies b) signs c) alters d) underlines
5. The hotel receptionist ... to the guest which services the hotel offers.
   a) teaches b) explains c) illustrates d) informs
6. The hotel guest, Mr. Morrow, seems to be very ... with the hotel.
   a) grateful b) joyful c) pleased d) lucky
7. The two ladies at the theatre think that £10 is too ... for one ticket.
   a) valuable b) much c) cheap d) little

And what about you?

8. Do you think it is advisable to take travellers' cheques instead of cash when you go abroad (*ins Ausland*)? Why?
9. When was the last time you stayed in a hotel?
10. What do you think the play *Amadeus* is about?

H Helping verbs (I): would like – can – will

Hilfsverben (I)

I'd (would) like to change these travellers' cheques, please.	Ich möchte bitte diese Reiseschecks einlösen.
Can we have two tickets, please?	Können wir bitte zwei Karten haben?
I'll take a single room.	Ich nehme ein Einzelzimmer.

- Im Englischen gibt es eine Reihe von **unvollständigen Hilfsverben**. Dazu gehören ***can, could, may, might, must, shall, should, will*** und ***would***. Sie sind unvollständig, weil sie u.a. die **dritte Person Einzahl ohne -s** bilden und nur **in Verbindung mit einem Vollverb** verwendet werden können *(Can she use your telephone?)*.
- Der Aussage eines Vollverbs wird durch Hilfsverben eine weitere Bedeutung hinzugefügt (z.B. ein **Angebot**, eine **Bitte**, eine **Fähigkeit**, eine **Aufforderung**, ein **Versprechen**, eine **Absicht**, eine **Möglichkeit**, eine **Erlaubnis**).
- Die **Frageform** dieser Hilfsverben wird durch **Umstellen** von **Subjekt** (Satzgegenstand) und **Hilfsverb** gebildet *(Can you speak English?)*. Zur Bildung der **Verneinung** verwendet man ***not*** *(I will not be there.)*.
- Nach ***would like*** folgt der **Infinitiv mit *to*** oder ein **Objekt**. Nach ***can*** und ***will*** kommt, wie nach den anderen unvollständigen Hilfsverben, ein **Infinitiv ohne *to***.

Exercises

I. Match sentences 1–5 with replies a–e to form mini-dialogues.

1. Can we use your dictionary?
2. Would you like something to drink?
3. I'll ring you later.
4. I can learn the new words later.
5. I'd like a cheese sandwich, please.

a. A cup of coffee, please.
b. OK. Anything else?
c. But the test is tomorrow.
d. Yes, of course.
e. Have you got my number?

II. Which meaning do the helping verbs in sentences 1–5 in exercise I express? Choose from the list below.

1. promise *(Versprechen)*
2. request *(Bitte)*
3. possibility *(Möglichkeit)*
4. offer *(Angebot)*
5. permission *(Erlaubnis)*

III. At a bank. Turn the tourist's sentences into English.

Clerk: Hello, how can I help you?
Tourist: *(Ich möchte bitte hundert Deutsche Mark in englische Pfund wechseln.)*
Clerk: Will tens and twenties be all right?
Tourist: *(Ja, danke, aber ich hätte gerne zehn Pfund in Ein-Pfund-Münzen.)*
Clerk: There you are and here's your receipt.
Tourist: *(Vielen Dank. Auf Wiedersehen.)*

IV. At a hotel. What does the guest say in English?

Receptionist: Good morning, can I help you?
Guest: *(Guten Morgen, ich hätte gerne ein Zweibettzimmer für eine Woche. Was kostet es?)*
Receptionist: Here are our prices.
Guest: *(Ja, in Ordnung. Bitte ein Doppelzimmer mit Bad für eine Woche.)*
Receptionist: Room 405. Do you have any luggage?
Guest: *(Nur eine kleine Tasche.)*

V. Word families. Fill in the table. Then complete the sentences (9–12) below.

	Verb	Noun
1.	change	change
2.	meet	...
3.	reserve	reservation
4.	sign	...
5.	say	...
6.	explain	...
7.	offer	offer
8.	help	...

9. Here are your tickets and one pound ... .
10. Would you like to make a ... for dinner?
11. Does the ... "Time is money" mean anything to you?
12. If you have lost your way, a policeman will probably offer you some ... .

2B

Travelling around ●●

The travellers in this module were asked two questions: What is the first thing you do when you visit a foreign country? And what do you take with you?

The two girls always go to the *tourist information office* first. They get *leaflets*, *brochures* and *street maps*. They do not take much luggage with them. They like to buy *clothes* when they're on holiday.
The first thing the woman does when she is on holiday is change some money. She takes travellers' cheques with her and changes them at a bank or *travel agent's*. She *travels light*. She takes a camera, a *guide book*, comfortable shoes and a *first aid kit*.
The *backpackers* always find somewhere to stay first. They go to a *campsite* or stay in a *youth hostel*. They take camping equipment with them: a *tent*, a *cooking stove*, waterproof clothes and good *walking boots*.
The young man and his girlfriend always *book* their accommodation *in advance*. The first thing they do is find a good restaurant. When he's *abroad*, the man takes his passport, credit cards and *mobile phone* with him. His girlfriend prefers to take her make-up, sunglasses and some *suntan lotion*. "Even in England," she says, smiling. "You never know."

The two girls at Tonbridge Castle

tourist information office	Fremden-verkehrsamt
leaflet	Faltblatt (*auch*: Flugblatt)
brochure	Broschüre
street map	Stadtplan
clothes /-z/, *pl*	Kleidung
travel agent's	Reisebüro
travel light	mit leichtem Gepäck reisen
guide book	Reiseführer
first aid kit	Verbandskasten
backpacker	„Rucksacktourist“
campsite	Zelt-, Campingplatz
youth hostel	Jugendherberge
tent	Zelt
pitch a tent	ein Zelt aufschlagen
cooking stove	(Camping-)Kocher
walking boots	Wanderstiefel
book in advance	im Voraus buchen
abroad	im, ins Ausland
mobile phone	Funktelefon (*Handy*)
suntan lotion	Sonnenschutzmittel

Understanding the text.

Identify the sentence (a-c) which completes the statements.

1. When the two girls first arrive in a foreign country they like to ...
   a) go to a good restaurant.
   b) change some money.
   c) get some information at the nearest tourist information office.
2. When the lady is on holiday she likes ...
   a) to travel light.
   b) to take along a lot of camping equipment.
   c) to buy expensive clothes.
3. The backpackers' rucksacks contain ...
   a) make-up and sunglasses.
   b) a mobile telephone.
   c) a tent.
4. When the young man and his girlfriend go on holiday ...
   a) they book a hotel before they leave home.
   b) they eat in a nice restaurant before they leave home.
   c) they get a suntan before they leave home.

Now answer these questions using full sentences.

5. What can you get at a tourist information office?
6. Why don't the two younger girls take much luggage?
7. Why are the other older girls called "backpackers"?
8. What does it mean when you say you "travel light"?
9. Why does the young man's girlfriend smile and say "even in England" when she talks about suntan lotion?

And what about you?

10. When and where was the last holiday you had?
11. How do you like to travel when you go abroad?
12. What is the first thing you do when you visit a foreign country?

H The present simple (II)

Die einfache Gegenwart (II)

They **always go** to the tourist information office first.	Sie gehen immer zuerst zum Fremdenverkehrsamt.
She **usually takes** travellers' cheques with her.	Normalerweise nimmt sie Reiseschecks mit.
He **often eats** in expensive restaurants.	Er isst oft in teuren Restaurants.

- **Häufigkeitsadverbien** *(adverbs of frequency)* wie ***always***, ***usually***, ***sometimes***, ***often***, ***rarely*** und ***never*** sind **Signalwörter** für die einfache Form der Gegenwart, weil sie **gewohnheitsmäßige Handlungen** beschreiben.
- Hierbei muß man besonders auf die **Wortstellung** im Englischen achten. Bei **Vollverben** kommen die Häufigkeitsadverbien, anders als im Deutschen, in der Regel vor dem Verb *(They always book a hotel in advance.)*. Bei **Hilfsverben** wie ***do/does/don't/doesn't*** oder ***can/would/will*** stehen die Häufigkeitsadverbien nach dem Hilfsverb und vor dem Vollverb *(They don't usually stay in youth hostels.)*. Bei ***to be*** dagegen kommen Häufigkeitsadverbien nach dem Verb *(She is never late.)*.

Exercises

I. Put the adverbs in their correct position. ●●

1. The two girls stay in youth hostels when they are in England. (often)
2. They have enough money for hotels. (never)
3. They are interested in clothes, music and boys. (always)
4. They speak English to each other. (rarely)
5. They have arguments. (sometimes)
6. They would do anything alone. (never)

The backpackers with their camping equipment

II. Ask the young man some questions in English.
The words in brackets will help you.

Fragen Sie ihn ...

1. ob er üblicherweise in teuren Hotels übernachtet (= *stay in*)?
2. ob er manchmal in Frühstückspensionen (= *bed and breakfasts*) ein Zimmer reserviert?
3. ob er immer sein Handy bei sich (= *with you*) hat?
4. ob er oft in Hotels mit Kreditkarte zahlen kann (= *can*)?
5. ob er nie zu faul (= *lazy*) ist, essen zu gehen (= *to eat out*)?
6. ob das Wetter in England immer so schlecht ist?

III. Remember the helping words "do", "don't", "does" and "doesn't"?
Which word is missing in these sentences?

1. The woman traveller asks: "... you want to know which cities I like best?"
2. She says she likes Verona, Brussels and Barcelona but she ... like London or Paris.
3. "I ... feel comfortable in big cities," she explains.
4. ... she travel abroad very often?
5. "I ... travel as much as I would like to," she says.
6. "It's expensive, and I ... really have the time."

H Possessive adjectives and possessive pronouns

Besitzanzeigende Eigenschaftswörter und Fürwörter

◆ Die **besitzanzeigenden Eigenschaftswörter** beziehen sich, wie echte Adjektive, immer auf Hauptwörter (Substantive).

my daughter	**my** daughters	(meine Tochter	meine Töchter)
your book	**your** books	(dein, Ihr Buch	deine, Ihre Bücher)
his sister	**his** sisters	(seine Schwester	seine Schwestern)
her brother	**her** brothers	(ihr Bruder	ihre Brüder)
its name	**its** names	(sein/ihr Name	seine/ihre Namen)
our child	**our** children	(unser Kind	unsere Kinder)
your car	**your** cars	(euer/Ihr Auto	eure/Ihre Autos)
their bike	**their** bikes	(ihr Fahrrad	ihre Fahrräder)

◆ Die **alleinstehenden besitzanzeigenden Fürwörter** (Pronomen) können, wie der Ausdruck besagt, für etwas alleine stehen. Auf die Frage *"Whose book is this?"* antwortet man üblicherweise mit *"It's mine."* (Es ist meines, das meinige.) oder *"It belongs to me."* (Es gehört mir.).

It's **mine**.	(= It belongs to me.)	It's **ours**.	(= It belongs to us.)
It's **yours**.	(= It belongs to you.)	It's **yours**.	(= It belongs to you.)
It's **his**.	(= It belongs to him.)	It's **theirs**.	(= It belongs to them.)
It's **hers**.	(= It belongs to her.)		

Eine alleinstehende Form *its* gibt es nicht.

IV. Use a possessive adjective to complete the mini-dialogues. ●●

1. Is your sister's car red?	No, ... car is white.
2. Are you 25 next week?	Yes, ... birthday is on Monday.
3. Is that woman John's sister?	No, it's ... mother.
4. The flat is large.	Is ... balcony big, too?
5. Joe and Terry are colleagues.	Oh, where is ... office?
6. Are you and Bill travelling together?	Yes, ... train leaves at 6.

V. Use a possessive pronoun to shorten the second sentence in each mini-dialogue.

1. Is this your bag?	Yes, it's my bag.
2. Her jacket is blue.	No, her jacket is white.
3. Peter has lost his dictionary.	This is his dictionary.
4. What's your telephone number?	And what's your number?
5. Our flat is very untidy.	You should see our flat!
6. The Greens like their new car.	My parents like their new car.

VI. Talking about prices.

British currency (*Währung*) is called **Sterling**. One hundred **pence** make a **pound**. The symbol for pounds is **£**, which is always written **before the amount** (*Betrag*): £5.99. British people don't usually say the word "pence" when they talk about how much something costs. They say **"p"** /pi:/. The amount £2.79 is "two pounds, seventy-nine p" or "two pounds, seventy-nine".

Read these prices out loud.

1. £4.50	3. £0.50	5. £9.99
2. £1.82	4. £6.05	6. £3.33

The following questions are useful in banks and shops. Link up the English (7–10) with a corresponding German version (a–d).

7. Do you take credit cards?	a. Kann ich bar bezahlen?
8. Can I pay with cash?	b. Wie ist der Wechselkurs?
9. What's the exchange rate?	c. Wie hoch ist die Umtauschgebühr?
10. How much is the commission?	d. Akzeptieren (Nehmen) Sie Kreditkarten?

2C

Liz Roberts – a tourist information officer

Listen to the interview with Liz Roberts, who works at a tourist information centre. Then answer the questions.

I. Which three things does Liz Roberts talk about?

She talks about ...
a) the people who come to the information centre.
b) her children.
c) English houses and castles.
d) what English people like to eat.
e) some popular tourist attractions.
f) why she likes her job.
g) which languages she is learning.

II. Identify the correct ending to the sentences by marking it with a cross.

1. A tourist information centre has information on ...
   a) places where you can stay.
   b) places where you can stay and places you can visit.
   c) places where you can change your money.
2. The cheapest places to spend the night are ...
   a) hotels. b) campsites. c) bed and breakfasts.

3. At a guest house you usually get ...
   a) breakfast only.
   b) breakfast and evening meal.
   c) breakfast, lunch and evening meal.
4. Mrs Roberts tells an interesting story about some visitors to Kent. They arrived at night and went to a bed and breakfast place. The next morning they went out to see some sights. In the evening they could not remember where they were staying. They could only remember ...
   a) the number of the house.
   b) the colour of the door.
   c) what they had for breakfast.
5. In the end a tourist information centre ...
   a) helped them find their accommodation.
   b) couldn't find their accommodation.
   c) found them some different accommodation.
6. Knole House is a stately home in Kent. It is the largest house in Britain which is ...
   a) owned by the state. b) owned privately. c) owned by foreigners.
7. The town of Rochester is famous for its Norman castle, its cathedral and one of Britain's most famous writers, ...
   a) Oliver Twist. b) Charles Dickens. c) Emily Dickinson.
8. Mrs Roberts notices how visitors to Britain ...
   a) always speak English very well.
   b) are never interested in Britain's history.
   c) buy lots of British antiques.

A pub in Rochester

Rochester Cathedral

2D

Meterman visits a stately home

I. Fill in the missing vowels to complete the text.

M_term_n is v_ry h_ppy b_c_use tod_y is a v_ry sp_cial d_y. He is going to r_ _d the m_t_r in on_ of the st_t_ly hom_s of Engl_nd.

H_ driv_s up to the b_ck _ntr_nc_ of the historic ho_s_. A gro_p of to_r_sts is st_nding in the *drive*. Met_rm_n *honks* his horn at th_m _nd _lmost *runs* th_m *down*. He s_ _ms to b_ _ngry. "To_rists _r_n't _llow_d to go in this w_y," h_ s_ys. "They h_v_ to go in by the front _ntr_nc_; b_y th_ g_id_ books; b_y th_ le_fl_ts; b_y the t_ck_ts; p_y the g_id_. In my job I c_n go ro_nd th_ b_ck. Engl_nd by the b_ck d_ _r!"

M_t_rm_n f_nds the m_t_r and r_ _ds it. H_ is sh_ck_d at the *amount of* _l_ctric_ty they _s_. He d_cid_s to f_nd o_t why th_y _s_ so m_ch. He f_ll_ws the *wiring* and c_m_s _cross th_ gro_p of to_rists _g_in. H_ c_rri_s on following th_ wiring. H_ go_s down on his h_nds _nd kn_ _s. P_opl_ f_ll ov_r him. A l_mp is kn_ck_d ov_r. Ev_nt_ _lly h_ is thrown o_t.

Th_ to_rists c_rry on w_th th_ir to_r. Slowly th_y climb th_ *oak* st_irc_s_ to th_ f_mo_s b_droom wh_r_ Q_ _ _n Eliz_b_th onc_ sl_pt. The g_id_ op_ns th_ door. Som_on_ is on th_ roy_l bed! It's M_t_rm_n! He is f_st _sl_ _p! On h_s *chest* th_r_ is a s_gn: "Do NOT to_ch the f_rnit_r_."

drive	Auffahrt	wiring (*uncount*)	(*elektrische*) Leitungen
honk	hupen	oak	Eiche; eichen
run down (ran, run)	überfahren	chest	Brust(korb)
amount (of)	Menge (an, von)		

II. The six sentences below contain expressions with the word "hand". Categorize the sentences into the three groups (a-c) below. There are two sentences in each category.

a. Helping someone or needing help.
b. Taking part in something.
c. Describing something that went wrong.

1. Could you give me a hand?
2. She had a hand in writing the report.
3. At the end of the evening the children got a bit out of hand and were sent to bed.
4. They were accused of having a hand in the robbery.
5. We lent him a hand to push his car from the road.
6. When the party got out of hand the police were called in.

III. Here are some more idiomatic expressions with "hand". Match them with their descriptions (a – e).

1. to bite the hand that feeds you
2. to have a free hand in something
3. to give someone a big hand
4. to keep your hand in
5. to be an old hand at something

a. to have the freedom to make your own decisions
b. to be ungrateful for something
c. to be very experienced at doing something
d. to practise skills so you do not lose them
e. to applaud enthusiastically

2E

Knole House

Look at the description of Knole House in the National Trust Handbook (see page 40). Then answer the questions below.

True or false? Put a cross in the correct column.

	True	False
1. Knole House is open only part of the year.		
2. It does not cost anything to go into the house.		
3. There is a shop, but no restaurant facilities at Knole.		
4. You cannot take dogs into Knole House.		
5. One of the most interesting aspects of Knole House are the important paintings which hang there.		

KNOLE

Sevenoaks TN15 0RP (01732) 450608

Knole is the largest private house in England and sits within a magnificent deer park owned by Lord Sackville. Dating from 1456, the house was enlarged in 1603 by Thomas Sackville, 1st Earl of Dorset, to whom it was granted by Elizabeth I. The 13 state rooms which are open to the public contain a collection of portraits, including works by Reynolds and Gainsborough, silver, tapestries and an important collection of 17th-century English furniture

House: April to end Oct: Wed, Fri, Sat, Sun & BH Mon 11–5; Thur 2–5. Last admissions 4. Pre-booked groups accepted on Wed, Fri & Sat 11–4, Thur 2–4. **Park:** open daily to pedestrians by courtesy of Lord Sackville. **Garden:** May to Sept: first Wed in each month only

£4. Pre-booked parties £3. Parking (NT members free) £2.50. Park free to pedestrians. Only vehicles carrying visitors to the house are allowed in the park

Guided tours for pre-booked parties on Thur 10–1 throughout season; no reduction

Shop open as house. Christmas shop, tel. Administrator for details

Access to Great Hall, Stone Court, Green Court, shop, restaurant, garden (only open on first Wed in month; May to end Sept) and park; WC near restaurant

Herb and wilderness garden, subject to limited opening, see above

Tea-room open as house. (Thur, open from 12). Light lunches available

In park only, on lead

At S end of Sevenoaks town; just E of A225 [188: TQ532543] *Bus:* From surrounding areas to bus station, ¾m (tel. (0800) 696996) *Station:* Sevenoaks 1½m

A FAMILY HOME

UNIT 3

3A

The Jones family

Hugh and Nick Jones with their parents

In this module we meet Hugh and Nick Jones, their parents and their grandmother.

"Hello. I'm Hugh. I'm sixteen. I like playing the guitar, I like windsurfing and I like playing with my dog. I've got one brother and no sisters. I get pocket money from my parents every month. I also earn extra money. For example, I do work in the garden. I quite like that. I don't like doing homework and I don't like doing *housework*."

"*Hi*. My name's Nick. I'm Hugh's brother. I'm fourteen years old. I like playing the *keyboard* and *drawing* on the computer. I also like playing cricket. I get pocket money every month from my parents. Sometimes I earn extra money. For example, I do work on the computer for my mum. That's all right but I don't much like cleaning the car."

"I am their grandmother and I live next door. I've got six grandchildren. They're all grandsons, I have no granddaughters."

"I'm Gill. I *grew up* here, in this house. I like gardening and I like going on holiday but I don't like cleaning the house and I don't like *ironing*."

Keith and his son, Nick, with the family pets

"I'm Keith. I grew up in *Wales*. My father was *Welsh*, my mother was English. I like *walking the dog* and listening to music. I don't like washing the cars. (Giving a *bucket* of water to his son.) Nick. The cars, please."

housework	Hausarbeit	Wales	*Land in GB*
hi	*Begrüßungsfloskel (umg.)*	Welsh	Walliser(in); wallisisch
keyboard	Tastatur, *hier*: elektrische Orgel, Keyboard	walk the dog	den Hund ausführen, mit dem Hund spazierengehen
draw (drew, drawn)	zeichnen		
grow up (grew, grown)	aufwachsen		
iron	bügeln	bucket	Eimer

Understanding the text.

1. Identify what Hugh likes doing by putting a cross next to the appropriate sentence(s). Hugh likes ...
   a) playing the keyboard. b) doing housework.
   c) playing with his dog. d) cleaning the cars.
2. Which of these things does Nick like doing? Nick likes ...
   a) doing his homework. b) playing music.
   c) drawing on the computer. d) gardening.

Answer these questions using full sentences.

3. Do Gill and Keith help their sons financially? If so, how?
4. How many of grandmother's grandchildren do not appear in module 3A?
5. What does Gill like better? Working in her house or working in her garden?
6. Is Keith English? Explain.

And what about you?

7. What do you like doing?
8. What do you not like doing?

H The verbs "have" and "have got"

haben, besitzen

I've (got) one brother and no sisters.	Ich habe einen Bruder und keine Schwestern.
Grandmother **hasn't got** any granddaughters. Grandmother **doesn't have** any granddaughters.	Großmutter hat keine Enkelinnen.
Have you **got** / **Do** you **have** any children?	Haben Sie (Hast du) Kinder?

- Beide Verben, ***have*** und ***have got***, entsprechen im Deutschen der Bedeutung **haben**, **besitzen**.
- Das Vollverb ***have*** verhält sich wie jedes andere Vollverb im Englischen. Um **Fragen** und **Verneinungen** in der einfachen Form der Gegenwart zu bilden, nimmt man ***do, does, don't*** und ***doesn't*** (*Do you have any English friends? I don't have a car.*).
- In der **Umgangssprache** (*colloquial English*) verwendet man meist ***have got*** anstelle von *have*. Bei *have got* werden **Fragen** und **Verneinungen ohne *do/does*** gebildet. Bei **Fragen** genügt ein bloßes **Umstellen** (*Have you got any English friends?*). Zur **Verneinung** brauchen wir lediglich ein ***not*** hinzuzufügen (*I haven't got any children.*).
- ***Have got*** wird in der **gesprochenen Sprache** oft **zusammengezogen**, so dass das Wort *has/have* fast verschwindet (*Grandmother's got six grandsons. They've got two sons.*).

Exercises

I. Put in "have (not) got" or "has (not) got".

1. The Joneses ... a large house.
2. Hugh ... his own dog.
3. Nick and Hugh ... a sister.
4. Gill ... a beautiful garden.
5. Keith ... a Welsh father and an English mother.
6. Nick and Gill ... computers in their rooms.

II. Change the "have" form into "have got" forms.

1. Hugh has his own surfboard.
2. Does Nick have a guitar?
3. Gill and Keith don't have a daughter.
4. Gill doesn't have much free time.
5. Keith and Gill have an old car.
6. Grandmother has her grandsons around her.

III. Shorten the "have got" forms to make them sound more colloquial.

1. I have not got a brother.
2. She has got an old computer.
3. They have got a lot of trees in their garden.
4. Tom has got a cat and Mark has got a dog.
5. You have not got the time, have you?
6. Sarah has got some English money.

IV. What does the 's stand for? Is it "is" or "has"?

1. Keith's from Wales.
2. Gill's a writer.
3. Hugh's got an electric guitar.
4. It's red and black.
5. Nick's hungry.
6. Grandmother's got six grandchildren.

V. You will need a form of the the verb "to do" to complete five of the sentences below, and a form of the verb "to make" to complete the other three. Which verb goes where? ●●

1. She doesn't like ... the ironing.
2. He doesn't want ... his homework now.
3. Can you ... the washing-up tonight, please?
4. It's so easy to ... a mistake, isn't it?
5. Would you like to ... a cake for her birthday?
6. Do you enjoy ... housework?
7. Can I ... a telephone call from here?
8. We must ... some work in the garden tomorrow.

VI. Don't mix up "I like + -ing form" – in a general sense – (ich mag, ich tue gerne) *and "I would like + to + infinitive" – in a specific situation –* (ich möchte gerne). *Complete the mini-dialogues below using the correct form of the words in brackets.* ●●

Examples:

... (you, like, swim)?	Do you like swimming?
Yes, but only outside in summer.	
... (you, like, have) a cup of tea?	Would you like to have a cup of tea?
Yes, please. No sugar, please.	

1. ... (you, like, come) to a party on Friday?
   Yes, that would be great. Whose party is it?
2. I ... (like, drive) my car but I ... (not, like, clean) it. ... (you, like, wash) it today?
   No, thanks. I've got no time.
3. ... (you, like, have) children one day?
   I'm not sure. I've never really thought about it.
4. ... (you, like, go jogging) with me tomorrow before breakfast?
   No, thanks. I ... (not, like, get up) early.

3B

A family visit ●●

Gill and Keith have got some visitors today. They are all from Gill's side of the family. Nick explains who has come: his *granny*, his uncle and *aunt*, and his two cousins. Timothy is six, ten years younger than Hugh. Simon is four. He's the youngest – and the *naughtiest* – of the cousins.

The family is in the garden. They are playing cricket. Nick is *batting*. Tim is *bowling*. Uncle Jonathan is *fielding*. Hugh and his mother are fielding while his aunt Ruth and his youngest cousin, Simon, are *keeping wicket*. Nick *is out* when his mother catches the ball. "Well caught!" shouts Keith, who is sitting on the garden *bench* with grandmother and relaxing.

After cricket the family sit down for tea. Gill has made a cake. Tim goes around and offers the others a piece: "Would you like some cake?"

Later the family *gathers in front of* the house for a photograph. Grandmother talks about the other members of the family: "I'm the grandmother. There are my daughter and my *son-in-law*, my son and my daughter-in-law and four grandsons." Keith describes the members of the family differently. He is with his wife, Gill, his mother-in-law, his brother-in-law, his sister-in-law, his two small *nephews* and his sons.

Playing cricket in the garden

Inside the house Gill looks at her grandparents' *wedding* photograph. There are the *bride*, the *bridegroom,* the *bridesmaids* and the *page*. Gill's grandmother *was born* in 1881. She *got married* in 1903 but *died* young, in 1916. Gill's parents got married in 1939. The bride *wore* a white dress and the bridegroom wore a *top hat* and *gloves*. Gill married Keith in 1977. The *photograph* Gill has in her hand *was taken* in the house she *still lives in*. "So there you have it," says Gill proudly. "Three generations of wedding photographs."

granny	Oma	bride	Braut
aunt	Tante	bridegroom	Bräutigam
naughty	frech	bridesmaid	Brautjungfer
bat (-ted, -ted)	(*den Ball*) schlagen	page	eigentlich *pageboy* – Pendant zu *bridesmaid*
bowl	(*den Ball*) werfen		
field	die Rolle des Feldspielers innehaben	be born (was, been)	geboren werden
keep wicket (kept, kept)	als Feldspieler hinter dem *wicket* (Tor) stehen	get married (got, got)	heiraten
		die (-d, -d)	sterben
be out (was, been)	ausgeschieden, „draußen" sein	wear (wore, worn)	tragen (*Kleidung*)
		top hat	Zylinderhut
bench	Bank	gloves	Handschuhe
gather	sich versammeln	take a photo (took, taken)	fotografieren
in front of	vor		
son-in-law	Schwiegersohn	still	(immer) noch
nephew	Neffe	live in	leben in, wohnen in, bewohnen
wedding	Hochzeit		

Understanding the text.

Read the first, second and the last paragraphs of text 3B carefully and complete this family tree with two dates and four names.

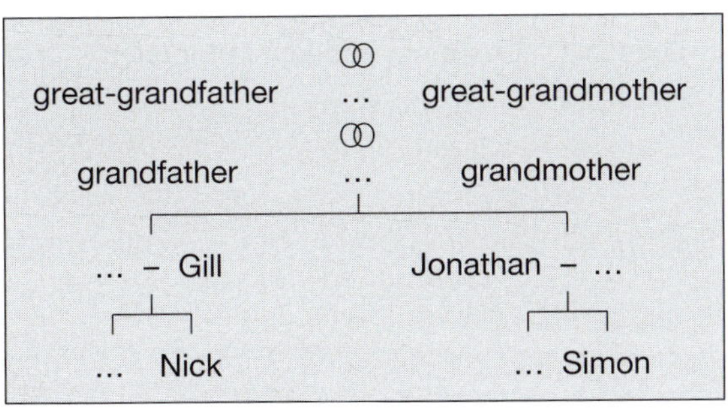

Find the English equivalents in the text for these German words. Then translate the sentences below into English.

1. Familienmitglieder
2. Schwiegermutter
3. Neffe
4. Enkel
5. Ehefrau
6. Bräutigam
7. Brautjungfer
8. Zylinder
9. stolz sein auf
10. Hochzeitsfotos
11. Hast du ein Foto von deiner Schwiegermutter?
12. Wie viele Enkelkinder hat dein Vater?
13. Mein Schwager lebt in Kalifornien.
14. Ist er stolz auf seine Frau?
15. Wo ist der Bräutigam? – Er spricht mit dem Fotografen.

H The comparison of adjectives

Die Steigerung der Adjektive

Eigenschaftswörter (auch **Adjektive** genannt) beschreiben Hauptwörter (Substantive). Sie haben eine **Grundstufe (Positiv)** und **zwei Steigerungsformen (Komparativ, Superlativ)**. Diese Formen werden im Englischen auf zweierlei Weise gebildet.

◆ **Einsilbige Adjektive** werden durch **Anhängen** von ***-er, -est*** gesteigert:

high	high**er**	the high**est**

◆ **Drei- und mehrsilbige Adjektive** steigert man durch ***more*** und ***most***:

expensive	**more** expensive	the **most** expensive
interesting	**more** interesting	the **most** interesting

◆ **Adjektive** mit **zwei Silben** bilden die schwierigste Gruppe, weil sie sowohl mit ***-er, -est*** als auch mit ***more, most*** gesteigert werden können. **Adjektive**, die auf ***-er, -le, -y*** und ***-ow*** enden, hängen meist ***-er, -est*** an:

clever	clever**er**	the clever**est**
happy	happi**er**	the happi**est**

Die **übrigen zweisilbigen Adjektive** steigert man mit ***more, most***:

famous	**more** famous	the **most** famous

◆ Es gibt auch **unregelmäßige Steigerungen**:

good	**better**	the **best**
bad	**worse**	the **worst**
much	**more**	the **most**
little	**less**	the **least**

Comparisons (Vergleichssätze)

Timothy is smaller **than** Hugh.	Timothy ist kleiner als Hugh.
Keith is taller **than** Jonathan.	Keith ist größer als Jonathan.
Ruth is **as** old **as** Gill.	Ruth ist so alt wie Gill.
Nick finds cricket **as** interesting **as** his father (does).	Nick findet Kricket genauso interessant wie sein Vater.

Das Englische ***than*** entspricht dem Deutschen **als**, das Englische ***as ... as*** dem Deutschen **so ... wie**.

Exercises

I. Look at the table below and put the adjectives in the correct column.

careful • easy • exciting • pretty • quick • hot • simple • difficult • big • tall • beautiful • small • dangerous • deep • boring • dirty • stupid • fast • wide • loud

one syllable	two syllables		three syllables
-er, -est	-er, -est	more, most	more, most
cold	clever	crowded	wonderful
⋮	⋮	⋮	⋮

II. Now use six different adjectives from exercise I to complete these sentences. ●●

1. A motorbike is ... than a bicycle.
2. Cairo is ... than Moscow.
3. Driving is ... than walking.
4. Learning English is ... than learning to dance.
5. Basketball players are ... than football players.
6. Heavy metal music is ... than classical music.

III. Add the superlative form of the adjective. ●●

1. It's an extremely fast car. It's ... car in the world.
2. The film was so boring. It's ... film I've ever seen.
3. She's a popular student. In fact she's ... student in class.
4. They're such a friendly couple. They're one of ... couples I know.
5. It's a really old house. People say it's ... house in the village.
6. It was an easy test. It was ... test we've done this year.

IV. There are two words missing in each sentence. Which are they? ●●

1. Mt. Everest is ... ... Mt. Blanc, isn't it?
2. Did you do ... or ... in the test than you expected?
3. Jörg ... Maths ... boring as Martina does.
4. Claudia has much ... hair ... you, hasn't she?
5. Isn't Sandra lucky! She got the ... mark in the test. She's the ... student in the class.
6. Is it ... expensive to stay on a campsite ... in a youth hostel?

H The past simple (I)

Die einfache Vergangenheit (I)

Gill's grandmother **was** born in 1881.	Gills Großmutter wurde 1881 geboren.
The bride **wore** a white dress.	Die Braut trug ein weißes Kleid.
Gill **married** Keith in 1977.	Gill heiratete Keith 1977.

◆ Die **einfache Form der Vergangenheit *(Past Simple)*** bezeichnet einen **in der Vergangenheit abgeschlossenen Vorgang.**

◆ **Regelmäßige Verben** bilden das *Past Simple* durch Anhängen von ***-ed***, z.B.:

work	–	worked	
repair	–	repaired	
smoke	–	smoked	
stay	–	stayed	
marry	–	married	("y" nach Konsonant wird zu "i")
die	–	died	(stummes "e" entfällt)
stop	–	stopped	(Der Endkonsonant wird nach kurzem, betontem Vokal verdoppelt)

◆ Eine große Zahl gebräuchlicher Verben bildet das *Past Simple* jedoch **unregelmäßig**, z.B.:

be	–	was, were (2 Formen!)	get	–	got
have	–	had	wear	–	wore
go	–	went	see	–	saw
do	–	did			

◆ **Fragen** werden mit ***did*** und der **Grundform** (dem **Infinitiv**) **des Verbs** gebildet (*Did you see Nick? Where did he go last night?*). Bei **Verneinungen** kommt zusätzlich ***not*** hinzu (*She did not (didn't) work on Friday.*). Mit ***did*** steht der Satz in der **Vergangenheit**. Das Verb selbst bleibt daher unverändert.

◆ Eine wichtige **Ausnahme** ist ***to be***: Hier werden **Fragen** durch **Umstellen** von **Subjekt** und ***was/were*** gebildet (*Were your parents in England with you? – No, they weren't.*).

◆ Manche Verben bestehen aus **zwei Teilen** (*to get married, to be born*). Hier wird **nur** die **Grundform** des Verbs geändert (*She got married in 1977. He was born in Wales.*). **Fragen** werden bei **Vollverben** wie *to get* mit ***did*** gebildet (*When did she get married?*), bei ***to be*** durch **Umstellen** von Subjekt und *was/were* (*Was he born in Wales?*).

V. Look at these infinitives and past tense forms. Which belong together?

INFINITIVE: be • have • grow • work • do • want • leave • hate • get • train • say • finish

PAST SIMPLE: worked • grew • hated • got • wanted • was • trained • left • had • said • finished • were • did

VI. Complete this text about Stephen by putting in the past tense of the verbs in brackets. ●●

"Hi. My name's Steve. I ... (be born) in London and ... (grow up) there. I ... (have) a great time as a child. My parents ... (be) not at home often because they ... (work) all day so my brother and I ... (do) what we ... (want) to most of the time!
At the age of sixteen I ... (leave) school. I ... (be) good at practical things but ... (hate) exams. I ... (get) a job in a company in my home town and there I ... (train) to become an electrician.
Two years ago my boss ... (say) I should go back to college and get more qualifications. It ... (be) a good idea. I ... (finish) my second year of the course last July. I hope to get a better job and earn more money in the future."

VII. Ask Joanna questions to get the information which is missing. (Be careful with question 6.) The question words are given in brackets. ●●

1. I was born in .?. in 1976.	(where?)
2. I left school when I was .?. years old.	(how old?)
3. My first job was in .?. .	(where?)
4. I stopped working there six months later because .?. .	(why?)
5. I got married in .?. .	(when?)
6. I've got .?. children.	(how many?)
7. Later I had a part-time job in a .?. .	(where?)
8. I did not want any more children because .?. .	(why?)

VIII. Write about your own family. The expressions below (and others in this module) will help you.

My mother/father was born ... .
They got married ... .
They had ? children ... .
I was born ... .

3C

Jonathan – a childhood at Merrimans

Listen to Jonathan talking about the house where he was born. Then answer the questions below.

I. Complete the sentences by choosing one of the alternatives (a – c).

1. Jonathan talks about ...
   a) the house and his parents.
   b) the house and his children.
   c) the house and its history.
2. Jonathan seems ...
   a) sad about what he is saying.
   b) interested in what he is saying.
   c) bored with what he is saying.
3. It looks as if Jonathan had ...
   a) a wonderful childhood.
   b) a terrible childhood.
   c) a lonely childhood.

II. Complete the text by choosing one of the expressions in each of the brackets.

Jonathan was born in a house called Merrimans in (1947/1957). The house was built in 1807 and has (never/often) been extended since then. Merrimans is in the county of Kent, which is (quite near to/a long way from) London where Jonathan and his family now live.

Jonathan often comes to Merrimans because his (brother/sister) lives there. The house has a very large garden with many trees and (horses/ponds) in it, which makes it very exciting for children. Many years ago the garden was not a garden but a farm, where nut trees grew. Today the nut trees are (still/no longer) there. After the terrible storm in (1978/1987) the (house/garden) was badly damaged. The electricity and the telephone were cut off for three (days/weeks).
Jonathan's room is still as it was when he was a boy. In fact the (wallpaper/computer) he had is still there! Obviously Jonathan has happy memories of (growing up/growing old) in Merrimans.

III. Around the house. Which words are missing? The number of lines corresponds to the number of letters.

1. The _ _ _ _ _ _ _ is where you prepare and cook food.
2. In the _ _ _ _ _ _ _ _ _ _ _ _ you sit, read or watch TV.
3. You sleep in the _ _ _ _ _ _ _.
4. The _ _ _ _ _ _ _ _ _ is the place where you wash and have a shower.
5. When you go up the _ _ _ _ _ _ you get to the first floor.
6. The cellar is _ _ _ _ _ the house.
7. The toilet is often the _ _ _ _ _ _ _ _ _ room in the house.
8. The English word for "Flur" is _ _ _ _ , not "floor".

3D

Meterman at Merrimans

I. Choose the appropriate words from the box below to complete the dialogue. Be careful, however. There are eight gaps in the text and ten words in the box.

audience • clever • day • idea • meter • moment • party • sayings • sure • window

Meterman is going to read the meter in Merrimans. He notices two young lads in an upstairs ... .

Meterman: Hello lads. Are your Mum and Dad in?
Nick: No. They're out at the ... .
Meterman: Well, I'm the Meterman. I've come to read the ... . Do you know where it is?

Nick:	Oh, I'm not ... . (To Douglas:) Do you know?
Douglas:	No ... .
Meterman:	Well, you'd better come down and find it for me, then! (Speaks to the ...:) Fancy not knowing where the meter is! I know where the meter is but I'm going to lead them a bit of a dance. That's one of our little ... . Lead them a bit of a dance. (To Nick:) Well, have you found the meter then?
Nick:	No.
Meterman:	Well you'd better go and find it. I haven't got all ... .

II. Link the expressions 1 and 2 with an appropriate explanation below (a–d).

1. Fancy not knowing that!
2. I'm going to lead them a bit of a dance!

a. I'm going to play a trick on them.
b. It's a shame that he is so ignorant.
c. I'm going to teach them something new.
d. It's surprising that he doesn't know that.

Now try to translate the expressions 1 and 2 into German.

III. Look at the underlined words in these pairs of sentences. In which pair or pairs of sentences are the underlined words pronounced in the same way?

1a. Did he <u>lead</u> you a bit of a dance?
1b. Can you buy petrol with <u>lead</u> in it today?

2a. His job is to read electricity <u>meters</u>.
2b. We live only a few <u>metres</u> away from your house.

3a. Do you have time to <u>read</u> books or magazines in English?
3b. I <u>read</u> a very interesting article last night.

4a. "<u>No</u>!" she said loudly and put down the phone.
4b. He didn't <u>know</u> what to say.

3E

Streets and houses

Streets and roads have names but people like to give houses names as well. Some names are historical, some are descriptive, some romantic. Some are named after their owners. Others are named after a holiday.

MY CAR HAS BROKEN DOWN UNIT 4

4A

What's wrong?

Kevin and his girlfriend are driving along a country road when their car suddenly stops.

Girlfriend:	What's the matter? Why are we stopping?
Kevin:	I don't know. I don't know what's wrong.
Girlfriend:	Well you can't stop here. There's someone behind us.

(Kevin gets out and opens the *bonnet*. The man in the car behind him gets out, too.)

Old man:	*What's up?*
Kevin:	I don't know. It just stopped.
Young woman:	What's wrong?
Girlfriend:	I don't know. I've no idea. It just stopped.
Young man:	*Maybe* it's *run out of* petrol.
Girlfriend:	Kevin. Have we run out of petrol?
Kevin:	No, we have not run out of petrol. Anyway, it's not petrol. It's diesel.
Old man:	Oh, diesel. Try it again.
Woman:	What's the matter?
Young man:	It won't start.

Kevin opens the bonnet to find out what's wrong

Old woman:	Maybe it's the battery.
Young woman:	Perhaps it's the *starter*.
Young man:	It could be the pump.
Old man:	Well, anyway, you can't stay here.
Girlfriend:	You'd better do something, Kevin.
Young man:	You'd better put your *hazard lights* on.
Young woman:	You'd better put your *warning triangle* out.
Old woman;	You'd better phone the *breakdown service*.
Old man:	You could telephone from over there.
Young man:	We could push ... . Come on.

break down (broke, broken)	*hier*: eine Panne haben	starter	Anlasser
bonnet	Motorhaube	hazard lights	Warnblinklicht
What's up? (*coll*)	Was ist los?	warning triangle	Warndreieck
maybe	vielleicht	breakdown service	Pannenhilfe
run out of sth (ran, run)	ausgehen		

Understanding the text. Which sentence (a–c) completes the statements best?

1. Kevin should not leave his car where it is because ...
   a) the traffic lights are green.
   b) there is another car behind him.
   c) a traffic sign forbids him to stop.
2. The best advice Kevin gets is to ...
   a) put his warning triangle out.
   b) phone the breakdown service.
   c) push his car to the side of the road.
3. Kevin's girlfriend ...
   a) is not very helpful.
   b) has some good ideas.
   c) wants to have an argument with the old man.
4. By the end of text 4A Kevin ...
   a) knows exactly what the problem is.
   b) does not know what the problem is.
   c) is not sure if there is a problem at all.

Further questions

5. Kevin uses the word "anyway" (line 14). What is the German equivalent for this word?
   a) übrigens b) gut c) trotzdem
6. The old man uses the word "anyway" (line 22). What is the German equivalent for this word?
   a) auf jeden Fall b) trotzdem c) übrigens
7. Which three expressions below (a–f) mean the same?
   a) What's the matter?
   b) What's your job?
   c) How are you?
   d) What's up?
   e) How are things?
   f) What's wrong?

Answer this question in complete sentences.

8. Why is it the old man who says (line 22) "you can't stay here"?

And what about you?

9. Do you drive a car? How often do you use it?
10. What sort of repairs can you do by yourself on a car?

H Helping verbs (II): can't/cannot – could

Hilfsverben (II)

You **can't** stop here.	Sie dürfen (Du darfst) hier nicht anhalten.
It **could** be the petrol pump.	Es könnte die Benzinpumpe sein.

Die unvollständigen Hilfsverben und ihre Funktion wurden im Modul 2A (vgl. Seite 27) zum ersten Mal erwähnt. Hier werden nun ***can't/cannot*** und ***could*** ausführlicher behandelt. In Fällen wie den oben genannten Beispielsätzen bringen sie ein **Verbot** und eine **Möglichkeit** zum Ausdruck.

Exercises

I. Explaining road signs. Write down what they mean. Start your explanations with "This sign means that you can't ... ."

1. 

2. 

3. 

4. 

II. Link the sentences 1–6 with a-f to form six mini-dialogues.

1. There's a traffic jam ahead.
2. He didn't pass his driving test the first time.
3. Her car's not working at the moment.
4. They don't like long car journeys.
5. Do you really want to go out when the roads are so icy?
6. Oh no! I've lost my car keys.

a. I don't mind. We could stay at home if you want.
b. They could always take the train, couldn't they?
c. Oh dear. It could be an accident.
d. Really? Couldn't she borrow her brother's?
e. You could phone your garage first. They might be able to help you.
f. It doesn't matter. He could do it again.

H "had better" + infinitive without "to"

You'**d better do** something.	Sie sollten (Du solltest) besser etwas machen.
We'**d better phone** my parents.	Wir sollten besser meine Eltern anrufen.
I'd better not **help** them.	Ich sollte ihnen lieber nicht helfen.

Mit der Konstruktion ***had better*** **+ Infinitiv ohne *to*** kann man jemandem einen **Rat** geben oder einen **Vorschlag** machen. In der **gesprochenen Sprache** wird das Wort ***had*** zu ***'d*** abgekürzt *(You'd better give me your telephone number.)*.

III. Giving advice. Read the situation and write a sentence with "had better" + (not) + infinitive without "to". ●●

1. Jessica feels ill. You think she should sit down.
2. You are going to dinner with a friend. The restaurant is busy so you want to book a table.
3. Mike is going for a walk. You see black clouds in the sky.
4. It's a warm day. You are near a river. Your friend suggests that you go for a swim in it. You don't want to because the water is dirty.
5. Kathy missed the bus so she will not get to the theatre on time. You suggest a taxi.
6. Your tooth hurts. You need to go to the dentist. What do you say to yourself?

IV. Choose the right question word from the box to complete the mini-dialogues. ●●

where • who • why • what • when • whose • which • who • how

1. ... is the matter?	The car's run out of petrol.
2. ... are you coming?	In about half an hour.
3. ... is the breakdown service?	It's in the town centre.
4. ... car is it?	It's mine of course.
5. ... is the best garage?	I've no idea.
6. ... is on the phone?	It's your mother.
7. ... did you just phone?	The breakdown service.
8. ... far is it to the garage?	About 2 miles from here.
9. ... are you stopping?	The car has broken down.

4B

Garage services ●●

That afternoon the breakdown service *tows* Kevin's car *back* to the garage. First the mechanic opens the bonnet and looks at the *engine*. Then he talks to Kevin.

Mechanic: Have you had this problem before?
Kevin: No, it's a very *reliable* car.
Mechanic: How long have you had the car?
Kevin: Three years.
Mechanic: We'll have a look at it for you. *Is* it *due for* a *service*?

Kevin: Yes, a service and an *MOT*.
Mechanic: We could do that at the same time.
Kevin: All right.
Mechanic: *Give us a ring* in the morning, will you?
Kevin: Right.
Mechanic: (sees lots of bags on the road:) Good heavens. You've done some shopping!

(Kevin's girlfriend has *unpacked* the *boot* and is looking at the bags.)

Girlfriend: The red one is yours. The blue one is mine. The small *purple* one is mine. The big black one is mine, too. The brown ones are yours.
Kevin: Yes, yes, all right. But what are we going to do with them?
Mechanic: You'd better take a taxi, sir. You can use the telephone.

The next morning the mechanic gives Kevin his MOT *certificate*. The lights, *brakes*, *seatbelts* and *tyres* are OK. The car *failed on* the *windscreen wiper*, which the mechanic *replaced*. He also changed the *fog light bulb*.
The mechanic tells Kevin exactly what he has done. "I've *carried out* a *major service*. I've changed the oil. I've cleaned the *injectors*. I've checked the tyre pressures and I've *topped up* the *windscreen washer*," he says. Then he gives Kevin a last *piece of advice*. "Put some diesel in," he says. "It's very *low*."

tow (back)	abschleppen, *hier*: zurückschleppen	fail on	versagen, was ... angeht; durchfallen
engine	Motor	windscreen wiper	Scheibenwischer
reliable	zuverlässig	replace	ersetzen, auswechseln
be due for	fällig sein, anstehen zu (*Wartung*)	fog light bulb	Birne für die Nebelleuchte
service	Wartung, Kundendienst	carry out	durchführen, ausführen
MOT (Ministry of Transport Test)	*entspricht in etwa dem deutschen TÜV*	major service	Hauptinspektion, großer Kundendienst
give sb a ring (gave, given)	jmdn. anrufen	injector	Einspritzdüse
unpack	leer machen, auspacken	top up	auffüllen
boot	Kofferraum	windscreen washer	Flüssigkeitsbehälter *(für die Scheibenwaschanlage)*
purple	lila(-farben)	piece of advice	Ratschlag
certificate	(TÜV-)Zertifikat	low	*hier*: knapp
brakes, *pl*	Bremsen		
seatbelt	Sicherheitsgurt		
tyre	Reifen		

The mechanic tells Kevin what he has done

Understanding the text.

Which sentence (a–c) completes the statements (1–3) best?

1. The mechanic thinks he can ...
   a) repair Kevin's car by the following morning.
   b) tell Kevin what's wrong with the car by the following morning.
   c) do a service and an MOT by the following morning.
2. Kevin's girlfriend seems to be more interested in ...
   a) the mechanic than she is in Kevin.
   b) her shopping than she is in the mechanic.
   c) Kevin's car than she is in her shopping.
3. It looks as if Kevin's problem was ...
   a) not enough diesel in the tank.
   b) not enough oil in the engine.
   c) low pressure in the tyres.

Answer these questions in complete sentences.

4. What exactly did the mechanic find wrong with Kevin's car?
5. Which work will Kevin pay for the next morning?

Further questions. Choose the right ending to the sentences. The answers are not in the text.

6. All in all the man at the garage seems to be ...
   a) a very good mechanic.
   b) a very good businessman.
   c) a very good driver.
7. The initials MOT probably mean ...
   a) Mind our Tests.
   b) Mechanics on Teabreak.
   c) Ministry of Transport Test.

And what about you?

8. Is there something like the MOT test in your country? Explain.

H The present perfect simple (I)

Die einfache Form des Perfekts (I)

I'**ve checked** the tyre pressure.	Ich habe den Reifendruck geprüft.
I **haven't had** the car long.	Ich habe das Auto noch nicht lange.
Have you **changed** the oil?	Haben Sie das Öl gewechselt?

- Das ***Present Perfect*** ist **keine Vergangenheitsform**. Wie der Name besagt, ist diese Form des Verbs eng mit der Gegenwart verbunden. Das Geschehen ist zwar vorbei, aber wir denken noch an die Folgen. *"I've changed the oil"* heißt, dass das Öl neu ist.
  Im Gegensatz dazu bezeichnet die ***Past Tense*** (**einfache Vergangenheit**) einen **in der Vergangenheit abgeschlossenen Vorgang,** der keinen Bezug zur Gegenwart hat *(I changed the oil last weekend.)*. (Vgl. auch Modul 3B, S. 51.)
- Die **einfache Form** des ***Present Perfect*** bildet man mit dem Hilfsverb ***have/has*** und dem **Partizip Perfekt** (der dritten Form des Verbs; *Past Participle*). Die **Frage** wird durch **Umstellung** gebildet *(Has he phoned?)*. Zur Bildung der **Verneinung** nimmt man das Wort ***not*** *(He has not left.)*.
- Die Kombination ***have + not*** und ***has + not*** wird in der **gesprochenen Sprache** üblicherweise **zusammengezogen** *(They haven't arrived.)*.

Exercises

I. Link up the infinitive, the past tense form and the past participle form of the verbs.

infinitive	past tense	past participle
be	saw	found
break	went	had
do	sold	seen
find	lost	broken
go	had	done
have	was, were	lost
lose	broke	sold
see	found	been
sell	did	gone

(It is important to learn irregular verbs by heart. See page 270 for complete list.)

II. Answer the questions using the present perfect simple of the verb in brackets. In sentences 5 and 6 you can add a small word. ●●

1. What have you done with your old mountain bike? (sell)
2. Where's your watch? (lose)
3. Why don't you want to watch *Summer* with us at the cinema? (see)
4. What has happened to your finger? (break)
5. Would you like a cup of coffee? (have)
6. We're going to lunch. Are you coming with us? (be)

III. Complete this dialogue between Julie and Richard using the present perfect form of the verbs in brackets. (Be careful. You also need one past tense form!) ●●

Richard: You seem worried, Julie. (anything, happen) ...?
Julie: Yes, I ... (lose) my car keys.
Richard: ... (you, look) in all your pockets?
Julie: Yes, I ... (search) everywhere.
Richard: ... (you, be) back to your car?
Julie: No, why?
Richard: Maybe you forgot to take them out of the ignition. I ... (often, do) that.
Julie: Wait a second. Here they are. I ... (find) them! They ... (be) in my bag all the time!

H The prop words "one" and "ones"
Die Stützwörter "one" und "ones"

Which of these T-shirts would you like?	Welches dieser T-Shirts möchtest du (möchten Sie) haben?
I'll have this **one**.	Ich möchte dieses.
Which **one**?	Welches?
The blue **one**.	Das blaue.

Die Stützwörter ***one*** und ***ones*** stehen für das entsprechende Substantiv. Man verwendet sie auch nach ***which***.

IV. Use the correct prop words to complete this paragraph. ●●

"Good heavens! How many bags are there? Six. One big ... and five small ... . What colour are they? There are two brown ..., one black ..., one purple ..., one blue ... and one red ... . Which ... are his and which ... are hers?"

V. Take out words and replace them with "one" or "ones". ●●

1. I'm having a drink. Would you like a drink?
2. The postcards from Canada arrived. The postcards from Ireland didn't.
3. The English apples are expensive but the apples from Spain are sweeter.
4. This dictionary is not very good. That dictionary is much better.
5. Are these cups clean? – No, use the cups over there.
6. Which car is yours? – The red car. – There are three red cars!

VI. Complete the text by using the words in the box. Put the verbs into their correct form. ●●

bonnet • certificate • cheque • engine • everything • how • low • MOT • to replace • ring • service • to top up

The mechanic looks under the ... . "I see," he says. "I think we'll have to look at the ... more carefully. Do you need a ... ? The best thing is if we do an ... as well. Just give us a ... tomorrow morning, will you?"
The next morning the mechanic hands Kevin his MOT ... . "I ... the brake fluid. It was very ... . And I ... your windscreen wiper, too. ... should be OK now. Right, ... would you like to pay – by credit card or by ... ?"

4C

Rick Bourne – the Morgan enthusiast

Listen to the interview with Rick Bourne and answer the questions below.

I. Choose an appropriate sentence (a-c) to complete these statements.

1. Rick Bourne is a ...
   a) motoring journalist. b) businessman. c) mechanic.
2. Rick Bourne's garage seems to be ...
   a) very successful. b) badly organized. c) chaotic.
3. Morgan cars are very special because they are ...
   a) extremely expensive. b) very old. c) built by hand.
4. Rick Bourne knows a lot about Morgan cars because he ...
   a) builds them. b) races them. c) designs them.
5. Morgan cars are raced ...
   a) all over Britain. b) all over Europe. c) all over the United States.

II. Listening for details. Write down the answers to these questions.

1. How many mechanics work in Mr Bourne's garage?
2. Which would you say is more important for Mr Bourne – looking after his Morgans or looking after his customers?

3. In which year did the Morgan Motor Company begin?
4. What two main things is a Morgan car made of?
5. In what weather conditions does Mr Bourne like to drive his own Morgan?

4D

Meterman on the road

I. Put the seven paragraphs (a – g) into the correct order to make up the story. Start with paragraph e.

a. "Aha! – what's going on here? A spot of *bother*? That's a saying, an expression we have. It means trouble, someone's got a problem. Now what's the problem here?"

b. He goes on. "There's a saying we have, you know? One good turn deserves another. Oh yes, indeed! People are very grateful to me. I'm always ready to help – and people like that."

c. Just at that moment Meterman *spots* a car at the side of the road. Its bonnet is up and a young lady is *peering* inside. There is a warning triangle in the road.

d. Meterman continues driving and talking. "You meet a lot of people in my job and I always take the opportunity to give a helping hand. Help other people and they'll help you, that's what I always say."

e. Meterman is driving along and talking. "There's one thing I enjoy in my job. Driving along a country road on a nice sunny day. I enjoy driving, you know. I expect you do too, don't you?"

f. Meterman gets out of the van and *approaches* the girl. "Good morning, good morning. Do we have a problem? Do we need some help and advice?" The girl has a mobile phone. "Oh no, thanks very much," she replies. "I'm just going to *ring* the breakdown service."

g. Suddenly a car *overtakes* him and *hoots* impatiently. "Now he is going too fast. He must be *exceeding* the speed limit by quite a bit."

bother	Ärger, Schererei	ring (rang, rung)	anrufen
spot (-ted, -ted)	entdecken, erspähen	overtake (overtook, overtaken)	überholen
peer	spähen, genau (hinein)schauen	hoot	hupen
approach	sich nähern, herantreten an	exceed	überschreiten, hinausgehen über

II. Use the four expressions in the box to complete the sentences below.

- the road to success
- the road to ruin
- the right road
- the road to nowhere

1. You're making good progress. You must be on ... .
2. Business is getting worse and worse for them. They're on ... .
3. Would you say that exercise is ... to beauty?
4. I don't think you'll ever succeed. You're on ... .

III. Look at these three examples of the word "spot". What do you think "spot" means? Choose one of the meanings (a – c).

1. Have you got a spot of trouble?
2. I think I'll do a spot of gardening.
3. How about a spot of lunch?

a. a small piece of
b. a large piece of
c. another piece of

4E

Traffic signs

I. Test your knowledge of British traffic signs. What do these signs mean? Choose one of the possibilities (a – c).

1. a. No snorkelling.
   b. No U-turns.
   c. Signwriter's mistake. Ignore sign.

2. a. Invisible man on bike.
   b. Village policeman on holiday.
   c. No cycling.

3. a. Two-way traffic crosses one-way road.
   b. Red Indian ambush ahead.
   c. Beware fallen palm trees.

4. a. Inflation warning.
   b. Big discounts on cheese.
   c. Steep hill upwards.

5. a. No vehicles.
   b. Danger. Balloons ahead.
   c. Oxygen shortage. Breathe deeply.

6. a. Sausages on road.
   b. Roundabout.
   c. Danger. Falling ashtrays.

II. On what side of the road do British people drive? Read the rhyme to find out.

The rule of the road is a paradox quite
In riding or driving along
If you go to the left you are sure to go right
If you go to the right you are wrong

FOOD AND DRINK UNIT 5

5A

Eating habits

Some English people were asked what they had for breakfast and lunch.

Interviewer: What do you have for breakfast?
First man: Usually I have toast or *cereal* and a cup of coffee as well.

Interviewer: What do you usually have for breakfast?
Second man: Sometimes I have toast for breakfast with tea, or cornflakes.

Interviewer: What do you usually have for breakfast?
First woman: Usually cereals or toast and sometimes eggs and bacon, a cooked breakfast.

Interviewer: What do you have for lunch?
Third man: Sometimes I have *stew* in this cold *weather* or maybe sandwiches in summer or salad.
Interviewer: What time do you usually have lunch?
Third man: About half-past twelve.

Interviewer: What would you normally have for lunch?
Fourth man: Normal for lunch would be a light lunch - *boiled* fish and a few *vegetables*.
Interviewer: What time do you normally eat lunch?
Fourth man: I eat at one o'clock.

Interviewer: What do you usually have for lunch?
Second woman: Lunch is usually sandwiches if it's at work and if I'm at home I usually cook myself something like soup or something like that.
Interviewer: What time do you usually have lunch?
Second woman: Always about twelve o'clock.

Interviewer: What do you have for lunch?
Fifth man: It varies. Something quick and easy.
Interviewer: Like?
Fifth man: Salad. You can see that I'm on a diet.

James asks his mother what's for dinner

We then see what happens in an English house when a meal is prepared for the whole family in the early evening.

While his wife is cooking, the husband *lays the table* – knives, forks, spoons and *serving spoons* as well as glasses and salt and pepper. Soon James, the son, comes in. The first thing he does is ask his mother what's for dinner. "It's *casserole* and *baked potatoes*," she replies. "Mmm," says James. "It smells good."

When Sarah comes home from college, her brother tells her what there is for dinner. "Anything else?" Sarah asks. The children's mother tells them that there are *peas* and *sweetcorn*. Sarah is thinking of pudding, however. "Yes," her mother goes on. "There's *apple crumble* and ice cream." Sarah is not so sure if she wants any. "It sounds good but *fattening*," she says. Her brother and father are quick to reply. "You don't have to eat any," they say. "There's more for us!"

Sarah talks about the sort of food the family eats. "In our family my mum does most of the cooking. We have traditional food like *shepherd's pie*, casserole and *lamb chops*." James adds, "We also eat burgers and chips and food from the *freezer*."

The children do not do much cooking themselves but Sarah enjoys making cakes for special *occasions* like birthdays. The children's mother likes cooking Sunday lunch, for example roast beef and Yorkshire pudding. Their father can't really cook at all, *although* he does say that he is very good at boiled eggs.

eating habits	Essgewohnheiten	baked potatoes	*vergleichbar mit Folienkartoffeln*
cereal	*Frühstückskost aus Weizen, Hafer etc., z.B. cornflakes*	pea	Erbse
		sweetcorn	Mais
stew	*Eintopfgericht*	apple crumble	*eine Art Apfelauflauf mit Streuseln*
weather	Wetter		
boil	kochen, sieden	fattening	dickmachend
vegetables	verschiedene Gemüsesorten	shepherd's pie	*Auflauf aus Hackfleisch und Kartoffelbrei*
lay the table (laid, laid)	den Tisch decken	lamb chops	Lammkottelets
serving spoon	Vorlege-, Servierlöffel	freezer	Gefrierschrank
casserole	*eine Art Schmortopfgericht (mit Fleisch)*	occasion	(besondere) Gelegenheit, Anlass
		although	obwohl

Understanding the text. Which sentence (a – c) completes the following statements best?

1. People in England ...
   a) never have a cooked breakfast in the morning.
   b) always have a cooked breakfast in the morning.
   c) sometimes have a cooked breakfast in the morning.
2. The word "lunch" normally describes ...
   a) the biggest meal of the day.
   b) a meal in the middle of the day.
   c) a cold meal.
3. The word "dinner" usually means ...
   a) a meal in the evening.
   b) a meal in the early afternoon.
   c) a light meal in the middle of the morning.

Complete these sentences using a word from text 5A.

4. You cut meat with a ... .
5. You put potatoes in your mouth with a ... .
6. You eat soup with a ... .
7. You drink wine out of ... .
8. To keep food for a long time you put it in a ... .

And what about you? (Write at least three sentences.)

9. What typically English food do you know?
10. Do you cook? If you do, do you like cooking? If you don't, why not?

H Quantifiers

Mengenbezeichnungen

We need **some** spoons.	Wir brauchen einige Löffel.
There's still **some** wine in the bottle.	Es ist noch etwas Wein in der Flasche.
Are there **any** potatoes left?	Sind noch Kartoffeln da?
We haven't got **any** ice-cream.	Wir haben kein Eis.

- Das kleine Wort ***some*** bedeutet „einige", „manche" und „etwas", d.h. eine **unbestimmte Menge**. In **Fragen** und **verneinten Sätzen** wird *some* in der Regel zu ***any***. Im Deutschen bleiben diese Wörter oft unübersetzt.
- Es gibt eine Reihe von **Wortzusammensetzungen** (***compounds***) mit ***some*** und ***any***:

somebody	**someone**	**something**	**somewhere**
anybody	**anyone**	**anything**	**anywhere**

Exercises

I. Choose one of the two words in the brackets to complete the sentences. ●●

1. There's ... at the door. Can you go? (someone/anyone)
2. Jane hasn't got ... brothers or sisters. (some/any)
3. We said hello but he didn't say ... to us. (something/anything)
4. I like ... English food, but not all of it. (some/any)
5. Did you take ... photographs at the party? (some/any)
6. We had a big breakfast so we're not having ... for lunch. (something/anything)
7. They spent the night at the station because they didn't have ... to sleep. (somewhere/anywhere)
8. Has ... seen Daniel this morning? (somebody/anybody)

Now translate these sentences into German.

II. Translate into English using "some" or "any" or their compounds. The words in brackets will help you.

1. Möchtest du etwas zu trinken?
2. Hat jemand für mich angerufen?
3. Ich habe keine Zeit.
4. Ist noch etwas Tee übrig? (*left*)
5. Nehmen Sie doch ein paar Kekse. (*biscuits*)
6. Wir haben nichts mitgebracht.

H The plural of nouns

Die Pluralbildung von Substantiven

Den **Plural** (die Mehrzahl) von **Substantiven** bildet man, indem man ein ***-s*** anhängt. Es gibt auch **Pluralformen mit *-es*** und, wie bei Verben, **unregelmäßige Formen**:

◆ **Plural** mit *-s*

book – book**s** /s/
road – road**s** /z/
office – office**s** /ɪz/

◆ **Plural** mit ***-es***

Bei Wörtern, die mit **f** enden:	leaf – lea**ves** /vz/	**f**	>	**ves**
Nach vielen Wörtern mit **o** am Schluss:	tomato – tomato**es** /əʊz/	**o**	+	**es**
Nach den Zischlauten **s**, **sh**, **ch**, **x**:	box – box**es** /ɪz/	**x**	+	**es**
Nach einem **Konsonanten + y**:	baby – bab**ies** /ɪz/	**y**	>	**ies**

Aber: boy – boys   disco – discos   roof – roofs

◆ **Unregelmäßige Formen**

man – men   woman – women   child – children
tooth – teeth   person – people   goose – geese

III. Write down the plural forms for these nouns.

1. family
2. address
3. secretary
4. six
5. knife
6. name
7. orange
8. language
9. potato
10. bush
11. pea
12. lorry

IV. Complete the sentences by using the plural form of the word in brackets. ●●

1. London ... (bus) are red but the ... (taxi) are black.
2. Are they wooden ... (roof) on those ... (house)?
3. Good evening, ... (lady), ... (gentleman) and hello to all you ... (child).
4. Most of the ... (person) here are ... (woman).
5. How many ... (page) are there in your ... (textbook)?
6. We bought ten ... (box) of ... (orange) for the party.

V. Food and cooking. Put the words in the box into the correct column. ●●

apple • boil • tomato • pear • cucumber • onion • fry • melon • beans • peas • raspberry • spinach • apricot • bake • gooseberry • peach • roast • lemon • grill • mushrooms • grapes • cherries • brussel sprouts

Vegetable	Fruit	Ways of cooking
tomato	apple	boil
⋮	⋮	⋮

5B

How to make Yorkshire pudding ●●

Roz Sampson teaches cookery and cooks for her family. She explains how to make Yorkshire pudding, which is eaten with roast beef and is a traditional English lunch.

What you need:

a large *bowl* (glass or *china*)
measuring jugs
a *wooden spoon*
and individual *baking tins*

Ingredients:

175 grams of *plain flour*
a teaspoon of salt

2 large eggs
175 ml of milk
110 ml of water

Instructions:

"First, *sift* the flour and salt into the bowl and make a *hollow* in the middle. Next, break the eggs into the flour. Now, with the wooden spoon, mix the eggs into the flour little by little, like this ... .

Now, add the milk a little at a time. *Draw* the flour slowly *into* the mixture. And now the water. Beat it for about five minutes if you can. Finally leave the mixture in a cold place for about an hour.

Meanwhile the beef is roasting in the *oven*. Now put some oil in the baking tins. Now put the tins in a very hot oven. When the oil is very hot, take the tins from the oven and place them on direct heat. Now *pour* in the mixture. Can you hear it *sizzling*? You can see it's beginning to cook. Put the Yorkshire puddings in the oven. Cook them for about ten minutes *until* they're nicely *risen* and lightly browned.

There you are! They're well risen and nicely browned. Serve them with roast beef, vegetables and hot *gravy*."

bowl	Schüssel
china	Porzellan
measuring jug	Messbecher
wooden spoon	Kochlöffel
baking tin	Backförmchen
ingredients	Zutaten
plain flour	gewöhnliches Mehl
instruction	Anweisung, Anleitung
sift	sieben
hollow	Kuhle, Mulde
draw into (drew, drawn)	unterziehen, einrühren
meanwhile	in der Zwischenzeit, mittlerweile
oven	Bratröhre
pour	(ein)gießen
sizzle	brutzeln
until	bis (*zeitl.*)
rise (rose, risen)	aufgehen
There you are!	Sehen Sie!
gravy	(Fleisch-)Soße

Understanding the text

Choose the most appropriate sentence (a–c) to complete the statements below.

1. Yorkshire pudding is something you eat ...
   a) after your main meal.
   b) before your main meal.
   c) with your main meal.
2. Yorkshire pudding is ...
   a) well-known in England.
   b) becoming unpopular in England.
   c) still quite rare in England.

Roz adds some milk to the flour

3. The English word “flour” sounds exactly like the word ...
   a) “floor”. b) “flower”. c) “flyer”.
4. The English word ”bowl” sounds like ...
   a) “hole”. b) “towel”. c) “oil”.
5. The first syllable (*Silbe*) in the word “oven” is pronounced like the first syllable in the word ...
   a) “over”. b) “other”. c) “otter”.
6. When an English person pronounces the word “vegetables” there are ...
   a) three syllables in it. b) four syllables in it. c) five syllables in it.

Further questions. Which sentence in the following pairs is correct?

7. a) A cooker is someone who likes cooking.
   b) A cook is someone who likes cooking.
8. a) Smell the meat! It’s already sizzling.
   b) Listen to the meat! It’s already sizzling.
9. a) Would you like some more gravy with your meat?
   b) Would you like some more gravy with your ice-cream?
10. a) Yorkshire is a country in England.
    b) Yorkshire is a county in England.

And what about you?

11. What mistake do you think visitors to Britain make when they hear that they are having Yorkshire pudding for lunch?
12. From listening to Roz Sampson’s description would you say that Yorkshire pudding is easy to make? Give some reasons for your answer.

H Adjectives and adverbs

Adjektive und Adverbien

He is a **slow** speaker.	Er ist ein langsamer Sprecher.
He speaks **slowly**.	Er spricht langsam.
She is an **aggressive** player.	Sie ist eine aggressive Spielerin.
She plays **aggressively**.	Sie spielt aggressiv.
I am a **careful** driver.	Ich bin ein vorsichtiger Fahrer.
I drive **carefully**.	Ich fahre vorsichtig.

- Im Modul 3B (Seite 49) haben wir gesehen, dass **Eigenschaftswörter** (auch **Adjektive** genannt) **Substantive beschreiben**. Das **Umstandswort** (auch **Adverb** genannt) wird vom Adjektiv abgeleitet. Man bildet es meist durch **Anhängen von *-ly***.
- Das **Adverb** ist eine **nähere Bestimmung** für ein **Verb**. Es beschreibt die Art und Weise, wie z.B. gesprochen, gespielt oder gefahren wird.

- Es gibt auch **unregelmäßige Formen**:

Adjektiv	Adverb	
She is a **good** cook.	She cooks **well**.	**(anderes Wort)**
Sie ist eine gute Köchin.	Sie kocht gut.	
He is a **fast** runner.	He runs **fast**.	**(gleiche Form)**
Er ist ein schneller Läufer.	Er läuft schnell.	
They like **hard** work.	They work **hard**.	**(gleiche Form)**
Sie mögen harte Arbeit.	Sie arbeiten hart.	
It is an **automatic** door.	It opens **automatically**.	**(*-ally* Endung)**
Es ist eine automatische Tür.	Sie öffnet sich automatisch.	

Das Wort ***hardly*** bedeutet „kaum“: *I hardly know him.* Ich kenne ihn kaum.

- Bei einer Reihe von Verben steht **kein Adverb**, weil sie keine echte Handlung ausdrücken:

to look (*aussehen*)	to feel (*sich fühlen*)	to seem (*scheinen*)
to smell (*riechen*)	to sound (*klingen*)	to taste (*schmecken*)

It sounds **good**.	Es klingt gut.
It smells **great**.	Es riecht toll.
It looks **wonderful**.	Es sieht wunderbar aus.

Exercises

I. Rewrite the sentences using an -ly adverb. ●●

1. David is a slow reader.
2. Anna is a brilliant singer.
3. Maud is a beautiful dancer.
4. Daniel is a quick worker.
5. Rachel is a dangerous cyclist.
6. Terry is an excellent swimmer.
7. Peter is a careful writer.
8. Gabriele is a perfect English speaker.

II. Try these sentences. You will need adjectives and adverbs to complete them. ●●

1. What do you think of this old typewriter? It worked ... (electronic).
2. Your English is very good. Where did you learn to speak it so ... (good)?
3. He drives ... (fast) and very ... (aggressive).
4. What are you baking? It smells ... (wonderful).
5. That CD sounds ... (brilliant). Who's the group?
6. They felt ... (happy) when she performed so ... (successful).
7. After playing the music ... (loud) we felt ... (great).

III. Look back at module 2B (page 31). Put the adverbs of frequency in the brackets into the correct position in the sentence. ●●

1. They go out for dinner. (seldom)
2. We have bacon and eggs for breakfast. (sometimes)
3. She has fish and chips. (occasionally)
4. I have a cooked breakfast. (rarely)
5. Have you eaten fast food? (never)
6. Is he on a diet? (normally)
7. My diet varies. (always)
8. She has vegetarian meals. (frequently)

IV. Translate the following sentences into English. The words in text 5B will help you. ●●

1. Möchten Sie etwas Soße zum Fleisch?
2. Könnte ich bitte einen Löffel haben?
3. Ich esse keine Eier.
4. Die Kirschen sind in der großen Schüssel.
5. Haben Sie "flour" oder "flower" gesagt?

V. Put the sentences (a – k) into the right order to form a dialogue between a waiter and a guest.

a. Guest: All right. I'll have that then.
b. Guest: Can you suggest anything?
c. Guest: I'd like a gin and tonic, please.
d. Waiter: Yes, the roast beef and Yorkshire pudding is delicious.
e. Waiter: A gin and tonic. Certainly, and what would you like to start with?
f. Waiter: Good evening. Would you like a drink? An aperitif?
g. Waiter: Would you like some vegetables to go with that?
h. Guest: The green bean soup, please.
i. Guest: Some brussel sprouts and boiled potatoes, please.
j. Waiter: And for your main course?
k. Waiter: Thank you.

VI. Schoolboy humour

Guest: Excuse me. What sort of soup is this, please?
Waiter: It's a bean soup, sir.
Guest: I don't want to know what it was. I want to know what it is!

5C

Beryl and Dave Stephens – a new home in the country

Listen to the interview with Beryl and answer the questions.

I. Complete the statements (1–4) below by choosing the most appropriate ending (a–c).

1. Beryl and Dave Stephens bought their house because they wanted ...
   a) to make their own beer in it.
   b) to be in the country.
   c) to live near a farm.
2. The kitchen in their house is very interesting because it ...
   a) is round.
   b) smells of hops.
   c) is always warm in winter.

Beryl and Dave's dining room, with a view of the pond

3. Beryl and Dave would like ...
   a) to make no changes to the house that they have bought.
   b) to make the house a very modern place.
   c) to make the house more comfortable to live in.
4. Beryl could imagine ...
   a) selling the house and buying another house in the country.
   b) living in the house for ever.
   c) moving back to the city.

II. Complete these sentences by using a word from the interview. The first letter of each word has been given.

1. Marmalade is made of oranges or lemons. J... is made of other fruits like strawberries or raspberries.
2. Lights in a room hang from the c... .
3. Putting new wallpaper and paint on walls in a house is called d... a house.
4. The room in a house where you keep your books and where you read, write and learn new things is called a s... .
5. A p... is a small area of water in a garden or field.
6. Hops give beer its special f... .

III. Find it out yourself. Look it up in a good dictionary.

1. What does a "do-it-yourself enthusiast" do?
2. What does "hustle and bustle" mean?

5D

Meterman the cook

I. In four of the five paragraphs below <u>one</u> sentence does not belong there. In one of the paragraphs <u>two</u> sentences do not belong there. Read through the text carefully and locate all six sentences.

"Oh hello. It's you again. Good to see you. I've just been looking at all those restaurants and *takeaways*. Chinese takeaways. Indian takeaways. Fish and chips. Secondhand clothes. Hamburgers. Pizzas. It's all quite *ridiculous* if you ask me. 'If you ask me'– that's one of our little sayings.

You buy it hot and you take it away. Who wants to take away Chinese food? Chinese food is the easiest food in the world to cook. At home! Tonight I have invited some friends to dinner and one of them is a very special friend! Two cups of tea, please. And I'm going to cook a Chinese meal."

Meterman gets out of the car carrying shopping bags. "Now you come along inside and watch me because I am an expert Chinese cook. Now *don't get under my feet*, because we haven't got much time, right? The time is four minutes past six and they are coming at seven. She doesn't smoke. Have I got everything? Let's go!"

He continues. "Now have I got all the ingredients? *Bamboo shoots*? *Garlic*? Red peppers? Mushrooms? Newspaper? *Spring onions*? *Almonds*? Birthday present? Soya sauce? Oil? Noodles? Rice? And most importantly, chicken?"

"And now for *the tools of the trade*, as we say. First and most importantly – the Wok. W.O.K. WOK! This is what the real Chinese people use to cook real Chinese food. The job is quite interesting. And to eat real Chinese food we use *chopsticks*."

takeaway	*Geschäft oder Restaurant mit Fertiggerichten zum Mitnehmen*
ridiculous	lächerlich
Don't get under my feet.	Kommen Sie (Komm) mir nicht in die Quere.
bamboo shoot	Bambussprosse
garlic	Knoblauch
spring onions	Frühlings-, Lauchzwiebeln
almond	Mandel
the tools of the trade	das Handwerkszeug
chopstick	Essstäbchen

II. Look at the verb "get" in these pairs of sentences. In which pair is "get" used to describe receiving something (to get = bekommen*)? In which pair is it used to describe movement (to get into/ off =* ein-/aussteigen*)? And in which pair is it used to describe change (to get =* werden*)?*

1a. She got into the car and drove away.
1b. Where do we get off the train?

2a. It's getting cold. Shall we go inside?
2b. Everything has got so expensive in the last few months.

3a. Where can I get a newspaper?
3b. Did you get the book you were looking for?

III. Look at these pairs of words. Can you pronounce them properly?

1. clothes – close
2. draft – giraffe
3. chess – jazz
4. won't – want
5. bad – bed
6. juice – shoes

5E

Weights and measures

I. Although the metric system (centimetres, litres etc.) is widely used in Britain, people still prefer the old system with inches, miles etc.
(The metric equivalents given in the table are only approximations.)

an inch	2.5 cm*)
a foot (12 inches)	30 cm
a yard (3 feet)	90 cm
a mile (1,760 yards)	1.6 km
an ounce	28 gm
a pound (16 ounces)	455 gm
a stone (14 pounds)	6.4 kg
a pint	568 cl
a gallon (8 pints)	4.55 l
° Fahrenheit	°C = (°F - 32) x 5/9 (eg. 86°F = (86 - 32) x 5/9 = 30°C)

*) Note the difference:
The English say "two **point** five centimetres".

Complete the sentences below with one of the words from the table on page 85.

1. The bank is really very near here. It's about 200 ... on the left. You can't miss it.
2. David has put on a lot of weight recently. He told me he weighs over 15 ... now.
3. It was one of the hottest summers we've ever had with temperatures over 80° ... for nearly a whole month.
4. The Channel Tunnel is 60 ... from where we live so it takes us a good hour to get there.
5. There's no more milk left? That's funny. I bought two ... yesterday.
6. We are now flying at an altitude of 28,000 ... .
7. Have you seen how tall Rachel's son is? He must be over six ... surely.
8. People say that this is one of the most economical cars you can buy. It can drive over 45 miles to the ... .

II. And what about you?

Can you say in British English how tall you are and how much you weigh? Do you know what size shoes you take?

AT THE HAIRDRESSER'S

UNIT 6

6A

A good place for a chat

Let's listen to some of the things people talk about when they go to the hairdresser's.

Holiday plans

– Did you make any plans for your holiday?
– Yes, we're going to Spain this year, in July.
– Oh, lovely. What part of Spain?
– Málaga. It's very nice there. We've been there before. How about you?
– We're going to Scotland in September.

The wedding

– So the wedding is tomorrow, is it?
– That's right, at 2.30.
– And what are you wearing?
– I'm wearing a new dress. Yellow, with a wide hat.
– Oh, lovely.

Moving house

– We're moving house, you know.
– Oh, really?
– Yes, we've sold our house.
– Oh? Where are you moving to?
– We're going up north, to Yorkshire.
– Oh, I'm sorry. When are you leaving?
– In June.

Leaving school

– How's your son?
– He's fine. He's leaving school this summer.
– Is he really? Doesn't time *fly*? How old is he now?
– He's nearly 18. He *takes* his *driving test* next week.

at the hairdresser's	beim Frisör
chat	Plauderei
move house	umziehen, ein neues Haus beziehen
leave school (left, left)	den Schulbesuch beenden, mit der Schule fertig werden
fly (flew, flown)	fliegen
take a driving test	die Führerscheinprüfung ablegen

Understanding the text. Choose a suitable ending for the statements.

1. In dialogue 1 the phrase "How about you?" (line 7) means:
   a) "How do you feel?"
   b) "What are your holiday plans?"
   c) "Do you know Spain?"
2. In dialogue 2 (line 10) a woman says "So the wedding is tomorrow, is it?". This woman ...
   a) doesn't know that there is a wedding tomorrow.
   b) is not sure if there is a wedding tomorrow.
   c) is well informed about the wedding tomorrow.
3. In dialogue 3 (line 21) the speaker says "I'm sorry". This means ...
   a) she is sad that she can't buy the woman's house.
   b) she is pleased that the woman has sold her house.
   c) she likes the other woman.
4. To be able to take a driving test in England you must be ...
   a) at least 17 years old. b) over 18 years old. c) 21 or older.

Write down the English for the following expressions.

5. Wir waren schon mal dort.
6. Wohin ziehen Sie?
7. Wie die Zeit vergeht!
8. Wir plaudern gerade.

And what about you?

9. How often do you have your hair cut?
10. Would you like to work in a hairdressing salon? Give some reasons for your answer.

H Future forms (I) – the present continuous

Zukunftsformen (I) – die Verlaufsform der Gegenwart

We'**re leaving** school this summer.	Diesen Sommer sind wir mit der Schule fertig.
Where **are** you **moving** to?	Wohin ziehen Sie (ziehst du)?
What **are** you **wearing** at the wedding?	Was ziehen Sie (ziehst du) zu der Hochzeit an?

- Es gibt **mehrere Zukunftsformen** im **Englischen**. Eine der **gebräuchlichsten Formen** ist die **Verlaufsform der Gegenwart**, die bereits im Modul 1A (Seite 11) behandelt wurde.
- Bei dieser Form werden **bereits festgelegte Pläne** oder **Vereinbarungen** ausgedrückt. Dabei erscheint oft eine **Zeitangabe** (*We're going to Scotland in September.*) oder ein **Fragewort der Zeit** (*When are you leaving?)* im Satz, um deutlich zu machen, dass es sich um etwas Zukünftiges – und nicht um etwas Gegenwärtiges – handelt. Diese Form wird oft als ***diary future*** (*diary* = Terminkalender) bezeichnet.

Exercises

I. John wants to play squash with Malcolm next week but Malcolm is too busy. Complete the dialogue using the correct form of the words in brackets. ●●

John:	What about Monday?
Malcolm:	Sorry. On Monday I ... (go) to the cinema with Tracy.
John:	And Tuesday?
Malcolm:	My parents ... (come) to have dinner with us.
John:	I see. And Wednesday?
Malcolm:	Let me see. Oh, yes. On Wednesday I ... (work) late, I'm afraid.
John:	But you must have time on Thursday?
Malcolm:	On Thursday I ... (babysit) for my sister.
John:	Really. Well, what about Friday?
Malcolm:	Oh dear. On Friday Tracy and I ... (drive) to her parents' place.
John:	... (you, come) back on Saturday?
Malcolm:	No, we ... (stay) the whole weekend. Sorry.

II. Talking about other people's plans. Look at the table below and complete the dialogues using the words in brackets. ●●

People	Plan	Leave	Return
Tom	go camping	July 25	July 31
Sally	fly to Spain	July 29	August 12
Peter and Sue	stay at home	---	---
Pam and Rick	visit Pam's sister	August 11	August 18

1. What ... (Tom, do) this summer?
   He ... .
   Really? When ... (he, come back)?
   He ... on ... .
2. ... (Sally, go away)?
   Yes, she is. She ... .
   That sounds nice.
   ... (go away) for long?
   I'm not sure. About ..., I think.
3. ... (Peter and Sue, have, holiday) this year?
   No, ...
   What ... (they, do)?
   They ... .
4. ... (Pam and Rick, do) anything this summer?
   Yes, they ... .
   Really? How long ... (they, stay)?
   Not long. ... , I think.

III. Everyday reactions. Match up the two halves of the mini-dialogues. ●●

1. My son's getting married next month.
2. Beautiful weather, isn't it?
3. How's work?
4. Cup of coffee?
5. Are you going away at all this year?
6. Thanks very much. That's lovely.

a. Not too bad.
b. Yes, to France.
c. You're welcome.
d. Is he really?
e. Oh, yes please.
f. Yes, lovely.

IV. Questions with prepositions at the end. Ask for the missing information. Use the question word in brackets. ●●

Example:
We are moving to .?. after Christmas. (where?)
Where are you moving to?

1. I was listening to .?. when you phoned. (what?)
2. I wrote a letter to .?. last week. (who?)
3. He paid for .?. while we were on holiday. (what?)
4. She's interested in .?. . (what?)
5. He's a member of the .?. club. (which?)
6. He ran away from .?. . (who?)

Now translate your sentences into German.

V. Complete the dialogue using a correct form of the words in brackets. If there is no bracket, think of the word yourself. (Sometimes more than one answer is possible.) ●●

– Hello. This is Jane speaking. I ... (like) to make an appointment with Charlotte, please.
– Yes, of course. When ... (you, want) to come?
– Tomorrow afternoon. ... (that, be) possible?
– Let me see. How about 2.30?
– 2.30. That ... (sound) fine.
– Sorry but I ... (not, catch) your name.
– Jane.
– Jane. ... (we, have got) your phone number?
– I think so. It's 512850.
– Thanks. And is it a wash, cut and dry?
– That's right.
– OK. Tomorrow ... 2.30. Thanks for ... (call). Bye now.
– Thanks very much. Bye.

6B

How would you like it?

In this module we find out more about what happens when people go to the hairdresser's.

Lee cuts men's hair, not women's. He has got an old-fashioned *barber shop* because he thinks that a lot of men prefer to have their hair cut (and their *beard trimmed*) in a shop where there are no women. Also men don't usually have their hair cut as often as women. "Some of my *customers* come *once a month*," says Lee. "Some of them come more often, say, *twice a month*."

'Blades' is a hairdressing salon where *both* men and women can have their hair cut. Here are some bits of conversation from the salon.

– How would you like your hair cut today?
– I'd like about *half an inch off*, but nothing off the *fringe*, please.
– So just a *tidy-up* really?
– Yes.

– Would you like it *turned up*, or would you like it *going under*?
– The top and sides under, please, but the back up.

– Do you have the *clippers*?
– Yes, all right.

– Do you have *grade* 1 or 2?
– Number 2, please.
– There you are. How's that?
– Yes. I really like it.
– Would you like some spray?
– Yes, please. Hmm. I think it really *suits* me.
– Here we are. Do you like it?
– I'm not sure. What do you think?
– I think it looks really good.
– Yes, I think I agree. Thank you very much. That's for you.
– Thank you very much.

Dee, the *owner* of 'Blades', talks about the *tools* he needs to do his job: *scissors*, *brushes*, *comb*, *clips* and *dryer*. He also has different types of shampoo for different types of hair, conditioner to *give body and shine* and various types of hair sprays and gels to *finish off*. And what about *tipping*? Dee has this to say: "*Clients* usually give a tip to their hair stylist, but unfortunately not always."

barber('s) shop	Herrenfrisörsalon
beard	Bart
trim	trimmen, stutzen
customer	Kunde, Kundin
once/twice a month	einmal/zweimal monatlich
both	sowohl ... als auch ...
half an inch off	um einen halben Zoll kürzen
fringe	*hier*: Ponyfransen
tidy-up, *n*	*hier*: „Säuberungsschnitt" um die Fasson wiederherzustellen, Fassonieren
turn up	*hier*: nach oben kämmen, ausrichten
go under	*hier*: nach unten kämmen, ausrichten
clipper	Schneidevorsatz (verschiedener Schnittlängen) für die Haarschneidemaschine
grade	Grad, Stufe; *hier*: Schnittlänge
suit sb	jmdm. stehen
owner	Besitzer(in)
tool	Werkzeug
scissors	Schere (*auch: a pair of ..., some ...*)
brush	Bürste
comb	Kamm
clip	(Haar-)Klammer
dryer	(Haar-)Trockner, Föhn
give body and shine	(*dem Haar*) Festigkeit und Glanz geben
finish off	beenden, letzte Hand anlegen
tip sb	jmdm. ein Trinkgeld geben
client	Klient(in), Kunde, Kundin

Dee talks about the tools he needs

Understanding the text. Which ending (a–c) is the most appropriate?

1. A "barber" is not the same as a "hairdressing salon" because a barber ...
   a) is cheaper. b) is only for men. c) is only located in the country.
2. An "inch" is about ...
   a) 1 cm. b) 2 cm. c) 4 cm.
3. Somebody who uses clippers probably has ...
   a) long hair. b) short hair. c) dry hair.
4. The expression "There you are" (line 21) means ...
   a) "I've finished cutting your hair."
   b) "Have a look at what I've done."
   c) "I want to go home now."
5. When the woman says "That's for you" (line 28) she ...
   a) gives the hairdresser some money.
   b) gives the hairdresser something to eat.
   c) gives the hairdresser something to read.
6. At the hairdresser's a natural response to the question "How would you like it?" is ...
   a) "Not too short, please."
   b) "Oh, it's fantastic."
   c) "Milk but no sugar, please."

7. At the hairdresser's a natural response to the question "How do you like it?" is ...
   a) "One inch all round, please."
   b) "That's lovely. Thank you."
   c) "Black but not too strong."

Find the English for the following expressions.

8. Es steht mir gut.
9. Es sieht gut aus.
10. Ich bin Ihrer Meinung.

And what about you?

11. Do you feel comfortable in a hairdressing salon where there are both men and women or do you prefer places for men only or women only? Why?
12. How do you feel about tipping at a hairdressing salon?

H to have + object + past participle

lassen, veranlassen

I'd like **to have my hair cut**.	Ich möchte mir die Haare schneiden lassen.
We didn't **have the room painted**.	Wir ließen das Zimmer nicht streichen.
Have you **had the photographs developed**?	Haben Sie (Hast du) die Fotos entwickeln lassen?

- Wenn man eine Handlung von anderen ausführen lässt, verwendet man oft die sogenannte ***have-something-done***-Konstruktion, d.h. ***to have*** **+ Objekt + Partizip Perfekt**.
- **Fragen** werden in der **einfachen Gegenwart** und **Vergangenheit** mit ***do*** gebildet (*Did she have her hair cut?*), zur **Verneinung** verwendet man ***not*** (*He didn't have his beard trimmed.*).
- Außerdem kann man die *have-something-done*-Konstruktion in **allen anderen Zeitformen** und in der **Verlaufsform** gebrauchen (*She hasn't had her hair cut. We're having the room painted.*).

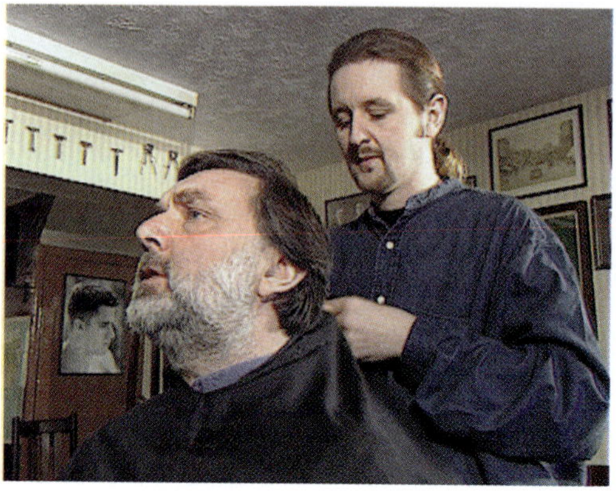

Lee in his barber's shop

Exercises

I. Answer the questions in the way shown in brackets using the have-something-done structure.

Example:
Did you build that cupboard yourself? (No, I ...)
No, I had it built.

1. Did they paint the room themselves? (No, they ... .)
2. Did you cut the trees down by yourselves? (No, we ... .)
3. Did your brother repair his bike himself? (No, he ... .)
4. Did your father cut his hair himself? (No, he ... .)
5. Did your boyfriend take that photo? (No, I ... .)
6. Did you clean that carpet yourself? (No, I ... .)

II. Rewrite the sentences using the have-something-done-structure.

Example:
A friend repaired our car for us.
We had our car repaired.

1. Mike painted our house for us.
2. Someone repaired my jacket for me.
3. Joan's cutting my hair next week.
4. Joe took the photos for them.
5. The company posted the tickets to us.
6. Craig has recorded the programme for me.

H Uncountable nouns

Nicht-zählbare Substantive

◆ Abweichend vom Deutschen sind **einige Substantive** im Englischen **nicht zählbar**. Sie haben **keine Pluralform** und das entsprechende **Verb** bleibt **im Singular**:

English **furniture** is expensive.	Englische Möbel sind teuer.
Her **knowledge** of English is excellent.	Ihre Englischkenntnisse sind hervorragend.

◆ Sie können **nicht** mit dem **unbestimmten Artikel** oder **Zahlwörtern** verbunden werden. Das kleine Wort ***some*** jedoch wird oft mit solchen Substantiven verwendet:

Could I have **some information** about trains to London, please?	Könnte ich bitte Auskunft über Züge nach London haben?
Would you give me **some advice** about where to have my hair cut?	Würden Sie (Würdest du) mir einen Rat geben, wo ich mir die Haare schneiden lassen soll?

◆ Das Hinzufügen von ***a piece of*** oder ***a bit of*** ist in den meisten Fällen aber möglich:

That was **a** difficult **piece of homework**, wasn't it?	Das war eine schwierige Hausaufgabe, oder?
Would you like **a bit of chewing gum**?	Möchten Sie (Möchtest du) einen Kaugummi?

◆ Einige Substantive werden, obwohl sie mit ***-s*** enden, als eine **Einheit** verstanden. Das **Verb** steht deshalb immer **im Singular**:

Here **is** the early evening **news** from the BBC.	Hier sind die Abendnachrichten der BBC.
The United States has won ten gold medals.	Die Vereinigten Staaten haben zehn Goldmedallien gewonnen.

◆ **Gegenstände**, die aus **zwei Teilen** bestehen, werden als **Mehrzahl** aufgefasst und verlangen die **Pluralform des Verbs**:

Where **are** my **scissors**?	Wo ist meine Schere?
These **are** my new **headphones**.	Dies ist mein neuer Kopfhörer.

III. Complete these sentences by using "are", "is", "do", "does", "have" or "has". ●●

1. ... the United Nations have its headquarters in New York?
2. Here ... the news from the BBC World Service.
3. All the important data ... on the hard disk.
4. The United States ... one of the richest countries in the world.
5. Do you know where my new trousers ... ?
6. Our new furniture ... from Italy.

IV. Translate into English. Use a dictionary if you need one. ●●

1. Hast du ein Fernglas?
2. Ich brauche eine neue Brille.
3. Die Schere geht nicht. (*to work*)
4. Ist das deine Kleidung in diesem Schrank?
5. Hast du diesen neuen Kopfhörer gesehen?
6. Die Nachricht kam zu spät.

6C

Pål Reynolds – hairdresser and designer

Listen carefully to Pål Reynolds talking about his work. Then answer the questions on page 99.

Pål works on a retail stand

I. What does Pål do? Tick the three sentences which apply to him.

a) He runs a hairdressing salon.
b) He repairs cars.
c) He designs furniture.
d) He holds seminars in chemical companies.
e) He advises banks.
f) He organizes photographic sessions.
g) He buys and sells houses and flats.

II. How would you describe Pål Reynolds? Choose one of the following sentences (a – d). Pål is a man ...

a) who would like to be famous.
b) who has lots of energy.
c) who wants to earn a lot of money.
d) who is bored with his job.

III. Pål Reynolds thinks there are two reasons why he has been so successful. Which two are they? Choose one answer (a – e) from below.

a) good luck and a good education
b) training and hard work
c) good public relations and interesting work
d) hard work and a variety of work
e) cost cutting and well-paid work

IV. Word families. Complete the table and use five of the words in the correct form in the sentences below.

	Verb	Noun
1.	differ	...
2.	...	satisfaction
3.	...	success
4.	invite	...
5.	...	plan
6.	prefer	...
7.	converse	...
8.	...	treatment

9. You get a sense of ... if you ... in your exams.
10. Did you get an ... to the party?
11. I'd like to practise my English ... .
12. Is there a ... between American and British English?

6D

Meterman at the hairdresser's

I. Use the verbs in brackets in an appropriate form to complete the text. Put any other words in the brackets in their correct position. If there is no word in a bracket after a gap, think of one yourself.

"Oh hello. You've just caught me in the act. I ... (just, look) at my reflection in the window. I ... (decide) I need a haircut."

"I always come here you know. This is a His and Hers hairdresser's. This is where I go. This is the His side. And this is Hers. Now what I ... (not, understand) is the difference in prices. It's far more expensive for ladies. Perhaps the service is better. Still I ... (always, want) to try the ladies' side. And perhaps today I ...!"

Receptionist:	Yes, sir, how can I help you?
Meterman:	Yes. Good morning. I ... (like) a dry cut, a *blow dry*, and a cut and blow dry and a shampoo and *set*.
Receptionist:	... (you, have) an appointment?
Meterman:	Of course not! I am known here.
Receptionist:	Yes, sir. Chris is available now. ... (you, like) to come through? This way to the gents, sir. This way.
Meterman:	If you ... (not, mind) I'd like to try the ladies' today.
Receptionist:	I think you'd be more comfortable in the gents. This way.
Meterman:	Equality of the sexes. We ... (not, want) any discrimination now my dear, ... we?
Receptionist:	Well, sir, if you insist! Then follow me. Lisa. I ... (have) a gentleman client for you.
Lisa:	Right. What can we do for you?
Meterman:	My dear. I would like the works! (That's one of our little sayings.) The works.

blow dry, *n/v*	(das) Föhnen; föhnen (*Haare*)
set, *n/v* (set, set)	*hier*: (das) Legen; legen (*Haare*)

II. Complete the sentences 1–5 by choosing one of the alternatives a–c.

1. The expression "you've just caught me in the act" means ...
   a) you saw me doing something funny.
   b) you saw me doing something I shouldn't really do.
   c) you saw me doing something embarrassing.

2. A "His and Hers Hairdresser" is ...
   a) a hairdresser's with one room for men and one room for women.
   b) one hairdressing salon for men and women.
   c) a hairdresssing salon with hairdressers who are male and female.
3. A "dry cut" means ...
   a) your hair is cut outside when it is sunny and warm.
   b) your hair is cut with dry scissors.
   c) your hair is cut when your hair is dry.
4. The expression "equality of the sexes" means that ...
   a) men and women are the same.
   b) men and women should be treated in the same way.
   c) men and women should have the same rights.
5. The expression "I would like the works" means ...
   a) "I would like everything."
   b) "I would like everything that works."
   c) "I would like the best you can do."

III. Make it sound English. Rewrite the sentences using apostrophes.

Example: shoes for men: men's shoes
a hat for a woman: a woman's hat

1. a bike for a boy
2. shoes for women
3. a toy for children
4. a jumper for a man
5. clothes for girls
6. a book for teachers

6E

Hair

If you're a man and you want an old fashioned haircut use your eyes and look for the barber's pole. It's a red and white pole. The red and white are symbolic. In the old days barbers didn't only cut your hair and trim your beard. They also shaved and even used to do the job of a *surgeon*. The red and white pole symbolized the blood and the bandages of the surgeon.

If there's no pole use your eyes and look for the window displays. You can learn a lot from the *window displays* – the hours of business, the products, the style of the salon.

Explaining what you want is sometimes a problem, but use your eyes: most salons have photographic displays to help you and many salons have style books with photographs.

Perhaps you are looking for something completely different? Use your eyes. Here is somewhere you can go to change the way you look almost completely. It's a *wig* shop! Why not go in and try on a wig?

surgeon	Chirurg
window display	Schaufensterdekoration
wig	Perücke

Match the idioms (1–4) with the meanings (a–d).

1. Keep your hair on.
2. Let your hair down.
3. Get out of my hair.
4. There's not a hair out of place.

a. Very neat and tidy.
b. Stop annoying me.
c. Relax and enjoy yourself.
d. Don't be so angry.

SPORT IN WINTER

UNIT 7

7A

Indoor and outdoor activities

Let's see what people talk about while they are doing sport and other outdoor activities.

Squash

Man: 9-4. That's my *game*, isn't it?
Woman: Yes.
Man: Let's *have a break*.
Woman: Good idea.
Woman: Have a drink.
Man: Great, thanks. Would you like one of these?
Woman: Er ... no thanks. Not just now. That was a good game, wasn't it?
Man: It certainly was. Your *backhand*'s improved, hasn't it?
Woman: Thanks. It's getting better. You wait till next time.

Cycling

1 Man: Let's have a rest.
2 Man: Good idea. We're nearly there, aren't we?

Cycling down a country lane

1 Man: Yes, it's not far now. Have a banana.
2 Man: OK, thanks.
1 Man: Would you like a banana?
3 Man: No, thanks. Not for me.
2 Man: Would you like a drink?
1 Man: Yes, please. (Handing back the bottle:) Thanks.
2 Man: Would you like a drink?
3 Man: Oh, thanks very much.

Using a map and binoculars to check where you are

Walking

1 Man: We're here, aren't we?
Woman: Yes, I see. Mmm. That's right. That's Shipbourne Forest over there, isn't it?
1 Man: And this is Wilmott Hill. We've walked about 8 miles, I think.
Woman: That's right. (To 2 man:) Have a sandwich.
2 Man: Oh, yes please.
Woman: (To 1 Man:) Sandwich?
1 Man: No, thanks. Not for me.
2 Man: (To woman:) *Would you like a go* – with the *binoculars*?
Woman: Oh yes. Thanks. (To 1 Man:) Do you want a go?
1 Man: Oh, yes please.

game	Spiel	Would you like a go?	Willst du (Wollen Sie) es einmal versuchen? (*hier*: durchsehen)
have a break	eine Pause machen		
backhand	Rückhand		
walking	(das) Wandern	binoculars	Fernglas

Understanding the text. Identify the right ending (a–c) for the statements.

1. The man in the squash court says, "That's my game" (line 5). This means ...
   a) he has made up new rules for the game.
   b) he has won the game.
   c) he has paid for the game.
2. "Your backhand has improved" (line 12) means ...
   a) your hand doesn't hurt any more.
   b) you are hitting the ball too hard.
   c) one of your strokes (*Schläge*) is better than it was.
3. When the woman says, "You wait till next time" (line 13) she means ...
   a) that her game will be better next time.
   b) that next time she's going to beat the man.
   c) that he should wait until she comes back for another game.
4. Eight miles (line 29) is about the same distance as ...
   a) 3 kilometres. b) 13 kilometres. c) 30 kilometres.
5. The man who is walking says, "Would you like a go with the binoculars?" (line 34). This means the same as:
   a) Would you like to take them and carry them?
   b) Would you like to see if they work?
   c) Would you like to look through them?

And what about you?

6. Which of the three sports - squash, cycling, walking - do you like best? Why?
7. Which other sports do you do in winter?
8. Do you like team sports or do you prefer individual sports? Why?

H Question tags

Frageanhängsel

Your backhand has improved, **hasn't it**?	Deine Rückhand hat sich verbessert, nicht wahr?
We're here, **aren't we**?	Wir sind da, oder?
You don't like cycling, **do you**?	Du fährst nicht gerne Fahrrad, oder?

- Es gibt im Englischen keine direkte Entsprechung für das deutsche „nicht wahr?", „oder?" und „nicht?" am Ende eines Satzes. Die **Form des Frageanhängsels** im Englischen (***question tag***) richtet sich nach dem Verb bzw. den Verben des vorausgehenden Satzes:
  - Das Verb ***to be*** und die **Hilfsverben** werden im *question tag* **wieder aufgenommen** (*She isn't right, is she? He's got a new bike, hasn't he? She can drive, can't she?*).
  - Steht im vorausgehenden Satz ein **Vollverb**, wird für das Frageanhängsel die entsprechende Form von ***do*** gewählt (*You play squash, don't you?*). Eine Form von ***do*** im *question tag* haben ferner die Verben ***to have to*** („müssen") und ***used to*** („pflegte zu"): *He has to improve his backhand, doesn't he? They used to play squash once a week, didn't they?*
- Auf einen bejahten Satz folgt in der Regel ein **verneinter** *question tag*, auf einen verneinten ein **bejahter** *question tag*.

Let's begin, **shall we**?	Sollen wir anfangen?
Have a seat, **will you**?	Nehmen Sie doch Platz.
I'm a bit fat, **aren't I**?	Ich bin etwas dick, oder?

- Es gibt einige **Ausnahmen** in der Form des Frageanhängsels. Nach dem Ausdruck ***"Let's ..."*** folgt ***"shall we?"***. Nach **Aufforderungen** und **Befehlen (Imperativ**) verwendet man ***"will you?"***. Statt *"am I not?"* sagt man ***"aren't I?"***.

Exercises

I. These statements are positive. Add the negative tags.

1. He plays squash well, ...?
2. That's Shipbourne Forest, ...?
3. We're nearly there, ...?
4. They enjoyed the game, ...?
5. She has always enjoyed walking, ...?
6. You are here tomorrow, ...?

II. These statements are negative. Add the positive tags.

1. They don't exercise regularly, ...?
2. You wouldn't go for a ride at night, ...?
3. It isn't far, ...?
4. She hasn't seen it before, ...?
5. You didn't ring earlier, ...?
6. We weren't sitting here last week, ...?

III. These sentences are both positive and negative. Add the appropriate tags.

1. John's father is from Germany, ...?
2. You weren't listening, ...?
3. You can ride a bike, ...?
4. You haven't got the time, ...?
5. Jackie might be able to help them, ...?
6. You eat onions, ...?

IV. These sentences are more difficult. Try them.

1. You don't have to get up early, ...?
2. I'm a bit overweight, ...?
3. Let's take a rest, ...?
4. You've got a mountain bike, ...?
5. They used to play football, ...?
6. We never have breakfast during the week, ...?

H Short answers

Kurzantworten

Are you from Germany? Kommen Sie (Kommst du) aus Deutschland?	Yes, I **am**. Ja.
Can you speak English? Können Sie (Kannst du) Englisch?	Yes, I **can**. Ja.
Do you come here often? Kommen Sie (Kommst du) oft hierher?	No, I **don't**. Nein.

- Da die bloße Antwort *"Yes"* oder *"No"* im Englischen oft als zu knapp und damit als unfreundlich empfunden wird, verwendet man gerne Kurzantworten mit einer Verbform. Bei der **Wahl der Verbform** gelten **dieselben Regeln** wie für **Frageanhängsel**.
- Zu beachten: Bei ***to be*** steht nur in **verneinten** Kurzantworten die **Kurzform** *(Are these your binoculars? – Yes, they are. / No, they're not. Or: No, they aren't.).*

V. Complete the short answers. The first word has been given. ●●

1.	Is he from Germany?	No, ...
2.	Can you speak English?	Yes, ...
3.	Would you like a drink?	Yes, ...
4.	Does she smoke?	No, ...
5.	Have they been here often?	No, ...
6.	Are you leaving soon?	Yes, ...
7.	Were you talking to me?	Yes, ...
8.	Didn't you see us?	Yes, ...
9.	May she come with us?	No, ...
10.	Will he be here later?	No, ...

VI. Fill in the gaps. Use the word "team(s)", "game(s)" or a form of the word "play".

Example:
Shall we ... this new ... ? It's called 'Labyrinth'.
Shall we play this new game? It's called 'Labyrinth'.

1. Every August the two village ... play their annual ... against each other.
2. Did you hear the result of yesterday's rugby ... ?

3. Do you know where the next Olympic ... are?
4. The first goal was scored in the second minute of the ... .
5. As it was raining the children had to stay indoors and ... .
6. Graf leads by two ... to one in the second set.
7. Can you believe Meterman wanted ... squash against a professional?

7B

How did the game go?

In this module three groups of people talk about what happened during the games they were watching or playing.

On the football pitch

John Warren does *football coaching* with children every Saturday morning. Normally the boys and girls play on one of the pitches but because of the snow they are having a game in the *playground* today.

John, a father of one of the children, doesn't coach because he has to. He enjoys working with the kids. He thinks Saturday morning football is important because during normal school there isn't enough time for sports.

Mike, who is also a *parent*, explains what happened during the game: "The Blues won by 4 *goals* to 1. The Reds scored first and then the goalkeeper *saved a shot* by the Blues. The Reds were doing really well at first, then the Blues woke up and scored three goals one after another. The Reds couldn't stop them. The score was 3–1 at half-time. In the second half the Blues scored again making the *final score* 4–1."

Saturday morning football

On the tennis court

1 Woman: I play here every week *even* in winter. There's a tennis coach and you can have lessons. The lessons cost £5 an hour. *That's good value.*

2 Woman: I *joined* the club three years ago. I play every Thursday. There's a group of us and we come regularly. It's great fun. We enjoy ourselves.

(A third woman joins them.)

3 Woman: Hi.
1 Woman: Hi.
2 Woman: Hi.
3 Woman: Well? How was your game?
2 Woman: Great.
3 Woman: Did you beat her?
2 Woman: No, Janice beat me.
1 Woman: But it was very *close*. You were playing very well. You were *serving* brilliantly.
2 Woman: Well, not at first. I served four double faults in the first game! She won the first *set* 6 games to 4, wasn't it?
2 Woman: That's right. I lost the second set 5 games to 7. In the third set I think I lost my concentration. I hit a ball right out of the court and we couldn't find it anywhere. I was playing really badly then. Janice won the third set. 6–3, wasn't it?
1 Woman: Yes.
3 Woman: Wasn't it cold?
2 Woman: It was quite cold. But we enjoyed it anyway.
3 Woman: Well, *it's my turn now. See you later.*
1/2 Women: Good luck!

At the ice hockey rink

The Medway Bears are *playing* the Bracknell Bees.

1 *Supporter*: I *support* the Medway Bears. I come to all their *matches*. We all do. Matches are good fun because of the atmosphere, the excitement, it's very *colourful*.
2 Supporter: There's a lot of noise, isn't there?
3 Supporter: It's *a good night out*. I enjoy it. Everyone does.

One of the supporters describes the game which she has just watched. "The Bears were playing the Bracknell Bees. The Bears weren't playing very well at first.

The Medway Bears supporters talk about the game

The other team were keeping the puck down their end. After about ten minutes things changed and the Bears scored three goals very quickly. After that the other side were in trouble. They didn't score at all in the second period. In the third period the Bears got four goals and the other side got two. The Bears were playing brilliantly. The *final total* was quite close; 7 goals to 6." After the game the supporters were celebrating: "Go Bears!"

pitch	Platz, Feld
football coaching	Fußballtraining
playground	(Kinder)Spielplatz
parent	Elternteil (Mutter od. Vater)
goal	Tor
save a shot	einen Torschuss halten, verhindern
final score	Endergebnis
even	selbst, sogar
that's good value	das ist es wert
join	*hier*: bei-, eintreten
close	*hier*: eng, knapp
serve	*hier*: aufschlagen
set	Satz (beim Tennis)
it's my turn now	ich bin jetzt dran, an der Reihe
see you later	bis später
rink	(Kunst-)Eislaufbahn
play sb	gegen jmdn. spielen
supporter	Anhänger, Fan
support	unterstützen
match	(Wett-, Einzel-) Spiel
colourful	farbig, lebendig, abwechslungsreich
have a good night out	einen schönen Abend verbringen
The other team were keeping the puck down their end.	Die andere Mannschaft hielt den Puck in der gegnerischen Hälfte.
final total	Endergebnis

Understanding the text. Correct any statements that are wrong.

1. John Warren coaches children on Sunday mornings.
2. John coaches children because he enjoys it.
3. The three women play tennis professionally.
4. They only play in summer when it's warm.
5. The group of ice hockey fans who appear in this module all support the same team.
6. These supporters were sad because their team lost.

Match the German expressions with the English ones (a–d). Add the one word which is missing in sentences a–d.

7. Sie hat gut aufgeschlagen, oder?
8. Sie haben das Spiel in der letzten Minute verloren.
9. Sie erzielten drei Tore hintereinander.
10. Sie gewann den dritten Satz 6 : 3.

a. They ... the game in the last minute.
b. She ... the third set, 6–3.
c. She ... very well, didn't she?
d. They ... three goals one after another.

Find the English for the following.

11. Es war knapp.
12. Ich bin jetzt dran.

And what about you?

13. Which kinds of sports do you not do well but enjoy playing?
14. Which sports do you like to watch rather than play?

H The past simple (II) and the past continuous

Die einfache Vergangenheit (II) und ihre Verlaufsform

I **lost** my concentration.	Ich verlor die Konzentration.
You **were playing** well.	Du hast gut gespielt.
The Reds **were doing** really well,	Die Roten haben sehr gut gespielt,
then the Blues **woke up**.	dann sind die Blauen aufgewacht.

◆ Im Modul 3B (Seite 51) wurde zum ersten Mal auf die einfache Form der Vergangenheit hingewiesen, vor allem auf die große Zahl unregelmäßiger Verben im Englischen. Auch im Text 7B kommen einige **unregelmäßige Vergangenheitsformen** vor, und zwar im Zusammenhang mit Sport:

infinitive	past tense	past participle
win	won	won
beat	beat	beat
lose	lost	lost
hit	hit	hit
get	got	got

◆ Es gibt auch eine **Verlaufsform der Vergangenheit** (***past continuous***). Diese Form betont, dass ein Vorgang in der Vergangenheit **längere Zeit angedauert** hat. Die **Verlaufsform** wird **häufig zusammen** mit der **einfachen Form der Vergangenheit** gebraucht. Die Verlaufsform drückt aus, dass eine Handlung bereits ablief („Hintergrundhandlung“), während eine neue (in der einfachen Vergangenheit) eintrat.

◆ Die **Verlaufsform** wird gebildet durch ***was/were* + -ing Form** des Verbs. Die **Frageform** wird durch das **Umstellen** von ***was/were*** und **Subjekt** gebildet *(Were you playing football?)*. Zur Bildung von **Verneinungen** nimmt man ***not*** *(We were not doing well.)*.

Exercises

I. Look at the list of things Tracy did yesterday. Now write out full sentences and say what she was doing at these times. You will need to add some of your own words, especially prepositions. ●●

Example: Between 7.30 and 8.00 she was taking the dog for a walk.

7.30 – 8.00:	take / dog / walk
8.00 – 8.15:	speak / secretary / tennis club
8.15 – 9.00:	read paper / have breakfast
9.00 – 9.30:	go shopping
9.30 – 10.00:	drive / tennis club
10.00 – 11.30:	have / tennis lesson
12.00 – 12.30:	talk / friends / club
12.30 – 13.00:	drive / sister's house
13.00 – 13.30:	have lunch / sister

II. At quarter past eight last night there was a power failure in Kemsing. What were these people doing at that time? Use the prompts to form sentences. ●●

Example:
Gemma / do / homework
Gemma was doing her homework.

1. Gregory / sit / bath / read / paper
2. Kate and her sister / watch / an American soap on TV
3. Jonathan / write / a letter / his ex-girlfriend
4. Meterman / repair / car
5. Jackie and her husband / have / argument
6. Rachel / bake / cake
7. Richard / read / children / story
8. Jane / talk / parents / on the phone

III. Fill in the gaps with the past tense forms of the verbs in brackets. You will need only one past continuous form. ●●

The coach for the Reds looks back at the match against the Blues.

"We ... (score) first. We ... (play) really well at first and ... (hit) the posts two times. Unfortunately after ten minutes the Blues ... (wake up) and ... (score) three goals one after the other. We ... (can, not) stop them. The score ... (be) 3–1 at half-time. In the second half the Blues ... (score) again making the final score 4–1."

IV. Mixed grammar passage. Complete the dialogue using the correct form of the words in brackets. (More than one answer is possible.)

1 player: Well, you two. How ... (be) your game?
2 player: Great.
3 player: Good.
1 player: ... (you, beat) her?
2 player: No, she ... (beat) me. But it ... (be) very close. She ... (play) very well. She ... (serve, excellent).
3 player: Well, not at first. I ... (have) a lot of problems in the first few games. You ... (win) the first three quite ... (easy), didn't you?
2 player: Yes, that's right. But I ... (lose) all the rest in the first set. I just ... (can, not) concentrate, I think.
1 player: Never mind. What ... (be) the final score?
3 player: I ... (win) both sets. By the way, when ... (your game, begin)?
1 player: I'm starting soon. ... (you, have) the time?
2 player: Yes, ten to four.
1 player: I'd better ... (go) then. See you later.
3 player: Bye.

V. Do you remember adverbs? Put them into the sentences. ●●

Example:
He doesn't play (bad) for a beginner.
He doesn't play badly for a beginner.

1. Arsenal scored the first goal very (quick).
2. Blackburn had to work (extreme) (hard) in the second half.
3. The teams took the game really (serious).
4. Blackburn's number 9 can head the ball (good), can't he?
5. Are football teams always so (colourful) dressed these days?
6. The names of the goal scorers appeared (automatic) on a big screen.
7. Arsenal (hard) had a chance, did they?
8. Would you say Blackburn won (easy)?

H Elliptic "do"

Stellvertretendes "do"

I like football. We all **do**. (= like football)
I come to all the team's matches. They all **do**. (= come to the team's matches)
I enjoy it. Everyone **does**. (= enjoys it)

Um **Wiederholungen** zu **vermeiden** wird ***do, does, did*** verwendet, wenn die **gleiche Person** oder **Sache** gemeint ist. Das **Hilfsverb** übernimmt die **Funktion** eines im vorhergehenden Satz verwendeten **Vollverbs**.

VI. Complete these mini-dialogues by using the elliptic "do/does". ●●

1. I love watching tennis.
   Well, if it's a good game everyone ... .
2. You don't have to wear white, do you?
   No, you don't but most people ... .
3. You have to book a court in advance, I think.
   It's never very busy so only a few ... .
4. She doesn't get enough time for sports.
   No, not as much time as most people ... .
5. They play at the weekends or after work, I believe.
   Yes, most of our friends ... as well.
6. They have lessons every week.
   I ..., too. Don't you?

7C

Tony Pulis – a life dedicated to football

Listen to the interview with Tony Pulis and answer the questions below.

I. Read through the following text. Three sentences in it are wrong. Can you find them?

Tony grew up in Wales and began his football career with Bristol Rovers when he was 16. After finishing his playing career he became a coach at Bournemouth and ended up being manager there. Then he left football for two years and decided to open up a pub. Now he is manager of Gillingham Football Club.

Gillingham Football Club was in serious financial difficulties until the Chairman invested a lot of money in the club. He sold his house in England and his villa in the south of France and gave all the money to the club. Now, after buying ten new players, the situation is much better. Now the matches are on television every week and the Chairman has become a well-known face throughout Britain. Gillingham are in the top three of the league. If they can finish in the top three, they will gain promotion to the next league.
Tony is optimistic for the future of the club and is working hard to maintain the success the club has had so far in the season.

dedicate widmen

II. Look at the underlined expressions in these sentences. What do they mean? Choose from the alternatives below.

1. It was touch and go whether the club was going to live on.
2. The gates were down to about 2,500.
3. We've taken great strides to stabilize the club.
4. They're players who have been through the mill.
5. We've got to get on with things.

a. earn a lot
b. It was not certain if
c. We've trained a lot
d. forget disappointments in the past
e. The hooligans pulled down
f. buy new players
g. We've worked hard
h. The numbers of spectators fell to
i. are very experienced

III. Words to do with football. Put the words in the box into the correct form and the right places in the text.

season • promotion • league • club • team • game

If a football ... does well, wins most of its ... and is one of the top three ... at the end of the ... then it will gain ... to the next ... .

7D

Meterman the sportsman

I. In each paragraph some words have been taken out. Which words are they? The first letters have been given.

Meterman drives up to a leisure c... . He speaks to the camera. "Hello there. I'm really glad you've come today because this place is really interesting. There's so much going on here. Now, while I read the m..., you take a look."
We see *facilities* for playing hockey, rugby, squash, tennis and c... . We hear some i... which are sung like a song to music. "Feel the rhythm *turning up the heat*. Change your body!"
Meterman returns. He is very excited. "It's absolutely a... . Hockey. Rugby.

Squash. Tennis. Swimming. Trampoline. Cricket. And Ladies' Aerobics. That sounds very i... ."

Meterman *is off* to join Ladies' Aerobics. He comes back in *tight* t... and still wearing his Meterman cap. He tries to go too fast stepping up and down a stair. The i... calls out: "Slow down! Slow down! Come on, sir! You have to slow down. Up up! Down down!" Meterman tries hard but soon collapses.

Later Meterman is e... a cup of tea by the poolside. "Those ladies were quite good but I don't think they were quite as good as me, do you? Step aerobics isn't quite *my cup of tea*! That's one of our little p... . Not quite my cup of tea. But badminton – that IS my cup of tea."

He is soon having a badminton l... . He actually hits the *shuttlecock* back. "It's a very easy game. You hit the shuttlecock with this simple r... ." He tries to demonstrate but misses the shuttlecock several times. Angrily he smashes his racket on the f... .

Off he goes again. This time he tries the trampoline.

facilities	Einrichtungen, Anlagen	tight	eng
turn up the heat	*hier*: aufheizen	That's not my cup of tea.	Das ist nichts für mich. Das liegt mir nicht.
be off	weggehen, sich davonmachen	shuttlecock	Federball

II. Link the sports (1–8) with the types of equipment (a–h).
Use a dictionary if you want.

Example: 6. squash – e. racket

1. athletics	a. board
2. badminton	b. club
3. golf	c. goggles
4. hockey	d. pistol
5. shooting	e. racket
6. squash	f. shuttlecock
7. surfing	g. spikes
8. swimming	h. stick

7E

Sporting headlines

Look at the following newspaper headlines. Which sports are they referring to? Choose from the box below.

athletics • boxing • cricket • football • golf • horse racing • motor racing • tennis

MUSIC IN MY LIFE

UNIT 8

8A

Different tastes in music

Some students in England were asked about what music means to them.

– Can I ask you a few questions?
– Yes.
– Do you like music?
– Yes, I do like music.
– Why do you like music?
– I like music because I find it relaxes me if I've had a hard day.

– What kind of music do you *play*?
– I play music by bands like Oasis and Blur.

– Do you listen to music much?
– I listen to it quite a lot.
– When do you listen to music?
– Erm ... in the mornings, in the evenings, any time of day really.
– Where do you listen to music?
– I listen to it at home, in people's cars, walking down the street, you know, listening to a walkman.

– Do you play an instrument?
– Yes, I do. I play the electric guitar.
– Which?
– Electric guitar. Lead or rhythm, *depending on* what mood I'm in.
– Is music important to you?
– Yes, music is important to me. *I wouldn't mind being a* professional musician. *If* my other studies here *don't work out*, I can always *fall back on* it.

– What music do you enjoy?
– I enjoy ... er ... the Beatles, Rolling Stones, Small Faces.

– What do you play?
– I play the bass guitar. Music is very important to me. I practise every day.
– Have you got your own guitar?
– Yeah, this is my guitar. It's a good one.

– And what do you play?
– I play the lead guitar. I practise a lot. I really enjoy playing music. We all do.
– And have you got your own guitar?
– Yeah. This is my guitar here. It's a very good one.

– Which instrument do you play?
– I play the *drums*.
– And does this *drum kit* belong to you?
– It belongs to the college.
– Do you have one of your own at home?
– Yes, I do.

– And which instrument do you play?
– I play *percussion*.

– And you play?
– I play the piano and other *keyboard instruments*.
– And who does this piano belong to?
– This piano belongs to the college.
– And what kind of music do you play?
– We play jazz rock but we play most of our own compositions.

play	spielen	drum	Trommel
depending on	je nach(dem)	drum kit	ein Satz von verschiedenen Trommel- oder Schlaginstrumenten
I wouldn't mind doing sth	es würde mir nichts ausmachen ... zu sein, ... zu tun	percussion	Schlag-, Trommelinstrument
if ... doesn't/ don't work out	wenn bei ... nichts herauskommt, die Erwartungen sich nicht erfüllen	keyboard instrument	Tasteninstrument
fall back on (fell, fallen)	zurückgreifen auf		

Understanding the text. Choose a suitable ending (a – c) for these statements.

1. In these short interviews ...
   a) some of the young people say they like music.
   b) most of the young people say they like music.
   c) all of the young people say they like music.
2. The young men in the band play music ...
   a) professionally.
   b) as part of their course at college.
   c) because their parents tell them to.

3. The expression "depending on what mood I'm in" (line 21) means in German ...
   a) abhängig von der Gage, die ich bekomme
   b) je nachdem, in welcher Stimmung ich bin
   c) von Tag zu Tag unterschiedlich
4. The word "studies" (line 24) means ...
   a) the room where you study.
   b) a job you do to earn money for your course.
   c) the course at college you are doing.
5. If you "fall back on" something (line 24) you ...
   a) ask somebody to help you in a difficult situation.
   b) do something because it is an easy thing for you to do (but not necessarily the best thing for you to do).
   c) stop doing something because you don't like it.

And what about you?

6. How important is music to you? Can you say why?
7. What kind of music do you like? Give some examples.
8. Do you play an instrument yourself? (If not, which instrument would you like to play and why?)

H Questions without question words

Entscheidungsfragen

Do you like music? Mögen Sie (Magst du) Musik?	Yes, I do. Very much. Ja, sehr.
Do you play an instrument? Spielen Sie (Spielst du) ein Instrument?	No, I don't unfortunately. Nein, leider nicht.
Do you listen to music much? Hören Sie (Hörst du) oft Musik?	Yes, every day. Ja, jeden Tag.

- Die Hilfsverben ***do***, ***does*** und ***did*** leisten viel Arbeit in der englischen Grammatik. Mit diesen **Hilfsverben** und dem **Infinitiv** können wir sogenannte **Entscheidungsfragen** in der **einfachen Gegenwart** und **Vergangenheit** stellen. Solche Fragen müssen zunächst einmal mit *"Yes"* oder *"No"* beantwortet werden.
- **Ausnahme**: Die Verben ***to be*** und ***to have got*** sowie die **unvollständigen Hilfsverben** (***can***, ***could*** etc.) bilden Fragen **ohne** *do*, *does* und *did* (*Has she got her own guitar?*).

Exercises

I. Put the words into the right order to make questions which begin with "do", "does" or "did". ●●

1. classical – do – like – many – music – people – young
2. a – concert – did – go – last – to – year – you
3. a – at – CDs – do – have – home – lot – of – you
4. a – do – instrument – musical – play – you – yourself

H Questions with question words

Ergänzungsfragen

What type of music do you like? Welche (Art von) Musik mögen Sie (magst du)?	I like jazz. Ich mag Jazz.
Which instruments can you play? Welche Instrumente spielen Sie (spielst du)?	I play the bass guitar. Ich spiele Bassguitarre.
When do you practise? Wann üben Sie (übst du)?	I practise in the evenings. Ich übe abends.

- Mit den **Fragepronomen** ***where*** (wo), ***when*** (wann), ***what*** (welche, was), ***who*** (wen, wem), ***which*** (welche), ***whose*** (wessen), ***why*** (warum) und ***how*** (wie) bilden wir sogenannte **Ergänzungsfragen**, die nicht mit einem einfachen *"Yes"* oder *"No"* beantwortet werden können.
- Zur **Bildung** der **Frage** brauchen wir auch hier die **Hilfsverben** ***do***, ***does*** und ***did***. (Zu den **Ausnahmen** vgl. Seite 123, „Entscheidungsfragen".)

II. Form questions with and without questions words. The answers will help you to choose the correct form. ●●

Example:

you / like / music? Do you like music?	Yes, I do.
1. you / like / music?	Because it relaxes me.
2. you / play / music?	I play music by groups like the Beatles.
3. you / listen to / music / much?	Quite a lot.
4. you / listen to / music?	Any time of the day really.
5. you / play / an instrument?	Yes, the electric guitar.

The students practise in one of the college rooms

6. music / be / important / to you? — Yes, very important.
7. you / music / enjoy? — Oh, the Small Faces, the Stones ...
8. you / have got / own guitar? — Yes, this is mine.

H Subject questions

Subjektfragen

Who plays a musical instrument?	Wer (von euch, von Ihnen) spielt ein Musikinstrument?
What sounds nicer? A saxophone or a violin?	Was klingt schöner? Saxophon oder Geige?
Which of you made that noise?	Wer von euch (Ihnen) hat das Geräusch gemacht?

Wenn nach dem Subjekt gefragt wird, tritt das **Fragewort** an die Stelle des **Subjekts**. Bei diesen sogenannten **Subjektfragen entfällt** die Umschreibung mit ***do/does/did***. Die **Wortstellung** bleibt **SVO** (Subjekt-Verb-Objekt).

III. Make subject questions with the question word "who" or "what". ●●

Example:

Someone phoned. Who phoned?

1. Someone is playing their music very loudly.
2. Something woke him up.
3. Someone gave Simon a guitar for his birthday.
4. Something happened last night.
5. Someone phones Susan every evening.
6. Something fell off the table and broke.
7. Someone said something about Diana.
8. Somebody plays the keyboard really well.

IV. Look at this sentence and answer the questions below.

John saw Kate and Kate saw Tom.

1. Who saw Kate?
2. Who did Kate see?

V. Feelings. Match an adjective to a situation.

angry • bored • disappointed • embarrassed • irritated • lonely • sad

How would you feel if ...

1. it was grey for a month and you never saw the sun?
2. you said something horrible about somebody who was standing behind you?
3. you had no friends at work?
4. you really wanted to go on holiday but you didn't have any money?
5. somebody stole your new car?
6. somebody at a concert talked very loudly during the whole performance?
7. you had English lessons all day for one year?

8B

Students of music ●●

These two young men are studying music technology. They are explaining what the studio equipment can do.

The first student describes the function of the keyboard. "The keyboard," he says, "is used to produce different sounds. It can produce 128 different instruments." When he *plays* a phrase *in* he can change the sounds of the instruments. A vibrophone, for example, can become a brass instrument by just pressing a *button*. "The advantage of the keyboard," the young student explains, "is that you don't have to use real instruments."

The computer is used to *record* the sounds. You can record up to 16 different *channels* or tracks. When you record something it is called an *"event"*. With the software you can *shift* the *pitch* and change the *length* of the note. If a note is too short, you can make it longer. If it is too long, you can make it shorter. You can also change the *volume* or produce a *pitch bend* or modulation.

The second student is sitting at a *mixing desk*. This is used to record music *onto tape*. It's not difficult to *operate*. With the volume *faders* you can make a track louder or *softer*. If a track is too loud, you can make it softer. If it is too soft, you can make it louder.

play sth in	einspielen, aufzeichnen
button	Knopf
record	aufzeichnen, speichern
channel	(elektromagnetischer) Kanal
event	*hier*: Einspielung
shift	verschieben, *hier*: verändern
pitch	Tonhöhe
length	Länge
volume	Lautstärke
pitch bend	Modulation in der Tonhöhe
mixing desk	Mischpult
record onto tape	auf Band aufzeichnen
operate	bedienen
fader	(Lautstärke-)Regler
soft	*hier*: leise

Understanding the text. Which sentence (a–c) completes the following statements best?

1. The keyboard which the student in the programme has in front of him ...
   a) is used to produce different songs.
   b) is a place for the students' car keys.
   c) produces the sounds of different instruments.
2. A "phrase" is another word for ...
   a) a single sound. b) a few notes. c) a CD.
3. The student says a vibrophone can become a brass instrument by just ...
   a) pressing a button. b) turning a switch. c) playing on the keys.
4. The computer is used to ...
   a) record the sounds. b) make the sounds. c) count the sounds.
5. To "shift the pitch of the note" (line 12) means ...
   a) to record it. b) to change it. c) to fix it.

Find words from the text to complete these sentences. Use the correct form. The first letter of each word has been provided.

6. Is there an a... in studying rather than working?
7. If you turn up the v... on a CD player you make the music louder.
8. The different songs on an LP are often called t... .
9. It is not always easy to e... the functions of a machine or instrument to somebody else.
10. In most jobs today you need to know how to o... a computer.

And what about you? Answer the questions in full sentences.

11. Can you imagine studying music? Why/Why not?
12. Would you like to be a professional musician? Give reasons for your answer.

H Passive forms (present, past, present perfect)

Das Passiv

The song	**is**	**recorded**.	(... wird aufgenommen.)
	is being		(... wird gerade aufgenommen.)
	was		(... wurde aufgenommen.)
	was being		(... wurde gerade aufgenommen.)
	has been		(... ist aufgenommen worden.)

- Das **Passiv** wird dann verwendet, wenn betont werden soll, dass mit einer **Person** oder einer **Sache etwas geschieht**. Daher auch die Bezeichnung **„(Er-)Leideform“**.
- Gebildet wird das Passiv mit **einer Form von *to be* + *past participle*** des jeweiligen Hauptverbs.

Exercises

I. How a record is made. Complete the sentences using the verbs in the box in the passive form of the present simple tense. ●●

advertise • design • make • mix • compose • produce • record • rehearse • sell • write

1. The music ... .
2. The lyrics ... .
3. Then the songs ... .
4. Later they ... in a studio.
5. The tracks ... .
6. A master tape ... .
7. At the same time a CD cover ... .
8. The CDs ... .
9. The product ... to record stores.
10. The new release ... in the media.

II. Past and present perfect passive forms. Complete the sentences by adding the past participle of a verb in the box. Be careful, though. There are nine verbs and only six sentences! ●●

ask • build • cancel • find • give • invite • sing • teach • tell

1. Have you ever been ... to sing in front of people?
2. Was the CD ... to you or did you buy it yourself?
3. Our college was ... over 30 years ago.
4. Was music ... to all the pupils at your school?
5. How many people have been ... that they did not pass the test?
6. The lesson was ... because the teacher was ill.

H Passive forms with helping verbs

Passivformen mit unvollständigen Hilfsverben

The music **must be rehearsed** first.	Die Musik muß zuerst geprobt werden.
The text **should be sung** in English.	Der Text sollte in Englisch gesungen werden.
The song **will be recorded** later.	Das Lied wird später aufgenommen werden.

Es gibt auch **Passivformen** mit den **unvollständigen Hilfsverben** (*can, could, must, shall, should, will, would, may, might*). Zur **Bildung** dieser Formen nimmt man das jeweilige **Hilfsverb + *be* + *past participle***.

III. Rewrite these sentences using passive forms with helping verbs. The first words in each sentence have been given. ●●

1. Someone must tell the teachers about the problem.
   The teachers ... .
2. They can't find the tickets anywhere.
   The tickets ... .
3. Students should not eat food in the classrooms.
   Food ... .
4. Somebody might steal your car if you leave it there.
   Your car ... .

5. They could not hold the open-air concert because of the bad weather.
   The open-air concert ... .
6. They will write the exams at the beginning of June.
   The exams ... .

IV. Choose the correct half-sentences (a – h) to complete the statements (1 – 6). ●●

1. Smoking ...
2. Drinks from the bar ...
3. The audience ...
4. Some tickets ...
5. Recording equipment ...
6. During the interval ...

a. must not be taken into the concert hall.
b. has been told not to applaud.
c. will be served in plastic cups.
d. CDs, T-shirts and caps can be bought.
e. is not permitted while the band is playing.
f. will be sold half an hour before the concert begins.

Now try to translate your sentences into German.

V. A quiz. Use a passive form of the verb in your answer.

1. Who composed the opera *Porgy and Bess*?
2. Who sang *Jailhouse Rock*?
3. Who first recorded the song *Help*?
4. Who wrote the *Jupiter Symphony*?
5. Which Shakespeare play is *West Side Story* based on?
6. Which famous Irish singer organized *Live Aid*, a project to help poor people in Africa?

8C

James, Alex and friends – future rockstars?

Listen to the interview with James Cox and answer the questions below.

I. Are these statements true or false?
Tick the appropriate box.

	True	False
1. The band are professional musicians.		
2. They write their own songs.		
3. They practise in their own homes.		
4. They want to play in churches because it doesn't cost anything.		
5. They would like to make their own album one day.		

II. Which word is missing from these sentences? The first letter has been given.

1. To move their equipment from one place to another the band h... a van.
2. James says that you need quite a lot of technical k... to set up the equipment.
3. To get a better sound from one of his drums James has cut a h... in it.
4. The band write their own music but they have a friend who writes the l... .
5. The band wants to r... as much as possible before it performs in p... .
6. The group is working hard and one day would like to get a recording d... with a well-known record company.

James sets up his drum kit

III. Here is a paragraph from the middle of the interview. Which sentence comes naturally after this text? Choose from sentences a-d below.

"I've got my own drum kit which I bought off my cousin a couple of years ago. James plays his own guitar which he bought and he has his own amp as well, and Sally borrows James's bass guitar."

a. We used to play in Alex's front living-room.
b. She doesn't actually have one of her own.
c. I quite actually enjoy doing that sort of thing.
d. We haven't got our own van for transport.

8D

Meterman the music lover

I. Read through the text on page 134. Which of the sentences below summarizes the story best?

a. Meterman thinks he knows a lot about music but shows that he is not at all informed.
b. Meterman tries to make a good impression on some young people but he makes a fool of himself.
c. Meterman wants to become a member of a band but discovers he is not good enough.

"Hello again. I am a great lover of music. I'm always *humming* a tune or singing a song. And I'm also a great romantic, a true romantic – that's me! 'If music be the food of love, play on,' ... as Shakespeare once said.
Of course, I don't like these walkmen. All the young people have walkmen these days. There's one over there now. He's in a world all of his own. If you talk to him he doesn't hear you. Of course, I do like listening to the radio. It's just a matter of finding what I like. Oh, dreadful! Call that music?
Ah well. Here's my next stop. More loud music. Teenagers!
"Good morning. I've come to read the meter. I've come to read the meter. Could you *turn* it *down* a little bit?"
Meterman reads the meter and then becomes interested in the music. He wants to play the drums. If they can do it, so can I, he thinks. But he finds it a little difficult. He tries to drum too quickly and he *ends up* on the carpet, his brown shoes waving in the air.
Meterman walks away. Now that wasn't my cup of tea at all, he says to himself.

hum	summen
turn down	leiser machen
end up	enden, „landen"

II. These sentences mean the same. Which word is missing in each? The first letter and the number of letters have been given.

1. I think I'm getting the h _ _ _ of it.
2. I've g _ _ the knack (*Dreh*) of it.
3. I t _ _ _ _ I've grasped it.
4. I'm slowly beginning to u _ _ _ _ _ _ _ _ _ it.

III. Meterman quotes Shakespeare: "If music be the food of love, play on." What do you think this means? Choose from the alternatives below.

a. If music puts you in the mood for love, then play some more.
b. The more you listen to romantic music, the more you feel like love.
c. If oysters be the food of love, keep swallowing.

8E

Listen to the radio

Look at the radio programme and answer the questions below.

1. On which station will you hear the most pop music – Radio One or Radio Three?
2. On which station will you hear more news – Radio Three or Radio Four?
3. What sort of music will you hear on Radio Three – classical or pop?
4. Which radio station would you listen to if you were a fisherman – Radio One or Radio Four?
5. Which station would you listen to if you were interested in books – Radio Two or Radio Four?
6. Which station would you listen to if you were awake all night – Radio Five or Radio Two?

TODAY'S LISTENING GUIDE

ONE 97.6-99.8MHz **6.30** Chris Evans **9.00** Simon Mayo **12.00** Lisa I'Anson **2.00** Kevin Greening **4.00** Mark Goodier **7.00** Evening Session **9.00** In Concert **10.00** Mark Lamarr **12.00** Claire Sturgess **4.00 - 6.30** Charlie Jordan

TWO 88-91MHz **6.00** Martin Kelner **7.30** Sarah Kennedy **9.30** Ken Bruce **11.30** Jimmy Young **1.30** Debbie Thrower **3.00** Ed Stewart **5.05** John Dunn **7.00** Steve Wright **7.30** Malcolm Laycock **8.30** Big Band **9.00** Humphrey Lyttelton **10.00** On the Air **10.30** Jamesons **12.05** Steve Madden **3.00 - 4.00** Alex Lester

THREE 90.2-92.4MHz **6.00** On Air **9.00** Morning Collection **10.00** Musical Encounters **12.00** Composer of the Week **12.55** Afternoon on Three **1.00** News; Proms Chamber Music 1996 **2.10** Dolly Suite **2.30** BBC Proms **3.10** Interval **3.30** Proms **4.30** Class of 86 **5.00** Music Machine **5.15** In Tune **7.30** BBC Proms **8.25** Takemitsu **8.45** Proms **10.00** Ensemble **10.45** Mixing It **11.30** Composers of the Week **12.30** Jazz Notes **1.00 - 6.00** Through the Night

FOUR FM: 92.4-94.6MHz LW: 198 **6.00** News Briefing **6.10** Farming Today **6.25** Prayer **6.30** Today **8.40** Golf Stories **9.00** News **9.05** Start the Week **10.00** News; Battling with the Past **10.30** Woman's Hour **11.30** Money Box Live **12.00** News; You and Yours **12.25** Brain of Britain 1996 **12.55** Weather **1.00** World at One **1.40** Archers **1.55** Shipping **2.00** News; The Last September **3.00** Afternoon Shift **4.00** News **4.05** Kaleidoscope **4.45** Short Story **5.00** PM **5.50** Shipping **5.55** Weather **6.00** News **6.30** News Quiz **7.00** News **7.05** Archers **7.20** Over the Counter **7.45** Monday Play **9.15** Uncle Mort's Celtic Fringe **9.30** Kaleidoscope **10.00** World Tonight **10.45** Book at Bedtime **11.00** Chain Reaction **11.40** Reading Aloud **12.00** News **12.30** Late Book **12.48** Shipping **1.00** World Service **5.50** Inshore Forecast **5.55 - 6.00** Shipping

FIVE 909, 693kHz **6.00** Breakfast **8.35** Magazine **12.00** Midday **2.05** Ruscoe on Five **4.00** John Inverdale **7.00** News Extra **7.35** Games That Changed Football **8.00** Monday Match **10.05** News Talk **11.00** Night Extra **12.05** Other Side of Midnight **2.05** Up All Night **5.00 - 6.00** Morning Reports

CLASSIC 100-102MHz **6.00** Nick Bailey **9.00** Henry Kelly **12.00**

LE SHUTTLE

UNIT 9

9A

Crossing the Channel

Some British people were asked how they travel across the Channel. Do they take a *ferry* or do they use the Channel Tunnel?

How does this English family cross the Channel?

Mother: We always prefer to go on the ferry. For me it's the real start of the holiday. You can relax, have a meal, walk around.

Father: You can go on the deck and enjoy the view. And you've got the fresh air.

Daughter: You can do some shopping at the duty-free shop.

Son: It's an exciting way to start the holiday. You really feel as if you're going abroad.

Here are some other travellers' comments.

- The Tunnel's much quicker of course.
- I don't like tunnels much but when the sea is rough I *don't* like that *either*.
- I certainly don't enjoy being *seasick*. OK, it's a fine day today but you certainly can't trust the English weather, can you?

- If you *get off to a good start* you could be in the south of France by the evening.
- It isn't *frightening*. It's exciting! You don't feel *as if* you're in a tunnel or under the sea.

What does the family think about going through the Channel Tunnel?

Mother: I wouldn't like to go through the Tunnel because I *suffer from claustrophobia*. I hate being in small spaces.

Father: You don't have time to relax. You can't get a meal so it's not really a break.

Daughter: Well, you don't feel as if you're going to a different country.

Son: Me? *Actually*, I'd really like to try the Shuttle. But (he looks at the rest of his family) ... they don't listen to me!

ferry	Fähre
not ... either	auch nicht
seasick	seekrank
get off to a good start	gut „durchkommen“
frightening	Angst einflößend, entsetzlich
as if	als ob
suffer from	leiden an
claustrophobia	Platzangst
actually	eigentlich

Understanding the text.

One of the endings (a–d) for the three statements is wrong. The others are right. Can you identify the wrong one and mark it with a cross?

1. The English family crosses the Channel on the ferry because ...
   a) it is exciting.
   b) it is quick.
   c) they can do some shopping.
   d) they enjoy the view.
2. The family doesn't take the train through the Channel because ...
   a) the mother hates being in small spaces.
   b) the father can't have something to eat.
   c) the daughter doesn't feel as if she's going abroad.
   d) the son can't smoke.
3. The other travellers also comment on the Channel Tunnel. They say the Tunnel ...
   a) is too expensive.
   b) is exciting.
   c) is good when the weather is bad.
   d) is quick.

Which word from the text is missing? Add it.

4. Sometimes the movement of the sea can make you feel ... . Then all you want to do is get off the ferry.
5. People who don't like small spaces have ... and may not like travelling through the Tunnel.
6. You can't ... the English weather. One day it's rainy, the next it's windy, the next it's sunny.
7. If you go to the top of a mountain on a clear day you will have a wonderful ... .
8. To work ... for a year is a wonderful experience for a young person and a great way to learn a foreign language.

And what about you?

9. Would you prefer to go to England by boat, plane or train? Why?
10. What do you do if you want to have a short break?

H The gerund (I)

Das Gerund (I)

I **hate being** in small spaces.	Ich hasse es, in engen Räumen zu sein.
I **don't like being** seasick.	Ich bin nicht gern seekrank.
I **enjoy having** a meal and **walking** around.	Ich genieße es, etwas zu essen und herumzuspazieren.

- Wenn **ein Verb** einem **anderen Verb** im Englischen **folgt**, verwendet man oft das sogenannte **Gerund**, das die **gleiche Form** wie die **-ing Form des Verbs** hat. Das Gerund ist dabei **Objekt** des Satzes.
- Zu den Verben, auf die üblicherweise ein Gerund folgt, gehören:

to admit (*zugeben*)
to avoid (*vermeiden*)
to consider (*sich überlegen*)
to dislike (*nicht mögen*)
to enjoy (*genießen, Spaß machen*)
to hate (*nicht mögen, hassen*)
to like (*mögen, gerne machen*)
to mind (*etwas dagegen haben*)
to suggest (*vorschlagen*)

Exercises

I. Use the prompts below to complete these mini-dialogues.

Example:
Why don't you like the Tunnel?
(I hate – be – in small spaces)
I hate being in small spaces.

1. Why do people prefer to go on the ferry?
   (They – enjoy – look – at the sea)
2. What are you doing next summer?
   (We – consider – drive – to England)*
3. Why does she never go by plane?
   (She – dislike – fly)
4. Do you use the ferry even in rough weather?
   (Yes – I – not mind – feel – a bit seasick)
5. He wants to cross the Channel by hovercraft.
   (We – suggest – book – early)
6. Are the ferries expensive?
   (Not if you can – avoid – go – during the day)

(* You need the continuous form of the full verb here.)

The Eurostar comes out of the Channel Tunnel

II. Complete these questions in the present tense using the correct forms of the words in brackets. ●●

1. ... (you, like, get up) early?
2. ... (he, enjoy, learn) a foreign language?
3. ... (they, suggest, make) a reservation?
4. ... (you, admit, say) that to them?
5. ... (you, mind, travel) alone?
6. ... (she, avoid, talk) to him?

III. European countries. Complete this table.

	The country is:	The people are:
1.	Spain	the Spanish
2.	Portugal	...
3.	...	the Greeks
4.	Turkey	...
5.	...	the Norwegians
6.	Belgium	...
7.	...	the Dutch
8.	Austria	...

Now try to complete these four sentences in an appropriate way.

9. The Spanish are famous for their ... and their ... .
10. One of my favourite countries in the list above is ... because ... .
11. I've never been to ... but I would like to go there because ... .
12. ... are really ... people. They ... .

IV. Adjectives which end with "-ing". Put an appropriate word from the box into the sentences below. ●●

exciting • worrying • confusing • frustrating • inspiring • depressing

1. It's ... when the telephone doesn't work, isn't it?
2. Do you find classical music ... ?
3. Rainy weather can be very ... .
4. Many people find it ... when they go to an interview for a new job.
5. It's ... when you don't know the results of a medical test.
6. This is a ... instruction. Do you turn this switch to the right or to the left?

V. Words which are said in the same way but spelt differently (homophones). Complete the table below.

1.	break	brake	breɪk
2.	bored	board	bɔ:d
3.	see	...	si:
4.	sail	...	seɪl
5.	war	...	wɔ:
6.	caught	...	kɔ:t
7.	piece	...	pi:s
8.	threw	...	θru:

VI. Schoolboy humour

What did the tomato say to the cucumber?
Let us (= lettuce) get married.

9B

Travelling on Le Shuttle

Mr and Mrs Taylor would like some information about the Channel Tunnel so they go into their local *travel agency*. The travel agent speaks to them.

– Hello. Can I help you?
– Yes, we'd like to make a reservation for the Channel Tunnel. Can you give us some information first?
– Please have a seat. Is it Eurostar or Le Shuttle you're interested in?
– Can you explain which is which?

The man tells Mr and Mrs Taylor that the Eurostar goes direct from London to Paris and Brussels and that if you want to take your car then you use Le Shuttle.
The Taylors want to take their car so they ask if they can make a reservation for Le Shuttle. The man says an *advanced booking* is enough. Normally, as Le Shuttle's slogan says, you just *turn up* and go. Mrs Taylor would like to know more about prices. She is told that the price depends on when you travel; the time of day and the time of year.
The Taylors will be away for two weeks so they have to pay the standard *fare* for the journey. The man asks them how they would like to pay. Mr Taylor replies.

– By card. (Taking one out of his *wallet*:) Do you take this?

Mr and Mrs Taylor buy their tickets for Le Shuttle

– That'll do nicely. Passport control and *customs* are on this side before you go on the train and you have to go through a security check too, of course. (Handing them their ticket:) Here you are. Have a nice holiday!
– Thanks.
– Bye.

A week later Mr and Mrs Taylor are driving down the *motorway*. It's the first day of their holiday. They're going to Dover to catch Le Shuttle. Mr Taylor isn't sure which exit on the motorway he should take so he asks his wife.

– We take Exit 11 from the motorway, don't we?
– No, it's Exit 11a actually. We've just passed Exit 11 so it must be the next one. Here it is.

Before they drive onto the train, the Taylors have to check in. At the check-in point they are asked the following questions.

– Could I just *confirm* you both have your passports with you?
– We have.
– Are you carrying any canisters of *gas*, any *firearms* or any animals?
– No.
– Great. I'll just print your tickets for you now. In here are your *passes for duty-free* and your ticket. (Looking up at a *board*:) The next departure will be *loading* in *approximately* 20 minutes so when I *raise* the *barrier* you can either go left for duty-free and *services* or *straight ahead* and wait for the next train to load. OK, then, have a good trip. Bye-bye.

Mrs Taylor has the last word on Le Shuttle: "If you want to know what it's like, you must try it for yourselves!"

travel agency	Reisebüro
advanced booking	*hier*: die Fahrkarte im Voraus kaufen
turn up	„auftauchen", erscheinen
fare	Fahrpreis
wallet	Brieftasche
customs	Zollabfertigung
motorway	Autobahn
confirm	*hier*: sich vergewissern
gas	Gas
firearms	Feuerwaffen
passes for duty-free	Berechtigungsscheine für den zollfreien Einkauf
board	Anzeigetafel
load	laden, beladen; *hier*: der Zug nimmt die Reisenden mit ihren Autos auf
approximately	ungefähr, etwa
raise	*hier*: aufmachen
barrier	Schranke
services	*hier*: (verschiedene) Gaststätten und Dienstleistungseinrichtungen
straight ahead	geradeaus

Understanding the text.

True or false? Tick the correct box.

	True	False
1. The Taylors are taking the Eurostar train to Europe.		
2. They pay for their tickets by credit card.		
3. They take the wrong turning on the motorway and don't have enough time for the duty-free shop.		

Complete the statements by identifying the correct sentence (a–c).

4. Advanced booking (line 12) means ...
   a) you use a computerized system to book.
   b) you make a reservation.
   c) you buy your ticket before travelling.
5. Le Shuttle's advertising slogan "Turn up and go" (line 13) means ...
   a) you must make a reservation in advance.
   b) advanced booking is only for people on foot.
   c) you can use the train without booking.
6. The fare for the Channel Tunnel trains depends on ...
   a) what time of day and of year you travel.
   b) whether the sea is rough or not.
   c) whether you are alone or in a group.

Further question

7. What do you do when you take Le Shuttle from England to France? Put the following items in the correct order using the numbers 1–7. Start with c.

   a. show passport
   b. go to duty-free shop
   c. make a reservation
   d. pay for ticket
   e. go through a security check
   f. drive to Dover
   g. drive car onto train

Find a word from the text which fits into these sentences. The number of letters is shown by the number of lines.

8. Women keep their money and credit cards in a purse. Men keep them in a _ _ _ _ _ _ .
9. The _ _ _ _ _ on British motorways have numbers so it is easy to know which one you have to take.
10. The time when a train or aeroplane leaves is called the _ _ _ _ _ _ _ _ _ time. The time when it arrives is called the arrival time.

And what about you?

11. Why do you think that a tunnel for trains and not a tunnel for cars was built between England and France?
12. Do you think the Channel Tunnel will bring Great Britain closer to Europe? Give reasons for your answer.

H Helping verbs (III): to have to – must

Hilfsverben (III)

I'm afraid I **must** go.	Ich muss leider gehen.
Must you leave now?	Müssen Sie (Musst du) jetzt gehen?
I **have to** be there before 9 o'clock.	Ich muss vor neun Uhr dort sein.
Did you **have to** say that?	Mussten Sie (Musstest du) das sagen?

- Die Verben ***must*** **+ Infinitiv** und ***to have to*** **+ Infinitiv** kann man im Englischen leicht durcheinander bringen. Für eine **subjektiv empfundene Verpflichtung** verwendet man das Hilfsverb ***must.*** Es hat die Bedeutung „Ich denke, dass es notwendig ist ...“. Wenn der **Zwang von außen** kommt, benutzt man ***to have to***. Dieses Verb hat die Bedeutung „Es ist notwendig, dass ...“.
- Das Verb ***must*** ist ein **unvollständiges Hilfsverb**. Es gibt **kein -s** in der **dritten Person Einzahl**. Die **Frageform** wird durch das **Umstellen** von Subjekt und Verb *(Must you go?)* gebildet. Das Verb ***to have to*** dagegen ist ein **Vollverb**. Die **dritte Person Einzahl** heisst ***has to***. Um **Fragen** zu bilden braucht man ***do/does/did***. Die **Vergangenheitsform** von beiden Verben (***must*** und ***to have to***) lautet ***had to***.
- Bei der **Verneinung** dieser Verben ist Vorsicht geboten. Die Form ***must not*** oder ***mustn't*** heisst **„nicht dürfen“.** Die Form ***don't have to/doesn't have to*** bedeutet dagegen **„nicht müssen/nicht brauchen“**.

Exercises

I. Complete the sentences using "must" or "have to" and the correct verb from the box below. ●●

ask • buy • go • pass • show • take

1. "Before we get on the train we ... through a security check," says Mrs Taylor.
2. "We ... the right exit on the motorway," says Mr Taylor.
3. "I ... some suntan lotion," says Mrs Taylor.
4. "You ... your passports and tickets here," says the woman.
5. "The woman ... us all these questions. It's her job," says Mr Taylor.
6. "We ... to our car now," says Mrs Taylor. "Our train's leaving soon."

II. Complete the questions using a form of the words in brackets. ●●

1. ... (we, have to, book) in advance?
2. ... (he, have to, give) us all that information?
3. ... (you, must, say) that in front of him?
4. ... (they, have to, book) the tickets before they drove down to Dover?
5. ... (they, must, charge) so much money to use Le Shuttle?
6. ... (I, have to, tell) you what time of day I'm travelling?

III. Use "must not"/"mustn't" or "don't have to" to complete the following sentences. ●●

1. You ... book a ticket in advance but you can.
2. You ... take animals with you on the train.
3. You ... pack canisters of gas or firearms in your luggage.
4. You ... go through the duty-free shop. You can go straight to the train if you want.
5. You ... pay by credit card but you may find it more convenient.
6. You ... leave your passports at home. If you do, they won't let you on the train.

IV. Check your comparisons. (Look back at module 3B, page 49, to remind yourself of the forms.) Use the correct form of the word in brackets and add a word if one is not given in brackets. ●●

1. Sometimes information about trains is ... (easy) to get at a local travel agency ... anywhere else.
2. A travel agent can be ... (helpful) and ... (understanding) ... a clerk at a railway station.
3. Over the years Le Shuttle has become just ... popular ... the Eurostar.
4. Which is the ... (quick) way of getting to France?
5. The ... (early) you book, the ... (sure) you can be of getting a seat.
6. If you stay away for ... (long) than two days you have to pay the standard fare.
7. Most British people find it ... (convenient) to pay by credit card ... in cash.
8. Security checks will be ... (thorough) on this side of the Channel ... on the other side.

V. Check your question tags. (Look back at module 7A, page 106, to remind yourself of the forms.) ●●

1. You want to take the Eurostar, ... ?
2. You don't accept credit cards, ... ?
3. You'd like to make a reservation, ... ?
4. You couldn't do me a favour, ... ?
5. You don't know the price of a ticket, ... ?
6. I'm not late, ... ?
7. Open your suitcase, ... ?
8. We'll have to say goodbye now, ... ?

VI. Don't mix up the verbs "bring" ((mit)bringen) *and "take"* ((hin)bringen) *in English. In the following sentences you need to use each verb two times. Complete them using the correct verbs in the correct form.* ●●

1. Do you think you can ... me to the airport on Saturday?
2. Would you ... me a newspaper when you go to the shops, please?
3. ... my glasses, would you. They're on the table in the kitchen.
4. I'm going to ... these letters to the post office. Have you got any post?

VII. Choose one of the words in brackets to form correct sentences. (Look back at module 6B, page 97, to revise the forms.) ●●

1. The clerk gave them (a/some) very good advice.
2. Have you got (any/a) hand luggage?
3. We've got (some/a) good news for you.
4. He had (a /-) very good weather during the crossing.

9C

John Noulton – Head of Eurotunnel's Public Affairs Department

John Noulton talks about the Channel Tunnel. Listen carefully and answer the questions below.

I. John Noulton talks about four things during the interview. Which four are they? Choose from the list (a–f) below.

a. Some of the problems which the engineers had while constructing the Tunnel.
b. The effect of the Channel Tunnel on holidaymakers.
c. Some cultural differences between France and England.

d. The influence of the Channel Tunnel on the future European community.
e. The day the French and British engineers met in the middle under the Channel.
f. The day the Channel Tunnel was officially opened by the Queen and President Mitterrand.

II. Complete these sentences by using a word from the interview. The first letter has been given.

1. One of the most difficult problems for the French and English engineers was how to m... in the middle.
2. The enormous crossover cabins in the Tunnel make it possible for trains to s... from one line to another.
3. The British workers had to work under strict r... : they had to wear breathing equipment and could not drink alcohol or smoke.
4. The French workers had more freedom in the Tunnel. They were even allowed to have w... with their lunch.
5. December 1, 1990 was a memorable day because it was the day of the first u... breakthrough.
6. When the Channel Tunnel was finished many people in Britain were afraid that their splendid i... was over.

III. What does John Noulton personally think of the Channel Tunnel? Choose one of the alternatives in each of the brackets to complete the paragraph.

John Noulton thinks the Channel Tunnel is the (greatest/most expensive) building project of the last (decade/century) in (England/Britain/Europe). He believes it is a (wonderful/dangerous) piece of (infrastructure/information) that will help to (join together/force apart) the European (community/commuters) in the coming years.

Britain and France are linked by a tunnel

9D

Meterman in Dover

I. Twelve words have been taken out of the text. For each gap three alternatives have been given in brackets. Choose the one which is most appropriate.

"Hello. The white cliffs of Dover. Now these cliffs played a very important part in England's ... (future/history/achievements). Well. England used to end there! But not anymore. Not since the Channel Tunnel ... (opened/became official/collapsed). You come with me. Now if you are interested in our island history this is the very best place to come – the White Cliffs Experience in Dover!"

"I love learning about history. I mean look at these primitive *cave men*. *Savages*. Defending themselves against wild ... (tanks/dinosaurs/animals). Covered in blue paint and dressed in – well – I don't know! Looking out to sea. Ready to *fight* the *invader*. More savages I expect!"

(One of the group of sculptures comes to life and frightens Meterman.)

"Oi! I am not a primitive cave man. I am Colin the Celt. A very *ferocious* barbarian."
"Oh, how do you do. I'm Meterman."
"Apart from being a barbarian I also tell people all about ... (Britain/the Channel Tunnel/London). Now, today we're doing all about invasions. Do you want to come?"

"Well. Will it take long? I've got a meter to read, you know!"
"Oh, I should have thought about 2000 ... (seconds!/years!/days!)"

(The clock is *turned back* to 55 *BC*. The Romans are invading. Meterman is unhappy with all the *spears*, etc.)

"I'm off."
"Where are you going?"
"I'm not getting mixed up with this little *lot*!"
"Why not?"
"You Celts can fight your own ... (battles/friends/people). Anyway I know who won and it wasn't us!"

(The clock is turned back to 1066.)

"Come on. We're going to miss the next invasion. It's the French. 1066!"

(Meterman *pretends to be* the Saxon king who dies with an *arrow* in his eye.)

"Why," asks Meterman, "do we always have to ... (say no?/lose?/cook?)"
"Well, here's one we did win," replies Colin the Celt. "Thanks to Queen Elizabeth I. The Spanish Armada 1588."

(The clock turns back to 1805. The battle of Trafalgar. The war with Napoleon.)

"Good. The French again. This time we won."

(Meterman pretends to be the English ... (king/magician/hero), Admiral Nelson. Nelson only had one eye. At an important moment in the battle, Nelson put his telescope to it and said he could see no ... (birds/danger/*lighthouses*) and then, very riskily, *went on to* win the battle.)

"That was Lord Admiral Horatio Nelson," says Meterman,
"No", says Colin the Celt. "It was Admiral Lord Horatio Nelson."
"I'll *turn a blind eye* to that ... (word/comment/song)," says Meterman. "That's one of our little phrases. To turn a blind eye. Now I'd better get out of here before they kill me."

(The sound of a siren.)

"Here we are in *wartime* Dover," says Meterman, "and I am a member of the Home Guard."
"Well, if you're Britain's last line of ... (defence/shopkeepers/metermen), we're in a lot of trouble."
"My dear Colin. Perhaps you would like to go to the *underground air raid shelter*?"

"Oh, that's very kind of you!"
(Meterman watches him go. He picks up a ... (letter/book/noticeboard). It announces: DANGER! UNEXPLODED BOMB! It explodes.)

Meterman comes out from the White Cliffs Experience.

"After all our *struggles* to keep the foreigners off our island we are now encouraging them to ... (invade/sit down/pay more tax). And here come the French again." He shakes hands with the tourists, smiles and *mutters*, "Foreigners!"

cave man	(urzeitlicher) Höhlenmensch	arrow	Pfeil
savage	Wilder	lighthouse	Leuchtturm
fight sb	jmdn. bekämpfen, gegen jmdn. kämpfen	go on to do sth	dazu übergehen, etw. anderes zu tun; etw. als Nächstes tun
invader	Eindringling	turn a blind eye to sth	über etw. hinwegsehen, etw. (bewusst) ignorieren
ferocious	wild, grausam	wartime, *adj*	zu Kriegszeiten, während des Krieges
turn back	zurückdrehen (*Uhr*, *Zeit*)	underground air raid shelter	Luftschutzkeller
BC (= before Christ)	vor Christi Geburt	struggle	Kampf, Mühe, Anstrengung
spear	Speer	mutter	murmeln
lot	Haufen		
pretend to be	vortäuschen, vorgeben zu sein, so tun als ob		

II. Little words and expressions can make a lot of difference to natural speech. Look at the four in the box. Which dialogue do they go into?

Anyway • Let me see • Look • Well

- I need to repair my bike and I haven't got the right tools.
- ..., why don't you let me repair it for you?

- What's your new telephone number?
- ..., I've written it down somewhere.

- So you live in Sevenoaks, do you?
- ..., near Sevenoaks, actually.

- I'm afraid I can't come to your party next week.
- Oh dear. That's a pity.
- ..., thanks for the invitation.

9E

The lion and the cock

Look at the cartoon below. Why is the cock chasing the lion? Who is the lion? Who is the cock?

BED AND BREAKFAST

UNIT 10

10A

Finding somewhere to stay

A young *couple* from France wrote to the Wateringbury Hotel in England to reserve a room there. When they arrived at the hotel, however, they *discovered* that something had gone wrong.

Man: But didn't you get our letter?
Receptionist: I'm afraid not.
Woman: But this is terrible.
Man (to woman): Did you *post the letter*?
Woman: Of course I posted the letter.
Man (to receptionist): Can you suggest anything?
Receptionist: Well, most of the hotels are full this week, like us, but why not try bed and breakfast?

Later that day the French couple went to a tea room. They sat down at a table next to an English couple.

French woman: What are we going to do now? We must find a place.

French man: Don't worry. Have some tea and we'll think of something.

English woman: Excuse me, but why don't you try a bed and breakfast?

French woman: Have you ever stayed at a bed and breakfast?

English woman: Yes, many times.

French woman: How can we find out about bed and breakfasts?

English woman: Why not go along to the tourist information office? They would *probably* give you a *booklet*. Or you could phone from here.

French woman: *I'd prefer to* go there.

At the same time the two men were getting into conversation.

English man: What about trying a bed and breakfast?

French man: Have you ever tried one?

English man: Oh yes, of course. Often.

French man: Is it alright?

English man: Yes, they're fine. If you want to meet English people it's a good idea. The best thing for you to do is to go on to the tourist information office, or why not telephone from here?

French man: *I'd rather* go there.

The couple take the English people's advice and go to the nearest tourist information centre. The woman behind the desk tells them about bed and breakfast.

Receptionist: We have bed and breakfasts in the town and *in the countryside*.

French woman: We'd rather be in the town.

French man: No, we'd prefer to be in the country - a *farmhouse* perhaps.

Receptionist: (*pointing to* a picture of a bed and breakfast in a brochure:) This one is very *popular*. The house is a *converted barn*. I could telephone for you if you like.

French man: Yes, please do.

French woman: (to her husband:) Let's book one night to start with and then if we like it we can stay longer.

couple	(Ehe-)Paar
discover	*hier*: feststellen, herausfinden
post a letter	einen Brief aufgeben
probably	vielleicht, möglicherweise
booklet	Broschüre
I'd (I would) prefer (to do)	ich würde, möchte lieber ...
I'd (I would) rather (do)	ich würde, möchte lieber ...
in the countryside	auf dem Land
farmhouse	Bauernhof
point to	zeigen auf
popular	beliebt
convert	*hier*: umbauen
barn	Scheune

Understanding the text.

Answer the following questions.

1. These seven sentences (a–g) make up the story about the French couple. Put them into the correct order. Start with sentence a.

    a. A French couple arrive at a hotel in England.
    b. They book a room in a bed and breakfast place.
    c. They find out that they don't have a room.
    d. They get some good advice from them.
    e. They go to a tourist information centre.
    f. They meet an English couple.
    g. They go to a tea room to think things over.

Use complete sentences to answer the following questions.

2. Why is the French couple surprised when they arrive at the Wateringbury Hotel?
3. Who speaks to who first in the tea room? Why?
4. What is interesting about the way the young French couple decide where to book a room?

Find an English equivalent in the text for the following German words or expressions.

5. Leider nicht.
6. Können Sie einen Vorschlag machen?
7. Mach dir keine Sorgen.
8. Ich würde lieber hingehen.

And what about you?

9. Why do you think tourists to Britain like bed and breakfasts?
10. Which type of accommodation would you choose for yourself if you were on holiday in England?

H The present perfect simple (II)
Die einfache Form des Perfekts (II)

Have you **ever tried** bed and breakfast?	Haben Sie (Hast du) es schon einmal mit *Bed and Breakfast* (mit einer Frühstückspension) versucht?
We **have just arrived**.	Wir sind gerade angekommen.
I've never been here before.	Ich war noch nie hier.
Have you **told** your wife **yet**?	Haben Sie (Hast du) schon mit Ihrer (deiner) Frau gesprochen?
I **haven't seen** her **yet**.	Ich habe sie noch nicht gesehen.

- Im Modul 4B (Seite 64) wurde das ***Present Perfect*** als eine Form des Verbs vorgestellt, die **eng** mit der **Gegenwart verbunden** ist.
- In diesem Modul sehen wir, dass die **einfache Form** des ***Present Perfect*** oft mit kleinen Wörtern wie ***ever*** (jemals, schon einmal), ***just*** (gerade, eben, bereits), ***never*** (nie), ***not ... yet*** (noch nicht) und ***yet?*** (schon, bereits) vorkommt. Wir nennen diese Wörter **Signalwörter** für das *Present Perfect*. Denken Sie in diesem Zusammenhang an JENNY: Just, Ever, Never, Not ... Yet!

Exercises

I. Have you ever ...? Complete the questions using the present perfect with "ever". ●●

1. ... (you, ever, see) your name in a newspaper?
2. ... (you, ever, be) to Australia?
3. ... (you, ever, meet) a famous person in the street?
4. ... (you, ever, break) an arm or a leg?
5. ... (you, ever, have) a sleepless night in a hotel?
6. ... (you, ever, work) all through the night?
7. ... (you, ever, stay) in hospital for more than a week?
8. ... (you, ever, be involved) in a car accident?

II. Complete the mini-dialogues using the present perfect and "not ... yet" in the answer. ●●

1. What do you think of the new Spielberg film?
   I ... (not yet, see, it).

2. What does his boss say?
   He ... (not yet, speak, to him).
3. How much does it cost?
   We ... (not yet, ask, them).
4. Has he got the job?
   He ... (not yet, receive, an answer).
5. How do you like England?
   We ... (not yet, be to, that many places).
6. Are there any letters for me?
   The post ... (not yet, arrive).
7. Is it OK?
   I don't know. I ... (not yet, taste, it).
8. What did his parents say?
   He ... (not yet, tell, them).

III. Look at the word "just" in these sentences and answer the questions below.

He's **just** arrived so could you ring back in five minutes?
The way he behaved showed what a **just** man he is.
I **just** had a small sandwich for lunch so I'm still hungry.

1. Give three different German words for "just" in these sentences.
2. Think of another English word for "just" in the second and third sentences.

IV. Use four words in the box below to complete these mini-dialogues. ●●

already • never • once • twice • yet

1. Have you ever been to Canada?
   No, I've ... been there, I'm afraid.
2. Have you been to London?
   Yes, I've been there ... : this year and last year.
3. Have you ever had real English tea?
   Yes, I tried it ... but I didn't like it.
4. Have you been through the Channel Tunnel?
   No, I'm afraid I haven't been through it ... .

V. Put these sentences into English. Don't translate word for word. Exercises 1–4 on page 157 will help you. ●●

1. Waren Sie schon einmal in Großbritannien?
2. Wir wollten immer schon nach Irland.
3. Mein Bruder war schon zweimal in Schottland.
4. Ich bin noch nie in einem englischsprachigen Land gewesen.

VI. The expression "Have you tried ... + gerund" (Haben Sie (Hast du) schon versucht ... zu) *or "Why not try ... + gerund"*(Warum versuchen Sie (versuchst du) nicht ... zu) *are often used to give advice. Look at the example below and then use the prompts to give some advice yourself.* ●●

Example:
We can't find anywhere to stay.
(try / ask / at a tourist information centre)
Have you tried asking at a tourist information centre?
Why not try asking at a tourist information centre?

1. What can we do with our suitcases?
(try / leave / them at the railway station for a day)
2. What shall we do if it's raining?
(try / look / around the National Gallery)
3. The taxis are very expensive, aren't they?
(try / go / sightseeing by bus)
4. We don't want to go to restaurants every evening.
(try / have / fish and chips)
5. Do we have to take cash with us all the time?
(try / pay / by credit card)
6. The English are very reserved.
(try / get into / conversation in a pub)

VII. The two expressions "I'd rather + infinitive without to" and "I'd prefer + infinitive with to" have the same meaning (Ich würde, möchte lieber ...). *You use these expressions to say what you want to do in a particular situation. Look at the examples and then form sentences using the prompts. You will need to add some words yourself.*

Example:
Shall we go to the museum this afternoon?
(prefer / go shopping) (rather / go shopping)
I'd prefer to go shopping. I'd rather go shopping.

1. Shall we try bed and breakfast? (rather / stay / hotel)
2. Do you want to go for a walk? (prefer / go / boat trip)
3. Shall we go to a pub? (rather / have / Indian food)
4. How about a swim? (prefer / sit / beach)
5. A game of darts? (rather / play / cards)
6. Shall we go to the cinema? (prefer / go / theatre)

10B

Looking after guests

Jean and John Trasillion offer bed and breakfast at their home in the English countryside.

This is what John says: "We offer bed and breakfast and we always enjoy meeting new guests. We're not a hotel. We're a family home and guests live more as part of the family. We always like to explain things to them. Usually my wife takes them round the house and shows the *facilities* to them."

This is what Jean says to a couple who have just arrived. "This is your room. It's a *twin room*. (Pointing to the *wardrobe*:) You can hang your clothes here. Do ask if there's anything you need. There's a no-smoking *rule* in the bedrooms, oh ... and we'd rather you didn't bring food *upstairs*."

Jean goes on to show the guests the bathroom. "Do *have a* bath or *shower* any time you want," she says. Downstairs she *mentions* breakfast. "Breakfast will be at 8.30 *unless* you'd like it earlier. Would you like a cooked breakfast?"

In the sitting room Jean asks the visitors to *make themselves at home*. Over tea the couples start talking.

Woman: How long have you lived here?
John: Let's see. We've lived here for about eight years now.

John: How far have you come today?
Man: We've come from Norwich. About 150 miles.
John: You live in Norwich?
Woman: That's right. We *used to* live in Nottingham and we moved to Norwich three years ago.

Man: You have a very pretty garden. It looks lovely in the frost. Do you look after it yourselves?

Jean: Yes, it *keeps us busy*. Are you interested in gardening?
Woman: I love it.

John: Before I *retired* I used to teach languages.
Woman: Oh! How many languages do you speak?
John: French and German and a bit of Italian. And you? *Are you a linguist*?
Woman: Not really. I speak a little Spanish.

look after	sich kümmern um
facilities	*hier*: örtliche Gegebenheiten
twin room	Doppelzimmer
wardrobe	Kleiderschrank
rule	Regelung, Bestimmung
upstairs	nach oben
have a shower	duschen
mention	erwähnen, auf ... zu sprechen kommen
unless	es sei denn, falls ... nicht, wenn ... nicht
make oneself at home	es sich gemütlich machen, sich wie zu Hause fühlen
we used to /ju:stə/ live in ...	wir haben früher in ... gelebt, wir lebten früher in ...
keep sb busy	jmdn. in Trab halten, jmdn. (sehr) beschäftigen
retire	in den Ruhestand gehen
a linguist	jmd., der Fremdsprachen lernt bzw. beherrscht
Are you a linguist?	Sprechen Sie irgendwelche Fremdsprachen?

Understanding the text.
Look at these statements and indicate which are true and which are false.

	True	False
1. Guests cannot smoke in their rooms.		
2. Guests must have breakfast in bed.		
3. Baths can only be taken in the morning.		
4. Breakfast is always at 8.30.		
5. Guests can have a cooked breakfast if they want.		

Answer the questions using full sentences.

6. What do the two women in this module have in common?
7. How do you know that John no longer works?

Find the English for the following expressions.

8. ... es sei denn ...
9. Wie lange wohnen Sie schon da?
10. Kümmern Sie sich selbst darum?

And what about you?

11. Why do you think people like John and Jean open their houses for tourists and have a bed and breakfast place?
12. The English couples in this module are very good at "small talk". What in your opinion is "small talk" exactly?

H The present perfect continuous

Die Verlaufsform des Perfekts

How long **have** you **been working** here?	Wie lange arbeiten Sie (arbeitest du) schon hier?
She**'s been waiting** all afternoon.	Sie wartet schon den ganzen Nachmittag.
They **haven't been living** here very long.	Sie wohnen noch nicht sehr lange hier.

- Wie bei der Gegenwart und bei der Vergangenheit gibt es auch beim *Present Perfect* sowohl eine einfache Form als auch eine Verlaufsform. Die **Verlaufsform** des ***Present Perfect*** drückt aus, dass eine **Handlung noch nicht beendet** ist oder **eben erst beendet** wurde.
- Die Verlaufsform des *Present Perfect* wird mit ***have/has*** **+** ***been*** **+ -ing Form** des Verbs gebildet.

Exercises

I. Why ...? Find the reason (a–f) and complete the verb form in the present perfect continuous. ●●

1. Why is he so tired?
2. Why are his hands so dirty?
3. Why hasn't she got any money?
4. Why is the grass wet?
5. Why are you so red in the face?
6. Why are you crying?

a. She ... (shop) all afternoon.
b. I ... (run).
c. He ... (work) all night.
d. It ... (rain) of course!
e. We ... (watch) a very sad film.
f. He ... (repair) his motorbike.

II. In each of these pairs of sentences you need a present perfect simple form and a present perfect continuous form of the verb. Decide which is which and complete the sentences. ●●

to write

1a. He ... three letters today.

1b. She ... letters all morning.

to cycle

2a. ... you ever ... down a mountain?

2b. I'm very hot because I ... .

to talk

3a. I've nearly lost my voice because I ... all afternoon.

3b. They are going to help us. We ... to them.

to repair

4a. He ... his car and it's OK now.

4b. He ... his car today and he'll have to do some more work on it tomorrow.

to learn

5a. She ... French. Now she's learning Spanish.

5b. She ... all week because there's a test on Friday.

H The present perfect with "since" and "for"

Das Perfekt mit "since" und "for"

How long have you **lived** here?	Wie lange wohnen Sie (wohnst du) schon hier?
We**'ve lived** here **for** eight years (**since** July 1990) now.	Wir wohnen jetzt schon seit acht Jahren (seit Juli 1990) hier.

Sehr häufig nimmt man das ***Present Perfect*** (sowohl die **einfache Form** als auch die **Verlaufsform**) in Verbindung mit ***since*** (seit) und ***for*** (seit). Das Wort ***for*** bezeichnet einen **Zeitraum** *(I've been here for three hours.),* das Wort ***since*** dagegen einen **Zeitpunkt** *(I've been here since lunchtime.).* Hier liegt eine Schwierigkeit für Lernende, die Deutsch als Muttersprache haben, da in diesen Fällen im Deutschen meist die Gegenwart verwendet wird (Ich bin seit drei Stunden hier.).

III. A point in time or a period of time? Put in "for" or "since" to complete the sentences. ●●

We have been here
1. ... two months.
2. ... ten minutes.
3. ... August last year.
4. ... we were children.
5. ... yesterday.
6. ... just over three weeks.
7. ... the beginning of the year.
8. ... many years.

IV. Complete the text using the correct form of the words in brackets. If there is no word in brackets, add it yourself. ●●

James Williams was born in Sevenoaks, a small town near London.

He ... (live) there ... he was a child. He ... (work) as a teacher of English ... the last five years. James is well known in Sevenoaks. He ... (be) a member of the local cricket club ... nearly ten years. "I ... (be) mad about cricket ... I was about six years old," he explains. "In fact my wife always tells me that cricket and teaching are, and will always be, my favourite sports."

H The present perfect and the past

Das Perfekt und die Vergangenheit

Im Deutschen macht es häufig keinen Unterschied, ob man sagt „ich ging" oder „ich bin gegangen". Im **Englischen** sind die **beiden Formen** jedoch genau **voneinander abgegrenzt**. Das ***Past Tense*** ist eine **Vergangenheitsform**. Das ***Present Perfect*** ist **eng** mit der **Gegenwart verbunden**. Signalwörter können Ihnen helfen, zwischen diesen Formen zu unterscheiden:

Signalwörter

Past Simple	Present Perfect
• yesterday	• JENNY (just, ever, never, not ... yet)
• last week/month/year	• for (+ Zeitraum)
• ... ago	• since (+ Zeitpunkt)
• when I was a child/younger	• How long ...?
• in 1996	• until now
• When ...?	• so far

V. Complete these three dialogues using the present perfect or the past simple of the verbs in brackets. If there is no word in brackets, put it in yourself. ●●

1. Computers
   - Have you got your own computer?
   - Yes, I have.
   - How long ... you ... (have) it?
   - ... about two years.
   - How much ... it ...?
   - About £400, I think.

2. Homes
   - Do you live in London?
   - Yes, we do.
   - How long ... you ... (live) there?
   - ... 1992.
   - Really? And where ... you ... (live) before that?
   - Oh, we ... (have) a small house in Oxford before.

3. Work
   - ... you ... (work) in a post office long?
   - ... I was 22.
   - So long? And what ... you ... (do) before that?
   - I ... (work) in a travel agency.
   - ... you ... (like) the work?
   - Not very much. That's why I ... (leave).

VI. The expression "used to + infinitive" has one form and can only be used in the past. It describes a past habit (Gewohnheit)*. The sentence "We used to live in Nottingham" means: "In the past we lived in Nottingham but now we live somewhere else."* („Wir lebten früher ...“)*. Look at the example below and rewrite sentences 1–8 with the "used to" construction.* ●●

Example:
He has stopped teaching languages.
He used to teach languages.

1. He has stopped going for a walk twice a day.
2. She has stopped playing tennis regularly.
3. They have stopped going to the pub before noon.
4. She has stopped smoking a packet a day.
5. We have stopped going to bed late.

6. They have stopped travelling to Greece in the summer.
7. He has stopped eating meat every day.
8. She has stopped biting her nails.

VII. Words written in the same way but with different meanings.
Give the German for the words underlined.

1. John and Jean live / lɪv / in Kent.
2. This programme is coming live / laɪv / from Atlanta.
3. I used to / ju:stə / live in the country.
4. I used / ju:zd / a dictionary to do the last exercise.
5. They like / laɪk / living in the country.
6. This book is not like / laɪk / other books.
7. How long does the performance last / lɑ:st /?
8. Are these your last / lɑ:st / exams?
9. The weather is going to be fine / faɪn / today.
10. Oh no! We've got a parking fine / faɪn /.

10C

Lynn Redgrave – the B&B expert

Listen to what Lynn Redgrave, a Tourism Development Officer in Maidstone, says about her work. Then answer the questions below.

I. What has Lynn done since she left school?
Put the following sentences into the correct order (1–5).

a. She got a job with the English Tourist Board.
b. She left school at sixteen.
c. She went to Britain and worked in sales.
d. She went to Switzerland to learn languages.
e. She worked abroad as a tour guide.

II. What is Lynn's job? Tick one sentence which best describes what Lynn does.

a. She writes about bed and breakfast places in newspapers.
b. She checks that the bed and breakfast places are clean.
c. She collects information about bed and breakfast places.
d. She gives advice to tourists about where they can stay.

Lynn sits on board the Captain Webb

III. Lynn mentions two types of unusual bed and breakfast places (B&B) in her interview. Which are they? Tick the right answer.

a. A B&B on the top of a mountain and a B&B in a bus.
b. A B&B on a boat and a B&B with electric cars for guests.
c. A B&B on a boat and a B&B with bikes for the guests.
d. A B&B on an island and a B&B owned by a famous writer.

IV. Lynn talks about her surname "Redgrave". Why is this name such a problem for her? Tick the right answer.

a. Nobody can pronounce or write the name properly.
b. Everybody thinks Lynn is a member of a famous acting family with the same name.
c. Nobody believes that Lynn has that surname.
d. Everybody asks Lynn whether she is married to Mr Redgrave.

V. How does Lynn feel about the future of tourism in Britain? Tick the sentence which reflects Lynn's view best.

a. Tourism and tourists are boring for most British people.
b. Tourism is becoming more and more important for Britain and Britain's economy.
c. Tourism is a good way for people to earn some extra money.
d. Tourism is an interesting area to work in Britain but it's more fun in Switzerland.

On her way to another B&B

VI. Lynn talks about the time when she lived in the Lake District. Complete this text using the words in the box.

close • compact • good • mountainous • northwest • spare

"Before moving to Maidstone I lived and worked in the Lake District. The Lake District is in the ... of England and it's quite ... to Scotland. It's like Scotland in as much as it is a very ..., beautiful countryside but a lot smaller, a lot more ... , and as the word suggests, there are a lot of lakes.
I enjoy in my ... time visiting restaurants, pubs, tea places. That's probably why I like working in tourism because I like the ... things of life."

Talking to a proprietor

10D

Meterman stays at a B&B

I. Read through the text about Meterman's visit to a B&B. How does the lady react to Meterman's comments? Choose from the alternatives (a – c) below.

a) impatiently and aggressively
b) angrily but politely
c) calmly and kindly

"Hello there. I've just left a note for my milkman. No milk for two weeks. I'm off on a little holiday. I've got my *fishing rods* and my suitcases all ready in the back of Molly, my van. I've got my bed and breakfast book and I'm going to find a nice little farmhouse in the country, do a spot of fishing, relax and forget all about my work. Take my advice and forget your work, like me."

Meterman arrives at a Bed and Breakfast in the country later that morning. A lady opens the door.
"Good morning."
"Good morning."
"Are you the Bed and Breakfast?"
"Yes, we are."
"And are you open?"
"Well, not exactly. But - have you stayed in a bed and breakfast before?"
"Oh yes, indeed. In fact I'm something of an expert at bed and breakfast. I might be able to give you some *hints*."
"Well. That would be nice."
"I'll only stay a few nights."

"This is your room. Your *towel*'s here. And you can make your own tea in the morning." "That's very nice," says Meterman. "Now if I were you, I'd put a vase of flowers over there and arrange the *duvet* like this. And a little *bowl* of chocolates makes a good impression." The lady is getting quite *cross*. "I see. The bathroom's this way."

Meterman talks to the viewer. "You see what I mean? A few good ideas. Hints or tips as we call them. She'll find them very useful."

"There's plenty of hot water and you can *bath* or *shower* when you like."
"Good. Good. Excellent! Now, if you want my advice, you'll use the very best

soap in the bathroom. English lavender is what I find most suitable. This soap is all right but – and some *talcum powder* to *go with* it."
"I see. Well, I hope you can *make do with* this today!" And she pushes the bar of soap into Meterman's mouth.

fishing rod	Angelrute	bath	baden, ein Bad nehmen
hint	Hinweis, Tip	shower	duschen
towel	Handtuch	talcum powder	Körperpuder
duvet / ˈdjuːveɪ /	Feder-, Daunenbett	go with sth	zu etwas passen
bowl	Schale	make do with sth	mit etw. auskommen, sich mit etw. behelfen
cross	ärgerlich, verdrießlich		

II. Complete the sentences below using the words in the box.

work • fishing • all • away • farmhouse • fishing • holiday

1. Meterman is getting ... from it ... .
2. He's off on a little ... .
3. He's going to find a nice little ... in the country.
4. He's got his ... rods.
5. He's going to do a spot of ... .
6. He's going to forget all about his ... .

III. In Meterman's opinion, which three things are missing from the landlady's breakfast?

"An excellent breakfast – very good indeed. Nine points out of ten for the breakfast! I can give you one or two tips - little ideas. Bacon, eggs and sausages are fine, but there should be mushrooms as well. Now toast and butter and marmalade, that's all quite correct, but what kind of jam is this, I ask you? Oh dear me – the jam should always be home-made! I'm sure you can make your own jam! Well, home-made in future please and there should be honey as well. That makes the complete breakfast. That will give you ten out of ten."

10E

A request letter

67 Weston Close,
Rotherby,
Leicestershire
LE65 3 FB
7 June, 19...

Dear Anna,
When we left your house last week we unfortunately left behind a pair of spectacles belonging to my husband. They have silver frames and were in a brown case. I think he left them in the breakfast room. If you found them, I should be most grateful if you could post them to me at this address. I shall, of course, refund the postage.
We had a very pleasant stay at your house and enjoyed visiting your part of England.

Yours sincerely

Janice Whitting

KEEPING FIT UNIT 11

11A

In the fitness studio

Some young people get into conversation while they are exercising in a fitness studio.

- *How're you getting on*?
- Fine. I've done 3 *sets* of 12 today. And that's my record.
- *Well done! Keep going*!

- How are you finding the machine?
- It's hard work.
- Mmm. That's what I found. Don't *give up*!

- I *lifted* 50 kilos last week.
- Brilliant! *Keep it up*!

Three of them were asked how often they come to the studio.

1 Man: I train here twice a week. Why? Because I want to get fit, of course! I sit in an office and work behind a desk, so this year I've decided I need to get some exercise, so I train here twice a week and I play football every Saturday. I do feel a lot better.

2 Man: I come here *every other day*. I started last month. I'm trying to *lose weight* so I decided to do this. And walk to work and back. It does help. I've lost a kilo already.

Woman: I come here as often as I can. I want to keep fit. And I just enjoy it. It's fun. You meet people here and make good friends. It's good.

How're you getting on?	Wie läuft's?	give up	aufgeben
set	*hier*: Übungsblock	lift	heben, *hier*: stemmen
Well done!	Toll!	Keep it up!	Mach weiter so!
Keep going!	(Nur) Weiter so!	every other day	jeden zweiten Tag
		lose weight	(Gewicht) abnehmen

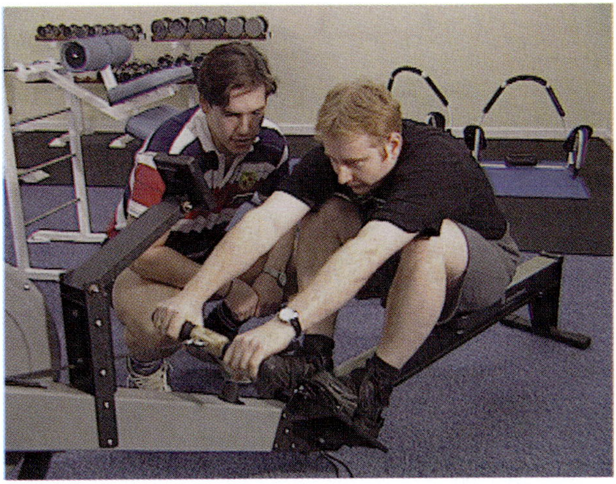

The trainer gives some advice

Understanding the text. Why do the three young people go to the fitness studio? Tick the sentence (a – c) which finishes the statements best.

1. The first man visits a fitness studio because he wants to ...
   a) meet lots of girls. b) feel better. c) lose weight.
2. The second man is in the studio because he would like to ...
   a) be a professional weightlifter.
   b) work better.
   c) get thinner.
3. The woman goes to the fitness studio because ...
   a) her boyfriend trains there.
   b) it's fun.
   c) she has nothing better to do.

Find an English equivalent for these German expressions.

4. Wie läuft's?
5. So ist es mir auch gegangen.
6. Toll!
7. zweimal pro Woche
8. jeden zweiten Tag

And what about you?

9. Would you go to a fitness studio? Why/Why not?
10. Do you think going to a fitness studio is a good way of getting fit? Give reasons for your answer.

H Three important verbs: "be", "do" and "have"

Drei wichtige Verben: "be", "do" und "have"

Die drei Verben ***be, do*** und ***have*** zählen zu den wichtigsten Verben im Englischen. Sie haben zweierlei Funktionen.

◆ Sie sind eigenständige **Vollverben**:

What do you **do**?	Was machen Sie (machst du) beruflich?
How many children did she **have**?	Wie viele Kinder hat sie gehabt?
Where have you **been**?	Wo sind Sie (bist du) gewesen? (Wo waren Sie (warst du)?)

◆ Als **Hilfsverben** spielen ***be, do*** und ***have*** eine zentrale Rolle in der englischen Grammatik:

- Mit dem **Hilfsverb *be*** beispielsweise werden alle **Verlaufsformen** *(She is working today.)* und alle **Passivformen** (*It is used to record music.)* gebildet.
- Das **Hilfsverb *do*** zum Beispiel wird verwendet, um **Fragen** *(Do you come from Germany?)* und **Verneinungen** *(We didn't see you at the party.)* zu bilden.
- Mit dem **Hilfsverb *have*** können wir das ***Present Perfect*** *(He has just come back from Canada.)* bilden.

Exercises

I. Put the correct form of the verb "to be" into the text. ●●

It has ... shown in a recent study that babies ... faster learners than adults thought they ... . Now every parent can ... sure that their baby will one day ... a superbaby. Today parents ... told to speak and read to very young children as much as possible even if the children ... as young as two. So if there ... a baby in your house you can start today. Perhaps in a few weeks the baby will ... reading this to you.

II. Look at the eight sentences (a–h). Change the two sentences below in the same way. Make any other changes where necessary.

a. I play squash.
b. I don't play squash.
c. Do you play squash?
d. My sister plays squash.
e. My brother doesn't play squash.
f. Does your brother play squash?
g. We didn't play squash last week.
h. Did you play squash last week?

1. I speak English.
2. I work in a computer company.

III. The word "have". Is the word "have" or "having" a full verb or a helping verb in the following sentences? Tick the correct box.

1. Are you having a shower?
2. You haven't introduced me to your brother.
3. How long have you been waiting?
4. The phone rang while she was having a shower.
5. Have you had something to eat?
6. Where have you been so long?

FULL	HELPING

IV. Fill in the gaps with "because" (weil) *or "so"* (und deshalb).

1. Why do you train here twice a week? – I train here ... I want to get fit.
2. I sit in an office and work behind a desk ... I've decided to get some exercise.
3. I train here twice a week ... I feel a lot better now.
4. How have you managed to lose a kilo already? ... I walk to work and back and come here every other day.
5. I'm trying to lose weight ... I walk to work and back.
6. Why do you come here as often as you can? ... you meet people here and make friends.

V. Fill in the gaps with "so as not to" (um nicht ... zu), *"so that"* (damit) *or "to"* (um ... zu). ●●

1. We train here twice a week ... get fit.
2. I come here every other day ... I can lose some weight.
3. She plays football every Saturday ... get some exercise.
4. He walks to work and back ... put on weight.
5. I come here as often as I can ... have a bit of fun.
6. We come quite early ... we can go out for a drink later.

11B

Getting to know the exercise machines ●●

When a new client comes into the fitness studio, the trainer *weighs* them, takes their *blood pressure* and pulse and then makes them a training programme. He shows them the different exercise machines and what to do.

– Would you like to get on the *scales*? OK. I'll put this on your arm. OK?
– So, what's normal?
– The *average* is about 120 over 80 and a pulse of about 70.
– And what's mine?
– 138 over 96 and a pulse of 84.
– So I need to exercise.
– (Smiling) A little bit.

The trainer shows the man the *rowing machine*. "You put your feet on here. Hold the *handles*. You *lean forward* and you *pull back*," he says. "That's it. Keep pulling. Don't stop!"

Next the trainer shows the man how to use the *leg press*. He explains that it develops your leg *muscles* and your general fitness. "This is the *weight stack* and you set it to where you *require*," he says. The man pushes up with his legs while the trainer gives him some more advice. "Try to keep a regular rhythm and don't forget to *breathe* deeply."

Then the trainer walks around the studio to *make sure* everybody is OK.

– Excuse me. Could you help me change the weights, please?
– Yes, of course. If you could put the *bar* down ...

– Would you show me what to do here?
– Alright. This is for your *stomach* muscles.

– Is everything OK?
– Could you put more weight on, please?
– Certainly. There you are.
– Thanks.

– Would you mind doing this for me?
– *Not at all*. How's that?
– Great.

get to know	kennen lernen, sich vertraut machen mit
exercise machines	Übungsgeräte
weigh	wiegen
blood pressure	Blutdruck
scales	Waage
average	Durchschnitt
(on an average)	(durchschnittlich)
rowing machine	Rudergerät
handles	Griffe
lean forward	sich nach vorne lehnen
pull back	nach hinten ziehen
leg press	Fußhantel
muscle	Muskel
stack	Stapel
weight stack	Scheibensatz von Gewichten
require	benötigen
breathe	atmen
make sure	sichergehen
bar	Stange
stomach	*hier*: Bauch
not at all	überhaupt nicht, ganz und gar nicht, *hier:* gerne

Understanding the text. Choose one of the sentences (a–c) to complete the statements.

1. The trainer carries out some checks on the client because he would like to ...
   a) find out how fit the client is.
   b) show the client how much he (the trainer) knows about fitness.
   c) see if he's fitter than his client.
2. On the rowing machine the trainer gives the client ...
   a) a bit of advice. b) some encouragement. c) a lot of criticism.
3. When they get to the leg press the trainer is ...
   a) helpful. b) aggressive. c) critical.
4. Walking around the studio later the trainer seems to ...
   a) get on well with the clients.
   b) dislike the clients.
   c) be uninterested in the clients.

Find an English word or expression which matches these German ones.

5. Blutdruck
6. Waage
7. tief atmen
8. Bitte schön.
9. Selbstverständlich.
10. Gerne.

And what about you?

11. Could you imagine being a trainer in a fitness studio? Why/Why not?
12. Today people no longer do exhausting physical work because there are machines to do it for them. At the same time they build machines for fitness centres so that they can get the exercise they want. What do you think about this? Write 40–50 words giving your personal view.

H Future forms (II) – to be going to

Zukunftsformen (II)

I'm going to weigh you.	Ich werde Sie jetzt wiegen.
Are you **going to** show me the machines?	Zeigen Sie mir die Geräte?
We**'re not going to** exercise every day.	Wir werden nicht jeden Tag trainieren.

- Im Modul 6A (vgl. S. 89) wurde eine der zahlreichen Zukunftsformen des Englischen geübt: das *Present Continuous*. In diesem Modul beschäftigen wir uns mit einer weiteren Form, die neben dem *Present Continuous* zu den gebräuchlichsten gehört: ***to be going to* + Infinitiv**.
- Das Verb ***to be going to* + Infinitiv** wird verwendet, um **bereits gefasste Absichten** oder **bereits in Gang gesetzte Ereignisse** zum Ausdruck zu bringen. Bei dieser Form ist für den Sprecher etwas Zukünftiges bereits in der Gegenwart erkennbar.

Exercises

1. Look at the pictures and write down a sentence with "to be going to" + infinitive.

II. Match up the two halves of the sentences. ●●

1. Be careful of that dog, won't you?	a. He's going to get fat, isn't he?
2. What a lovely morning.	b. I'm going to sneeze!
3. Your brother's eating a lot.	c. It's going to be a beautiful day.
4. Ah, ah, ah	d. It's going to bite.
5. Watch out.	e. She's going to resign soon.
6. She is not very happy in her job.	f. The book's going to fall off the shelf.

III. Complete these mini-dialogues using the "be going to" form of the verb in brackets. ●●

1. Have you really decided to go to the fitness studio?
   Yes, I ... (start) my training programme tomorrow.
2. Shall I take you to the youth club this evening?
   No thanks, mum. Dad says he ... (take) me.
3. I ... (get) some food on my way back from training. Do you want anything?
   Not today, but thanks anyway.
4. What ... (we, have) for lunch?
   Wait and see. It's a surprise.
5. Are you driving to Italy again this year?
   No, we ... (take) the train. It's easier.
6. Be careful!
   What's the matter?
   You ... (spill) honey on your shirt.

H The English "they"/"them"/"their"
Verallgemeinerndes "they"/"them"/"their"

If somebody rings, ask **them** to call back.	Wenn jemand anruft, bitten Sie (bitte) ihn, zurückzurufen.
When a new client comes in, I weigh **them**.	Wenn ein neuer Kunde hereinkommt, wiege ich ihn.

Das englische ***they/them/their*** kann **verallgemeinernd** für ***he/his*** und ***she/her*** stehen, auch in Verbindung mit unbestimmten Pronomen wie ***anybody***, ***somebody*** und ***everybody*** oder Substantiven, die im Singular gebraucht werden.

IV. What does the trainer do when a new client comes in? Add "they", "them" or "their".

1. I weigh ... .
2. I take ... blood pressure.
3. I measure ... pulse.
4. I make ... a training programme.
5. I show ... the machines.
6. Then ... are sent a bill.

V. Put "they", "them" or "their" into the following sentences.

1. Someone told you, didn't ...?
2. If anybody calls, tell ... to ring again later.
3. Who has left ... keys on the table?
4. Does everybody have to make ... own coffee here?
5. Somebody should know her address, shouldn't ... ?
6. I think someone is knocking at the door. ... want to come in.

11C

Richard and Simon Suthers – fit for the national championships

Listen carefully to Richard Suthers and his son Simon talking about rowing. Then answer the questions below.

I. Choose the sentence (a – c) which best completes the statements.

1. Richard Suthers is a ...
   a) rower. b) rowing coach. c) rowing champion.
2. Richard Suthers has ...
   a) two sons. b) one son. c) three sons.
3. Simon Suthers would like to be ...
   a) a rowing coach. b) a rowing champion. c) a fitness freak.

II. Which is which? Complete sentences 1 and 2 by choosing the correct ending (a – d).

1. Aerobic training is ...
2. Anaerobic training is ...

a. building up your resistance level.
b. stretching your muscles.
c. learning how to relax.
d. training your lung capacity.

III. At the end of the interview what impression does Simon give us of his father as a coach? Tick the most appropriate sentence.

1. His father is hard but fair as a coach.
2. His father is too hard as a coach.
3. His father is too old for the job of coach.

IV. Complete these paragraphs using the words from the box below.

improve • older • see • times • tiring • training • weekends • while

Son: I keep records of my ... because I just want to ... what I've done, and how I can ... . I've kept them for quite a ... .

Father: The boys and girls practise three ... a week. They will also be competing on Saturday or Sunday, most ... throughout the year. The job of coach is extremely ... , especially as one gets ... .

11D

Meterman joins the army

I. Fill in words which are missing in the text. The first letter is given.

We see Meterman singing as he drives along.

"Oh the grand old Duke of York
He had 10,000 men,
He marched them up to the top of the h...
And he marched them down again.

Now if you're wondering why I'm singing that s... it's because today we're going to the Duke of York's Royal Military School. It's a real school but it's *run* by the a... . The children here learn their 3Rs – Reading, Writing and Arithmetic – but there's also a fine military tradition of training, fitness and d... ."

Meterman talks to Molly, his car. "Now Molly today we have to be very s... . Tie straight. Jacket straight. Hat straight. What you need is some spit and polish – one of our rather nasty little phrases – spit and polish!" Meterman demonstrates by spitting on Molly and polishing her with his e... .

We hear the cadets marching. Meterman marches too, holding his *duster* like a military *cane*. He finds the meters in an old b... .

"Now, this is where the meters are. It's a great h... and privilege to read such meters as these. They are *the very pinnacle of efficiency*. They are simply the very b... meters. *Pukka* meters."

As he is speaking the Regimental Sergeant Major arrives.

RSM: You 'orrible little man! What do you think you are doing creeping around in a high security a...! This area is *out of bounds*.

MM: Just a routine inspection, Sergeant.

RSM: Sergeant! Sergeant! I'm a Sergeant Major!

MM: I do apologize Sergeant Major. But everything's in very good order. I shall be making an excellent r... to your superior officer (taps RSM on shoulder).

RSM: Don't t... me. Superior Officer! Superior Officer! Cadets! *Secure* this man.

Meterman is led out of the building.

MM: A simple misunderstanding. An easy m... to make. You were just doing your j... . I'm glad to see you keep the boys nice and fit, Sergeant Major. You do plenty of *press-ups*, do you? Training, cold s..., *cross country running*. Of course there can be no softies in the army. I myself I'm very fit. We *chaps* in u... , we know all about fitness.

Cadet: Excuse me, sir, perhaps you could teach us a few things about f...? Would you like to join in our training?

MM: Well, I'm in a bit of a h... actually. I've some i... work to do.

RSM: Well, let's see how fit you are! Get him in line here. Left, Right, Left, Right, Left, Right, Left ... .

After some vigorous training, Meterman has collapsed in a sand *pit*.

RSM: Hey, Mr Meterman. Do you think you're fit? You're fit for n...!

run (a business, organization, school etc.)	(einen Betrieb, eine Organisation, eine Schule etc.) leiten, führen, verwalten
duster	Staubwedel
cane	(Rohr-)Stock
pinnacle	Gipfel, Spitze
the very pinnacle of efficiency	*hier im Sinne von*: das Brauchbarste, Leistungsfähigste, das es gibt
pukka (*veraltet*)	echt, wirklich
out of bounds	Zutritt verboten
secure	festnehmen
press-up	Liegestütz
cross country running	Querfeldein-, Geländelauf
chaps	„Jungs"
pit	Grube

II. Join sentences 1–5 with a–e to form natural links.

1. The school is run by the army.
2. The car is running.
3. He runs a course for teachers.
4. A fridge doesn't cost much to run.
5. He runs three miles every morning.

a. The engine is switched on.
b. He organizes the course.
c. He runs around the park four times.
d. The running costs of a fridge are low.
e. The army is in charge of the school.

11E

At the doctor's

These expressions have been taken from posters and leaflets in a doctor's waiting room. Match them to the explanations below.

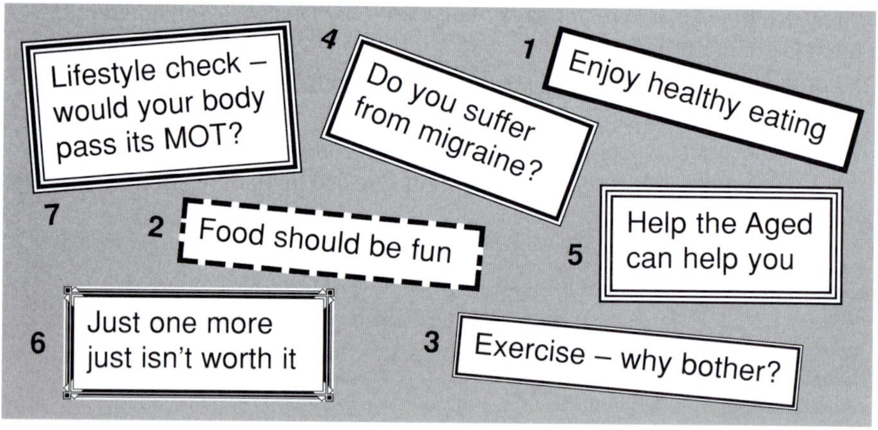

a. Drinking and driving wrecks lives.
b. When did you last go to the doctor's to have a check-up?
c. Eat what you want to eat – not what you think you should eat.
d. This organization can support you when you are older.
e. A healthy diet is important.
f. Is there any point in doing sport?
g. We can help you if you get very bad headaches.

TALKING ABOUT THE FUTURE UNIT 12

12A

Looking for a job

1 young woman: I'*m looking forward to* starting my *career* as an actress. I'm hoping *to land a part in* a West End musical in London. I'*m worried about* getting a job. Acting's a hard career.

Young man: I'm studying *performing arts* because I want to become an actor. I'm finishing my course in June and *eventually* I'd like to work in the theatre. If I get a good job, I'll move to a *flat* in London.

2 young woman: I'm studying hairdressing because I'd like to become a stylist. I'm worried about *failing my exams*. I'm taking them in June and if I *pass* I'll get a job with a hairdresser's. Eventually I'd like to have my own salon.

3 young woman: I'm studying *child care* because I want to become a *children's nurse*. I'm going to an *interview* next week at a London hospital. If I'm successful, then I'll *train for three years*. Eventually I hope to have children of my own.

look forward to doing sth	sich auf etw. freuen	flat	(Miet-)Wohnung
career	(berufliche) Laufbahn, Karriere	fail/pass (an exam)	durchfallen/bestehen (Prüfung)
land a part in	eine Rolle in ... „kriegen“, „ergattern“	child care	Kinderpflege
be worried about (+ *-ing or noun*)	beunruhigt, besorgt sein wegen; sich Gedanken, Sorgen machen wegen	children's nurse	Kinder(kranken)-schwester
performing arts	darstellende Künste	interview	*hier*: Vorstellungsgespräch
eventually	schließlich, endlich	train for three years	eine dreijährige Ausbildung machen, absolvieren

Understanding the text.

Complete the statements by choosing one of the sentences a – c.

1. The first young woman in this module ...
   a) would like to become a professional actress.
   b) has just been given a part in a musical.
   c) is a famous actress.
2. The young man ...
   a) will never work in the theatre.
   b) is not sure if he wants to work in the theatre.
   c) wants to become an actor.
3. The second young woman ...
   a) has got a job.
   b) will get a good job soon.
   c) will get a job if she passes her exams.
4. The third young woman ...
   a) is hoping to train to become a nurse.
   b) is still at school.
   c) wants to find a husband soon.

Answer the questions. Use full sentences and your own words as far as possible.

5. What are the first and second women worried about?
6. What plans does the young man have?
7. What long-term plans does the third woman have?

Write down an English expression for these German ones. The text will help you.

8. Ich schreibe bald Prüfungen.

9. Ich werde eine dreijährige Ausbildung machen.
10. Ich werde mein Studium im Juni abschließen.

And what about you?

11. What are your career aims?
12. What qualifications and experience do you need to get the job you want?

H The gerund (II)

Das Gerund (II)

He **is dreaming about becoming** an actor.	Er träumt davon, Schauspieler zu werden.
I'm looking forward to starting my career.	Ich freue mich darauf, meine Karriere zu beginnen.

◆ Im Modul 9A (vgl. S. 138) haben wir gelernt, dass wir im Englischen häufig ein Gerund (= -ing Form) verwenden, wenn auf ein Verb ein anderes Verb folgt (z.B. *I enjoy flying.*). Hier kommt nun eine weitere wichtige Regel hinzu: Folgt auf die **Verbindung Verb + Präposition** ein **anderes Verb**, steht **immer** das **Gerund**. (Auch das Wort ***to*** ist manchmal eine Präposition, z.B. *I'm looking forward to seeing you.*)
Im Folgenden eine kleine Auswahl besonders häufig gebrauchter Verbindungen:

to apologize for (*sich entschuldigen für*)
to congratulate sb on (*jmdm. gratulieren zu*)
to dream about (*träumen von*)
to insist on (*bestehen auf*)
to look forward to (*sich freuen auf*)
to object to (*dagegen sein*)
to rely on (*sich verlassen auf*)
to succeed in (*Erfolg haben mit, gelingen*)
to talk about (*sprechen von*)
to thank sb for (*jmdm. danken für*)
to think of (*denken an*)

Acting is a hard career.	Die Schauspielerei ist eine schwere Laufbahn.
Nursing is an interesting profession.	Krankenschwester zu sein ist ein interessanter Beruf.

◆ Wie die oben genannten Beispielsätze zeigen, kann das **Gerund** aber auch alleinstehend als **Subjekt eines Satzes** verwendet werden.

Exercises

I. The gerund as subject and object. Complete the sentences using the correct form of the words in brackets. (In one sentence you must use an infinitive.) ●●

1. (Work) from home is becoming popular nowadays.
2. Do you mind (stay) at home on Sundays?
3. (Cycle) is better for you than (drive).
4. Do you like (watch) football on TV?
5. What would you like (do) when you have finished your course?
6. (Be) an actor or actress is not as easy as it sounds.

II. Complete these sentences by using a gerund. In four of the sentences you must also add a preposition. ●●

1. He hates ... (get up) early at the weekend.
2. We're thinking ... (go) on a safari.
3. Why do you insist ... (talk) when I'm talking?
4. He objects ... (sit) in smoky restaurants.
5. She is talking ... (leave) her husband.
6. Please stop ... (shout), will you!

III. Join the two sentences into one. Start with the second sentence. You may need to add a preposition. ●●

Example:
Dan plays computer chess. He's really interested in it.
Dan's really interested in playing computer chess.

1. We'll go to their party. We're looking forward to it.
2. He'd like to live in Paris. He often dreams about it.
3. I didn't ring you yesterday. I apologize for it.
4. She paid for the coffee. She insisted.
5. We're glad you came. Thank you.
6. She passed the exams. She succeeded.

H If-pattern 1

Bedingungssätze (Konditionalsätze), Typ 1

If she**'s** successful, she**'ll train** for three years.	Wenn sie erfolgreich ist, wird sie eine dreijährige Ausbildung machen.
If I **pass**, **I'll get** a job with a hairdresser's.	Wenn ich die Prüfungen bestehe, werde ich eine Stelle bei einem Frisör bekommen.
Tom **will move** to a flat in London **if** he **gets** a job.	Tom wird in eine Wohnung in London ziehen, wenn er eine Stelle bekommt.

- Hier geht es um für die Sprecher **erfüllbare Bedingungen**. So ist es durchaus möglich, dass die erste junge Frau Erfolg hat, dass die zweite ihre Prüfungen besteht und dass Tom eine Arbeitsstelle findet.
- Im Satzteil nach ***if*** steht die **einfache Form der Gegenwart**. Im **Hauptsatz** (***main clause***) steht ***will*** **+ Infinitiv** oder ein anderes Hilfsverb, wie z.B. ***can*** oder ***must*** **+ Infinitiv** (*If you want to become a stylist, you must pass your exams first.*).
- Das Wort ***will*** wird im **Modul 12B** (vgl. S. 193) als eine Form der Zukunft ausführlicher behandelt.

IV. Link the two halves of the sentences together.

1. He'll get a part in a West End musical ...
2. ... he can't move to a flat in London.
3. ... she'll get a good job.
4. She'll open her own salon ...
5. She'll get a job as a children's nurse ...

a. ... if she can find the right place for a shop.
b. ... if the interview at the hospital goes as well as she hopes.
c. ... if he tries hard at acting school.
d. If his new job doesn't pay well enough, ...
e. If she passes her exams, ...

V. Complete the sentences using the correct form of the words in brackets. ●●

1. If she ... (want) to get the job, she ... (have to) work much harder.
2. We ... (be) there in the early afternoon if all ... (go) well.
3. If you ... (not, mind), I ... (sit) in this chair.
4. If you ... (be) not there by ten, we ... (go) without you.
5. We ... (take) the bikes if it ... (not, rain).
6. If we ... (not, hurry), we ... (miss) the bus.

VI. Complete these sentences using the correct form of the verbs in the box. ●●

be • buy • fail • get • have to • be • turn • pass • spend • need

1. If it ... a nice day tomorrow, we ... the afternoon in the park.
2. We ... something warm to wear if the weather ... bad.
3. If she ... the exam, she ... take them again, won't she?
4. If she ... the job, she ... so pleased.
5. He ... a car if he ... his driving test.

VII. Words in German and English which look the same but have a different meaning are called "false friends". Fill in the table below. Use a dictionary if you wish.

German ←	English	German →	English
...	eventually	eventuell	...
...	to become	bekommen	...
...	must not	muss nicht	...
...	meaning	Meinung	...
...	chef	Chef	...
...	will not	will nicht	...

12B

Planning an expedition ●●

James Grey is an expedition leader. He leads trekking groups up Africa's highest mountain – Mount Kilimanjaro. Today he's in Britain where he's talking to a group of people about the plans he has made for their trip to Tanzania.

"We will meet at Jomo Kenyatta Airport, Nairobi at 9 o'clock on 20 February. We will drive to the *border point* at Namanga. There we will *complete* passport formalities for Tanzania."

He goes on to tell them that they will be *spending* the first night in a hotel and that the next morning they will drive to the south-western side of Kilimanjaro to begin their *climb*.

James continues: "We will be travelling in a group. There will be a cook to prepare our meals and there will be *porters* to carry most of our luggage. We will have to be prepared for changes in climate."

Some of the group have questions: "What will we have to take in our rucksacks?" – "How far will we be walking in a day?" – "What *footwear* do you suggest?" – "What about money? Will we need much ready cash with us?" – "Will there be many animals along the route?"

James tells the group that they will *need* waterproof clothing for the jungle and light *cotton clothing* for the climb. He explains to them that they will be walking for approximately 5–6 hours a day so they will need *a* strong *pair of leather walking boots* to *avoid sprained ankles* on the difficult terrain. He advises them to take some money as they will probably want to *tip* the porters at the end of the trek. However, he is not too optimistic about seeing animals. “I’m afraid there won’t be many animals along the route,” he says. “But don’t *worry*, the *scenery* is *magnificent*!”

border point	Grenzübergang	avoid	vermeiden
complete	*hier*: erledigen	sprain	verstauchen
spend	verbringen	ankle	Knöchel
climb	Aufstieg	tip	Trinkgeld geben
porter	Träger	worry (worried, worried)	sich Sorgen machen, sich beunruhigen
footwear	Schuhwerk	scenery	*hier*: Landschaft
need	benötigen, brauchen	magnificent	großartig
cotton clothing	Bekleidung aus Baumwolle		
a pair of leather walking boots	ein Paar Wanderstiefel aus Leder		

Understanding the text.
Which of these statements is correct according to the text? Mark it with a tick.

1. It’s James’s job ...
   a) to show people slides about Tanzania.
   b) to lead expeditions to Tanzania.
   c) to write books about expeditions.

Which of these sentences is correct? Tick it.

2. The group ...
   a) will have their passport formalities completed at Nairobi airport.
   b) will spend their first night at a hotel in Tanzania.
   c) will have to be prepared to cook their own meals.

Compare this text with the last paragraph of Unit 12B. Construct the original text.

3. James explains to them that they will be walking for exactly 5–6 hours every other day so they will need a strong pair of leather climbing boots and white linen gloves to avoid bruised wrists on the difficult fields. He advises them to take along whips as they will probably want to beat the sherpas at the end of the trek.

Find an English word or expression for these German ones.

4. Grenzübergang
5. Aufstieg
6. wasserdichte Kleidung
7. verstauchte Knöchel
8. jedoch

And what about you?

9. Why do you think people want to take part in an expedition like this to Tanzania?
10. Which remote countries or places would you like to visit? Why?

H Future forms (III): "will"-future and future continuous

Zukunft mit "will" (einfache Form und Verlaufsform)

We **will drive** to the border point.	Wir werden zum Grenzübergang fahren.
Will there **be** many animals along the route?	Wird es entlang der Route viele Tiere geben?

◆ In den Modulen 6A (vgl. S. 89) und 11B (vgl. S. 178) wurden die Verlaufsform der Gegenwart und die Struktur *to be going to* als zwei Zukunftsformen im Englischen dargestellt. Hier treffen wir auf eine **dritte Zukunftsform: *will* + Infinitiv ohne *to*.**
Das **Hilfsverb *will* + Infinitiv** wird verwendet, um **sachlich** und **objektiv** über **zukünftige Ereignisse** oder **Situationen** zu sprechen. Diese Form der Zukunft wird deshalb oft als die ***neutrale Zukunft*** bezeichnet.

◆ Die **Verneinung** von ***will*** ist ***will not***, die als zusammengezogene Form ***won't*** geschrieben wird (*There won't be many animals along the route.*). Auch in der gesprochenen Sprache ist es wichtig, zwischen ***won't*** /wəʊnt/ und ***want*** /wɒnt/ sowohl in ihrer Bedeutung als auch in ihrer Aussprache zu **unterscheiden**.

They **will be spending** the first night in a hotel.	Sie werden die erste Nacht in einem Hotel verbringen.

◆ Es gibt auch eine **Verlaufsform der Zukunft** (***Future Continuous***). Mit ***will be* + -ing Form** des Verbs beschreibt man zunächst eine **Handlung**, die zu einer **bestimmten Zeit ablaufen** wird (*We will be arriving at nine o'clock.*). Man nimmt die Verlaufsform der Zukunft aber auch **ganz allgemein**, um ein **zukünftiges Geschehen zu schildern,** wobei der **Ablauf** des Geschehens **hervorgehoben** wird (*We will be spending the day together.*).

Exercises

I. Look at this paragraph from the text. Underline the five future forms.

We will meet at Jomo Kenyatta Airport on 20 February. Then we will be driving to the border point at Namanga. There we will complete passport formalities. We will be spending the first night in a hotel. The next morning we will travel on to Mt. Kilimanjaro.

II. Rewrite the text using negative forms of the verbs. Start like this ...

We won't meet ... .

III. Use the prompts and the "will"-future or the "will be + -ing"-future to ask James some questions about the trek. You will have to add some words. ●●

Question 1:	... (where / fly to?)
James:	To Nairobi.
Question 2:	... (when / meet?)
James:	At 9 o'clock on 20 February.
Question 3:	... (what / do / after that?)
James:	We'll go to the border point at Namanga.
Question 4:	... (go / bus?)
James:	No, by car.
Question 5:	... (stop / border?)
James:	Yes, we'll have to stop there for passport formalities.
Question 6:	... (where / spend / first night?)
James:	At a hotel in Tanzania.
Question 7:	... (where / start / climb?)
James:	At the south-western side of Kilimanjaro.
Question 8:	... (travel / groups?)
James:	Yes, we'll be travelling in one large group.
Question 9:	... (cook / own food?)
James:	No, there will be a cook with the group.
Question 10:	... (carry / own luggage?)
James:	No, there will be porters with us.

IV. The words "won't" (= "will not") and "want". Which word goes where? Complete the sentences below. Then translate them into German.

1. Where do you ... to go?
2. He ... be here yet, will he?
3. We ... be leaving tomorrow morning.
4. She doesn't ... to come with us.

V. Join column 1–8 with column a–h to form correct definitions.

1. An expedition is ...	a. a long journey on a ship or boat.
2. A trek is ...	b. a long walk over hills and mountains.
3. A voyage is ...	c. a short journey that you usually make for pleasure.
4. A trip is ...	d. an organized journey to explore unknown territories.
5. A drive is ...	e. getting somewhere on foot.
6. A hike is ...	f. going on a long and difficult journey on foot.
7. Hitchhiking is ...	g. going somewhere in a car.
8. A walk is ...	h. going somewhere by getting lifts in other people's cars.

12C

Bonnie Lamont – professional garden designer

Groombridge Place

Listen carefully to Bonnie Lamont talking about her work on the gardens at Groombridge. Then answer the questions below.

I. Complete the statements 1–7 by choosing one of the sentences a–c.

1. In the interview Bonnie talks about ...
   a) the different gardens you can see at Groombridge.
   b) why the gardens at Groombridge are so important for her.
   c) what problems she faced while working on the gardens at Groombridge.
2. The Spring of Life is ...
   a) a garden with a spring in it.
   b) water from the garden which visitors like to drink.
   c) a fishpond.
3. The Children's Garden will be ...
   a) a play area for children in a forest.
   b) a play area for children in the middle of a pond.
   c) an interesting garden for children to look at.
4. The Serpent's Lair is ...
   a) a mysterious garden based on a famous fairy tale.
   b) a mysterious garden based on a well known children's game.
   c) a mysterious garden based on a popular children's video.

5. The gardens at Groombridge ...
   a) are open to the public.
   b) will not be open to the public for some time.
   c) are opening soon.
6. The White Garden is special to Bonnie because she ...
   a) thought of the name for the garden.
   b) designed the garden.
   c) created the garden.
7. For Bonnie the most satisfying aspect of her work is ...
   a) being outside in the fresh air all the time.
   b) seeing the whole project develop step by step.
   c) smelling the different flowers all day.

II. Write down the English words for these German ones.

1. Forelle
2. Immergrün
3. Thymian
4. Laub
5. Molkerei
6. Scheune
7. Obstgarten
8. Rosmarin
9. Lavendel
10. Duft

12D

Meterman visits Madame Turufe

I. Ten adjectives have been taken out of the story. The first letters are given. Choose the correct word from the box below.

absurd • amazing • blonde • bright • colourful • confusing • darling • dear • plastic • purple • sad • strange • tall • terrific • ugly • useless • wet • wonderful • yellow • young

"I always look forward to reading the meter in this house. Of course I never know what I'm going to find here. It belongs to a very s... lady. She is a *fortune teller*. You can tell by her name: Madame Turufe. 'Turufe' is an *anagram* of 'Future'. Of course, I'm very interested in the future but people can't really *foresee* it, can they?"

Meanwhile inside the house the fortune teller is leaning over her crystal ball. She is a c... figure with *shawls* and *scarves*. With her is a young lady.

Madame Turufe: And, finally, my dear! It will be a year full of surprises.
Yes indeed! Starting with a tall dark stranger!
Oh to be y... again. Romance! I can see him coming soon.

Meanwhile Meterman, seeing the Please Enter sign, has entered and is looking for the meter.

Meterman: Now where is that meter?
Madame Turufe: That will be £5 please. Remember the t... dark stranger.
You will *bump into* him quite soon.
Young lady: Yes. Thank you. Thank you very much indeed.

The young lady comes out into the hallway where Meterman is on his knees looking for the meter. They bump into one another.

Meterman: My d... young lady. I do apologize.

He picks her up with much gallantry. She looks at him.

Young lady: A... . The tall dark stranger – and so soon.

Madame Turufe appears and takes Meterman into her *den*. Meterman protests. He has come to read the meter. She insists she reads the future.

Madame Turufe: Come! Look into my crystal ball. Hold my hand.
Together we will see the future! You will visit strange and w... places – a castle.
Meterman: No, no! That was last year.

Madame Turufe:	I see a b... lady – she is in terrible trouble – you will save her! She will love you for it!
Meterman:	You've got it wrong! That's not the future! That's the past! And she hated me for it. She said I was u... !
Madame Turufe:	Strange things will happen to you – you will change your appearance.
Meterman:	And that happened last year as well! Anyway, I'll never change my appearance again!
Madame Turufe:	Now I see! You will be going on a journey. Up hill, down hill. You will take a ship. A ship will bring you to an island.
Meterman:	An island? Whew, well that's fine! That's the Isle of Wight! Oh yes. I'll be going there this summer as usual. In fact, I've got my brochure here now. Very good indeed. You really can *foretell* the future. How much do I *owe* you?
Madame Turufe:	That will be £25.

Meterman leaves the house and bumps into the young lady. He sees she is interested in him. Perhaps she wants to be a metermaid? He asks her if she would like to wear a p... *grip* in her hair. It's a rather strange, multi-coloured grip. She runs off. Meterman decides his heart belongs to Molly. But he can't find Molly. He runs up and down the streets calling her name.

fortune teller	Wahrsager(in)	bump into	zusammenstoßen, zusammenprallen mit
anagram	Anagramm (*Umstellung der Buchstaben eines Wortes zur Bildung eines anderen Wortes*)	den	Höhle; „Bude“
		foretell (foretold, foretold)	vorher-, voraussagen
foresee (foresaw, foreseen)	voraussehen	owe	schulden, schuldig sein
shawl	Schal, Umhängetuch	grip	Haarreif, -spange
scarf, *pl*: scarves *or* scarfs	Hals-, Kopftuch, Schal		

II. Look at these two sentences carefully. What is unusual about them?

1. A man, a plan, a canal, Panama.
2. Was it a rat I saw?

12E

Signs around town

Which of these signs would you see ...

1. in a park?
2. near a railway station?
3. on the door of a large building?
4. in the centre of a town?
5. along a private road?

a)

b)

c)

d)

e)

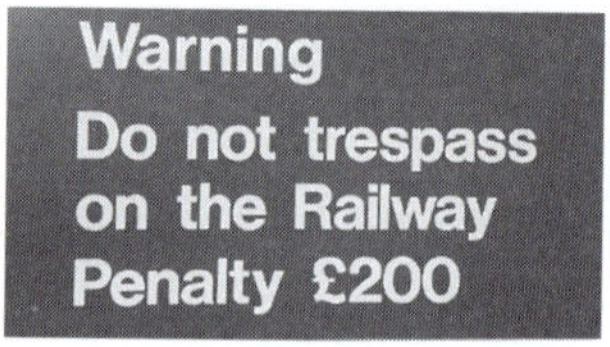

A GREAT DAY OUT

UNIT 13

13A

The car or the train?

Waiting for the next train

Four travellers were asked if people should take the car or use the train when they go out for the day.

1 Woman: I would say don't take your car. You should go by train.

1 Man: No, *definitely* don't go by car unless you have a very special reason. Go by train – that way you can relax.

2 Woman: You should *leave* your car at the station and take the train. You'll find it a lot more relaxing. You'll enjoy the day more.

2 Man: If you take my advice, you'll take the train – unless you want to spend half the day *stuck* in a *traffic jam*. It's madness to take the car!

Why should people take the train?

1 Woman: Why take the train? Well, the traffic is a problem. You *may* find yourself in a traffic jam. And when you do get there, you may not find anywhere to park. You could get a *parking ticket*. Then you have to pay a *fine*. You could even have your car *clamped*!

1 Man: Why go by train? Well, you could end up paying a *fortune* just to park the car.

2 Woman: Parking is a problem. And anyway, it's better for the *environment* to use *public transport.*

2 Man: I agree. More people *ought to* use public transport and leave the car at home. Anyway, it's quicker to go by train!

a day out	ein Tagesausflug	parking ticket	Strafzettel für Falschparken
definitely	entschieden, ganz bestimmt	fine	Geldstrafe, Bußgeld
leave at (left, left)	(stehen) lassen an, bei	clamp	eine Parkkralle anlegen
stick (stuck, stuck)	(fest)stecken	fortune	Vermögen (*viel Geld*)
traffic jam	Verkehrsstau	environment	Umwelt
may	*hier*: wird vielleicht, möglicherweise	public transport	öffentliche Verkehrsmittel
		ought to	sollte, müsste

Understanding the text. Complete the statements 1–3 by choosing the most suitable sentence below (a–d).

1. One main reason to take the train and not the car is that ...
   a) you meet friendly people on the train.
   b) you can have lunch on the train.
   c) parking your car is expensive.
   d) you can make phone calls from the train.
2. The expression "to go out for the day" (line 3) means ...
   a) to go out to celebrate a birthday.
   b) to go out to do some shopping.
   c) to go out to visit places of interest.
   d) to go out to discover something new.
3. The phrase "you could even have your car clamped" (line 15) means ...
   a) you could even find that your car has been broken into.
   b) you could even find somebody has towed your car away.
   c) you could even find that you can't drive your car away.
   d) you could even find a parking ticket on the windscreen.

Find the English for the following.

4. entspannend
5. Stau
6. Strafzettel
7. Umwelt
8. öffentliche Verkehrsmittel
9. es sei denn ...
10. Vermögen

And what about you?

11. Why do you think people still go to town by car rather than by bus or train?
12. Do you think cars should be banned from inner cities? Why/Why not?

H Helping verbs (IV): should

Hilfsverben (IV)

Why **should** people take the car?	Warum sollte man mit dem Auto fahren?
You **should** leave your car at the station.	Sie sollten Ihr (Du solltest dein/ Man sollte sein) Auto am Bahnhof stehen lassen.
You **should** go by train.	Man sollte mit dem Zug fahren.

Das **unvollständige Hilfsverb** ***should*** wird verwendet, um eine **Verpflichtung** auszudrücken oder einen **Rat** zu geben. Da es sich bei ***should*** (wie bei allen anderen unvollständigen Hilfsverben) um die **persönliche Einstellung und Meinung** des Sprechers handelt, wird diese Form oft mit *I think* ... oder *I don't think* ... eingeleitet.

Exercises

I. Translate the English sentences into German and the German sentences into English.

1. You should go by train.
2. You should leave your car at the station.
3. Mehr Menschen sollten öffentliche Verkehrsmittel benutzen.
4. Man sollte an die Umwelt denken.

II. Give some advice. Use the prompts below to form sentences with "should" or "shouldn't". You will have to add some words. ●●

1. My bike's been stolen.	(ring / police)
2. I bought this CD and it doesn't work.	(take back / shop)
3. My cough is getting worse.	(smoke / all day)
4. I'm getting fat.	(eat / so much)
5. He's always tired.	(have / a holiday)
6. My life's boring!	(moan / so much)

III. Ways of travelling. Fill in the table and complete the dialogues using words from the table. ●●

1.	air	plane	flight
2.	sea	...	crossing
3.	rail	...	journey
4.	...	car, bus	trip
5.	road	...	tour

6. – Did you have a good ... ?
   – We didn't fly this time. We came by ... . The crossing was excellent.
7. – Did the ... get to the station on time?
   – Actually we came by ... .
   – You cycled! How long did that take you?
8. – It's a long train ... from Germany to England, isn't it?
   – Yes, but if you go by ... it's just as long.
9. – Is that Philip over there?
   – Where? Is he in his ... ?
   – No, he's on his ... . Look! He's going to fall off.

IV. The word "unless" (es sei denn, außer) *is a very useful word when giving advice (e.g.: Don't go by car unless you have a good reason.).*
Look at the example and then join the two sentences below into one. ●●

Example:
Take the train. Or do you want to end up paying a fortune just to park?
You should take the train unless you want to end up paying a fortune to park.

1. Use public transport. Or do you want to get a parking ticket?
2. Leave your car at home. Or would you like to have it clamped?
3. Don't go by car. Or are you prepared to spend half a day in a traffic jam?
4. Take the train. Or would you prefer to get there even later?

V. Some verbs are easy to confuse.
Put a verb from the box into the sentences. ●●

borrow	•	lend
bring	•	take
fit	•	suit
remember	•	remind

1. These trousers don't ... me. They're too small.
2. Do you ... when we went on holiday to Greece four years ago?
3. Doesn't that woman over there ... you of my mother?
4. Can you ... me the newspaper, please? It's over there on the table.
5. Can I ... your car until tomorrow morning?
6. This jumper doesn't ... me at all. It's the wrong colour.
7. Can you ... us to the station on Sunday?
8. Can you ... me your laptop for a weekend?

Now try to translate your sentences into German.

13B

A day in Canterbury

Canterbury Cathedral

Mr and Mrs Spenser and their daughter Catherine have decided to go by train to Canterbury. After they have parked their car in the *station car park*, they buy their tickets. "Three cheap *day return tickets* to Canterbury, please. One under 15," says Mr Spenser.

Mr Spenser is not sure if they are on the right *platform*. He quickly asks another traveller. "Is this the right platform for Canterbury?" The man is able to help. "No," he says, pointing to the other side of the station. "You should be over there!"

Asking the way to the Cathedral

The Spensers run over the bridge to the other platform and only just *manage to* catch their train.

As soon as they have sat down, Catherine wants to know what they are going to do first when they get to Canterbury. "The Cathedral first, then some shopping, and then lunch," her father explains. Catherine has another idea. "And after that we'll go to *Canterbury Tales House*. That's the *Chaucer Exhibition*, right?"

At Canterbury station Mrs Spenser studies a map of the town. She wants to find the way to the Cathedral. "Well, we're here," she says. "So it's down here, turn left, keep straight on and turn left again here." As they walk through the centre of Canterbury the Spensers have to stop twice to *ask the way*. "Excuse me," says Mr Spenser to a young man who has just come out of a shop. "How do we get to the Cathedral?"

"Go *straight along* this street here, take the first *turning* on the left, and you'll see the Cathedral *straight ahead*," he replies. "You can't miss it."

After they have looked around the Cathedral, Mr Spenser suggests they do some shopping. Catherine, however, has had enough. "I've got a *blister*," she *complains*, "and a *headache*!" Her mother is quick to react. She asks a *passer-by* where there is a *chemist's*. "If you go down there and take the second turning on the right," he explains, "you'll find it on the left."

Catherine *is pleased* that there is still enough time after lunch to go to the Canterbury Tales House. She enjoys hearing about Chaucer's different stories and characters but it's hard work and she's very tired afterwards. "Can't we take a taxi back to the station?" she asks. Her father agrees.

"So we finished the day with a *taxi ride*," he explains. "It took us to the station and there we caught a train back to where we started. A really good day out!"

station car park	Parkplatz am Bahnhof
day return ticket	Tagesrückfahrkarte
platform	Bahnsteig
manage to do sth	es schaffen, etw. zu tun
as soon as	sobald, *hier*: kaum
Canterbury Tales House	*eine Art Museum, in dem die 'Canterbury Tales' von Chaucer mit lebensgroßen Puppen und in historischen Dekorationen nachgestellt werden*
Chaucer, Geoffrey	*engl. Dichter (um 1340–1400)*
exhibition	Ausstellung
ask the way	nach dem Weg fragen
straight along	gerade entlang, gerade weiter
turning	*hier*: Querstraße
straight ahead	geradeaus, direkt vor (sich)
blister	Blase (*Haut*)
complain	sich beschweren
headache	Kopfweh
passer-by	Passant(in)
chemist('s)	*in England: Drogerie und Apotheke*
be pleased	erfreut sein
taxi ride	Taxifahrt

Understanding the text.

True or false? Put a cross in the correct box.

	True	False
1. The Spensers go to Canterbury for a day.		
2. They almost miss their train.		
3. First they have lunch, then they go shopping.		
4. Catherine is bored and wants to go home early.		
5. A taxi takes them all the way back home.		

Select the right ending (a–c) for these sentences.

6. The phrase "Catherine has had enough" (line 23) means that ...
   a) she has done enough shopping.
   b) she is tired and doesn't want to go on.
   c) she has seen enough of the Cathedral.
7. The expression "you can't miss it" (line 21) means ...
   a) you won't like it.
   b) it is easy to find.
   c) it's no fun.

Find the English equivalent for the following.

8. Bahnsteig
9. nach dem Weg fragen
10. Gehen Sie geradeaus
11. Kopfweh
12. Passant(in)

On the way to the Canterbury Tales House

And what about you?

13. What would you do if you were in Canterbury for a day? The map in exercise III (see page 210) may help you.
14. What are the Canterbury Tales exactly? (If you don't know, try and find out!)

H Future forms (IV) – the present simple
Zukunftsformen (IV) – die einfache Gegenwart

The train **leaves** at 9.35.	Der Zug fährt um 9.35 Uhr ab.
The shops **close** at 8.30 this evening.	Die Geschäfte machen heute Abend um 20.30 Uhr zu.
When **does** the restaurant **open**?	Wann macht das Restaurant auf?

- Die vierte und letzte Zukunftsform ähnelt der ersten: Im Modul 6A (vgl. S. 89) wurde gezeigt, dass die Verlaufsform der Gegenwart verwendet wird, um bereits festgelegte Pläne oder Vereinbarungen auszudrücken (*We're leaving at six.*).
- In diesem Modul geht es um die **einfache Gegenwart**. Mit dieser Form will man ausdrücken, dass ein **zukünftiges Geschehen** durch einen **Fahrplan**, einen **Kalender** oder ein **Programm festgelegt** ist. Man spricht deshalb auch von der ***Timetable Future***. Verben wie ***arrive***, ***begin***, ***close***, ***leave***, ***open*** usw. werden oft so verwendet.

Exercises

I. Complete the sentences using the correct form of the words in brackets. ●●

1. The bus ... (leave) London in the morning and ... (arrive) in Glasgow the same evening.
2. When ... (the plane, leave)? ... (it, get) to Scotland much more quickly?
3. The football match ... (start) at 3 o'clock and ... (finish) at about 5.30. When ... (the film, begin)?
4. The new exhibition at the Tate Gallery ... (open) at the beginning of February. Do you know by any chance when it ... (end)?

II. Put the verbs into the present simple or the present continuous. ●●

1. We ... (have) a dinner party next Friday. ... (you, come)? We'd like to invite you.
2. Sally? Is it true that you ... (get) a new job next month?
3. Can you tell me when the next Eurostar for Brussels ... (leave)?
4. ... (the concert, really, start) at 6.30 tonight?

III. You have arrived at the bus station in Canterbury and you would like to go to the information centre. You ask a passer-by for directions. Complete the dialogue by choosing one of the words or expressions in each of the ten brackets. You will need to look at the map (see page 210) as you do the exercise. ●●

You: Excuse me. Could you (tell/say) me the way to the information centre, please?

Passer-by: Yes, certainly. You go down here – it's called Gravel (Walk/Way) – and at the end you turn (left/right) into Rose Lane.

You: Rose Lane.

Passer-by: Rose Lane bends round to the (left/right) and then you come into the High Street.

You: The High Street.

Passer-by: Then you go (straight along/straight away), past the (museum/hospital), over Stour Street and the information centre is on your right (after/before) you get to the (East Gate/West Gate).

You: Thanks very much. Is it far?

Passer-by: No. About (half a/one) mile I'd say.

You: Thank you.

Passer-by: (Please/You're welcome.)

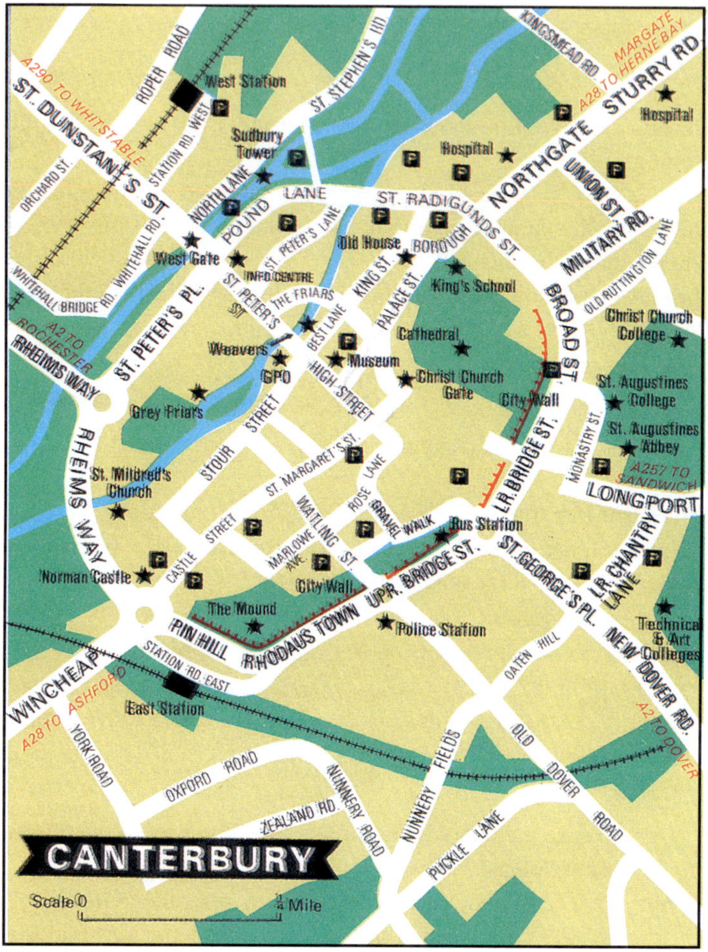
CANTERBURY
Scale 0 ¼ Mile
West Station
East Station
A290 TO WHITSTABLE
A28 TO MARGATE HERNE BAY
A2 TO ROCHESTER
A257 TO SANDWICH
A28 TO ASHFORD
A2 TO DOVER
ST. DUNSTAN'S ST.
NORTHGATE
STURRY RD
ST. RADIGUNDS ST.
BROAD ST.
MILITARY RD.
UNION ST.
LONGPORT
ST. PETER'S PL.
RHEIMS WAY
WINCHEAP
PIN HILL
RHODAUS TOWN
UPR. BRIDGE ST.
LR. BRIDGE ST.
ST. GEORGE'S PL.
NEW DOVER RD.
LR. CHANTRY LANE
OLD DOVER ROAD
NUNNERY FIELDS
OXFORD ROAD
YORK ROAD
ZEALAND RD.
NUNNERY ROAD
PUCKLE LANE
OATEN HILL
HIGH STREET
STOUR STREET
CASTLE STREET
WATLING ST.
GRAVEL WALK
ROSE LANE
BEST LANE
KING ST.
PALACE ST.
BOROUGH
POUND LANE
NORTH LANE
ST. STEPHEN'S HD
ROPER ROAD
STATION RD. WEST
STATION RD. EAST
ORCHARD ST.
WHITEHALL RD.
WHITEHALL BRIDGE RD.
KINGSMEAD RD.
OLD RUTTINGTON LANE
MONASTRY ST.
ST. MARGARET'S ST.
MARLOWE AVE.
THE FRIARS
ST. PETER'S LANE
ST. PETER'S ST.
Hospital
Sudbury Tower
West Gate
INFO CENTRE
Old House
King's School
Cathedral
Christ Church Gate
Christ Church College
St. Augustines College
St. Augustines Abbey
City Wall
Weavers
Museum
GPO
Grey Friars
St. Mildred's Church
Norman Castle
The Mound
Bus Station
Police Station
Technical & Art Colleges

IV. Complete this dialogue at a travel agency by using the correct form of the words in brackets. If there is no word in brackets, add it yourself.

- Good morning.
- Good morning. I ... (like) two tickets to Holyhead, please.
- Certainly. When ... (you, leave)?
- We ... (take) the 9 o'clock train tomorrow.
- I see. Single or ... ?
- Just single, please.
- First or second ... ?
- Second, please.
- Right. Two singles, Holyhead. That'll be £45.65, please.
- ... you are.
- Thank you. And £4.35 ... .
- Thank you.
- Have a good ... .
- Thanks.

V. Words which go together. Think of three words which would go well with the words below to form a compound noun (zusammengesetztes Wort). *Some of the exercise has been done for you.*

1. art	museum	2.	centre
3.	club	4. travel	agency

VI. Write a short paragraph in English about a city near you which might be of interest to tourists. Say where the city is, how big it is, what it is famous for and mention any other places of interest which you know.

13C

Sue Johnson – bad luck in Brighton

Listen carefully to what happened to Sue Johnson. Then answer the questions below.

I. What went wrong for Sue when she went to Brighton?
Cross the three things that did NOT go wrong.

a. She couldn't find her car keys.
b. She went the wrong way in the car.
c. She got stuck in a traffic jam.
d. She had an accident in her car.
e. Her handbag was stolen.
f. She had no change for the car park.
g. She lost an earring.
h. The theatre had reserved tickets for the wrong day.
i. They got to the theatre too late and missed the performance.
j. She got a parking fine.

II. What word from the text is missing? The first letter has been given.

1. If you are in a bad m... nobody can make you laugh.
2. The small money you need for coffee machines, underground tickets, newspapers is called c... .
3. We say the weather is "beautiful" or "lovely" but you can also say it is "g...".

4. If you look in shops and do not go in and buy anything it is called w... s... .
5. If you talk to a friend about what you have been doing and where you have been and who you have seen then you have a c... with him or her.
6. If you buy tickets for the cinema a few days before the film is shown, you order them in a... .

III. Write down the English for the following German expressions. They were all used in the story.

1. übrigens
2. sofort
3. laut Plan
4. kaum
5. etwas vereinbaren
6. Stell dir vor!

Brighton Pavilion

13D

Meterman goes to Laredo

I. Put these five sentences back into the text where they belong. They are the first sentences of paragraphs 1–5. The first sentence of the sixth paragraph is missing. Can you think of one yourself?

a. As he walks around Laredo Meterman *points out* some of the buildings.
b. Meterman can't find the meter anywhere but he doesn't give up.
c. Meterman finds it difficult to get into conversation with the *locals*.
d. The cowboys don't want anybody *interfering with* their lives.
e. Today Meterman has gone to Laredo, a Wild West town in the heart of the English countryside.

1. He talks to the camera: "Between you and me, there are no official records of electricity being *consumed* in this town. And I'm going to find out why."
2. Texas Rangers, the saloon, the gunsmith, the bank, the general store and an eating house. "You and I would call it a restaurant," he explains. "But these are primitive people."
3. Even the undertaker is too busy to say hello. However, in the Marshal's Office Meterman feels sure somebody will be there to help. "I don't suppose you know where the meter is, do you?" he asks the marshal politely.

4. "I *am determined to make* one of these cowboys *talk* to me," he says. *Gritting his teeth* he marches into the saloon and goes up to the barman. "The electricity consumption in this town is most irregular," he says in an official-sounding voice. "I must ask you to accompany me to headquarters."
5. Outside the saloon they fire at Meterman. He is hit in the chest, falls to the ground and dies. The undertaker arrives and Meterman is lifted into a *coffin*.
6. Slowly the *lid* of the coffin moves and Meterman appears. "Don't worry," he says removing a *bullet* from of his notebook. "I'm just keeping a low profile – that's one of our little phrases – keeping a low profile."

point out sth	hinweisen, aufmerksam machen auf etw.
locals	Ortsansässige, Einheimische
interfere with sth	sich in etw. einmischen
consume	verbrauchen
be determined to do sth	entschlossen sein, etw. zu tun
make sb do sth	jmdn. dazu bringen, etw. zu tun
grit one's teeth	die Zähne zusammenbeißen
coffin	Sarg
lid	Deckel
bullet	Kugel

II. Don't mix up words. Complete the sentences by using the words in the box. Think of the German translation for the words.

entrepreneur • undertaker

1. An ... is somebody whose job it is to organize funerals (*Begräbnisse*).
2. An ... is somebody who runs his or her own business.

sensible • sensitive

3. "Be ... . Don't buy a new motorbike if you've haven't got any money."
4. "Have you got any sun cream for ... skin?"

interfere • interrupt

5. "Do you always have to ... me when I'm in the middle of a sentence?"
6. "Do you like it when your parents ... with the education of your children?"

people • persons

7. How many ... live in Germany?
8. This lift will carry a maximum of eight ... .

locals • pubs

9. "When you are in England you really must go to some of the ... and try the beer there."
10. "We find it difficult getting to know the ... because we don't come from this part of the country."

III. Match the idiom (1–2) with its explanation (a–d).

1. Between you and me ... .
2. I'm keeping a low profile.

a. I'm telling you something which nobody else knows.
b. I'm making sure that nobody sees me.
c. I'm telling you something which you shouldn't tell anybody else.
d. I'm walking with my head down so nobody can see my face.

Now try to translate sentences 1 and 2 into German.

then just before we leave for the next race the car is again checked over and everything is *tightened* and all the *angles* are checked to make sure everything is correct. A lot of components on the car have a life, that is, we have experienced a part breaking after a certain length of time, and so we try to change the part before we know it's going to break.

The trophies are all ones that I have won. My favourite trophy is the one in the middle and that was on the Pirelli Classic Marathon in 1990 when we raced from London to Cortina in Italy, and it was the most spectacular race ever and we *came second overall*.

I do have another car for those horrible days when it's *pouring with rain* or snowing or I'm towing the Morgan to a motor racing circuit. But for those beautiful days when perhaps a little frost and the sun is shining, it has to be a Morgan."

run (a business, a shop etc.) (ran, run)	(ein Geschäft etc.) führen, leiten, betreiben
local community	örtliche Gemeinde
agent	Vertreter (einer Firma)
supply	liefern, ausliefern
service	warten, pflegen
restore	wiederherstellen, erneuern
cover	(be)decken, *hier*: die ganze Fläche erreichen
racing circuit	Rennstrecke
virtually	eigentlich, fast
formative	Aufbau-, Entwicklungs-
competition	Wettbewerb
dashboard	Armaturenbrett
dash	Abk. für *dashboard*
gauge	Anzeiger
switch	Schalter
fan	Ventilator, Lüftung
carry out	durchführen
consist of	bestehen aus
government testing (= MOT)	TÜV-Prüfung
on site	auf dem Gelände, *hier*: in der Werkstatt
achieve	erreichen, erringen, erzielen
be based in	seinen Standort haben in
retired	pensioniert, im Ruhestand
feel secure	sich sicher fühlen
apply to	*hier*: gelten für
craftsman	Handwerker, *hier*: Mechaniker
skill	Fertigkeit, Können
time after time	immer wieder
show off	demonstrieren, (her)zeigen
manufacturer	Produzent, Fabrikant, Hersteller
production run	Produktionslaufzeit
chassis	Chassis, Fahrgestell
body frame	Karosserie
be hand crafted	in Handarbeit hergestellt sein
fit sth	passen für etw.
adapt	anpassen, *hier*: vornehmen
cones	Kegel, *hier*: „Absperrhütchen" (*Straßenverkehr*)
marque	Automarke
tighten	festziehen, anziehen (*Schraube* etc.)
angle	Winkel(-eisen)
come second overall	*hier*: zweiter im Gesamtplacement, in der Gesamtwertung werden
pour with rain	in Strömen regnen, gießen, schütten

UNIT 5C

September is the month for making jam and *preserving fruit*. It's also the month when the *hops* are *harvested*. Hops are important for making beer. Beryl and Dave Stephens live in an unusual house called an *oast house*. For Beryl it is a very special place.

"We used to live nearer to London and we decided that we would like to have a place in the country and we were out looking. We found this oast house and it was in such an attractive setting that we just fell in love with it.

This is an oast house. It's used for *drying* hops. These are hops and they are used in the making of beer and they give beer their special *flavour*. This kitchen is special because it's round. In the old days this room was used for the drying of the hops. There was a huge fire in the centre and the smoke and the hot air rose to the *ceiling* and the hops were laid on the floor above and the hot air dried the hops.

My husband, Dave, is a do-it-yourself enthusiast. It's very *handy* to have someone like him in the home because there's a lot of work to be done here and he is doing a lot of the *decorating* and *converting*. The *roundel* is now used as a *study* for my husband and years ago it was used as a room for drying the hops that were laid on the floor and the heat from the fire from below would dry the hops.

This is the dining-room and it has a lovely view. You can see the duck pond. And we've kept a lot of the original *beams*, but the staircase we're hoping to change into a spiral staircase.

This is the *lounge* now and it was used for storing the sacks of hops after they'd been dried and before they went off in the wagons. I like living in the heart of the country for the *peace and quiet*, and without the *hustle and bustle* of being in London.

We plan to live here for the rest of our lives. It's a wonderful home for our grandchildren and it's a nice place for them to come and visit. We don't miss the city life at all, we know it's got fast food, the restaurants and cinemas and theatres, but we just like living in the peace of the country."

preserve fruit	Obst einkochen, einmachen
hops	Hopfen
harvest	ernten
oast house	Hopfendarre
dry	trocknen
flavour	Geschmack, Aroma
ceiling	Decke
handy	nützlich, praktisch
decorate	streichen, tapezieren
convert	*hier*: umbauen
roundel	*hier*: rundes Turmzimmer
study	Arbeitszimmer
beam	Balken
lounge	Wohnzimmer
peace and quiet	*wörtl.*: Friede und Ruhe, *hier*: Ruhe und Ungestörtheit
hustle and bustle	Trubel

UNIT 6C

Pål Reynolds runs a successful hairdresser's salon just off the busy high street. Why has he chosen such a small and *hidden* street? Hairdressing is not his only business. How are photography and *furniture* design connected to hairdressing? Find out what makes Paul successful and - where does he get his energy from?

"The satisfaction that one gets from making somebody look good never, never leaves you and it's something to this day that makes me still feel proud. I think that the salon used to be looked at as an *effeminate* place for men, yes, because if you remember, we did come from ..., hairdressing was in *cubicles at one stage*. The men went to the barbers, women were in their cubicles, a very private thing. And now we don't *treat* men any differently, there's nothing special for men or special for women, only the toilets.

When I started my business, I mean, I took the business plan to the bank, which they accepted, and I came straight out looking for a salon, and I found the salon and I *was after* a very cheap *rent*. I'm slightly off the main high street here but my rent is ten times less than the shop 25 yards away from me. You have to work very hard to get people in here because we are down an *alleyway* and so public relations plays a very large part in our company. For example, photo work. *We do lots of magazine work* to bring people in here because they're not going to *walk off the street*. We need to get that business in many other ways.

About three or four times a year we have a very big *photo shoot* where we drive up to a big studio in London and *hire* professional models from all the London agencies. It does *work out* very *expensive* but I have learned my lesson in doing cheap ones. Cheap photography does not work. Because a lot of hairdressing magazines are international, obviously they've seen it in other countries, *picked up on* it and that's how I became invited to going on to Germany and I've done lots and lots of seminars and shows over there now in Hamburg, Kiel, Neumünster and Cologne.

There are twelve staff in the salon and they are all trained here *to start with*, all the basic training is done here, and then, we then start sending them on *paid-for courses*. They come back with their little diploma which to them is their trophy and it makes me feel proud, makes them feel proud, and the clients like to see that we*'re* all *highly trained*. We're into design because we looked at the *retail* hairdressing *products* and found that they had lots of little *gaps* that I was interested to fill, as in *retail stands* for their products, why they weren't looking good and why they weren't working, and since then we've gone into designing some furniture and retail stands. So we actually designed one which was *flat packed* and so it *cut costs* for the company to import and export because most hairdressing retail products are worldwide. So the fact that they can send something smaller is going to save them a fortune.

The key to my success: I think the key to any success is hard work, but *linked in with* hard work I think it's variety. I wake up every morning and there's something different to do. I can come in here one day, I can go designing the next day, and do a photo shoot the next day. It keeps my *drive* strong, and if your drive is strong, the staff around you become strong too."

hide (hid, hidden)	verstecken
furniture	Einrichtung, Möbel
effeminate	unmännlich, eines Mannes unwürdig
cubicle	Kabine
stage	Phase, Zeitpunkt
at one stage	*hier im Sinne von*: früher
treat	behandeln, umgehen mit
be after	hinterher sein, suchen
rent	Miete
alleyway	(schmale) Gasse, Durchgang
We do lots of magazine work ...	Wir machen eine Menge Werbung in Illustrierten ...
walk off the street	die Straße verlassen, *hier*: abseits der Hauptstraße gehen
shoot	Aufnahme (*Foto, Film*)
photo shoot	Fototermin
hire	engagieren
it works out expensive	es kommt teuer
pick up on sth	etw. aufgreifen
to start with	zunächst
paid-for course	bezahlter Kurs
be highly trained	hervorragend ausgebildet, eine Spitzenkraft sein
retail products	Produkte für den Einzelhandel
gap	Lücke
retail stand	Verkaufsstand
flat packed	flach (= *raumsparend*) verpackt
cut costs	Kosten sparen
link in with	verbinden mit
drive	Motivation, Elan, Dynamik

UNIT 7C

Tony Pulis is the manager of Gillingham Football Club. The club were not doing very well when he joined them. What were the problems? What did Tony do to put things right? How are they doing now? Listen to Tony Pulis.

"I'm originally from South Wales and I was brought up not far from the docks in Newport. My father was a steel worker. I started my career at Bristol Rovers when I was sixteen and spent nine years there and then went off to Newport in Bournemouth. At the end of my career I got into the coaching and ended up coaching at Bournemouth. I became manager of Bournemouth and then I joined Gillingham as manager. For the last five seasons Gillingham Football *Club* had *finished in the bottom three of the third division* and *gates* were down to about 2,500, and when I took over the football club it was very, very important that we change the playing staff, and we brought ten new players into the football club.

Gillingham Football Club were in serious financial difficulties, they had the *receiver* in and *it was touch and go* whether the football club was going to live on, and the *Chairman* of the football club invested almost a million pounds to keep the club alive, and since then we've taken great *strides*, both on and off the field, not only to stabilize the club but to *push the club on*. It was very good to bring ten new players in, very important that the playing side was *strengthened*, and the players that the football club have brought in are very experienced players, they're not young players, they're players who *have been through the mill* and understand what's needed from them *week in and week out*. Because the season is a very long season, a very *gruelling* season where we almost play two games a week.

If we take a typical week, training will *commence* on Monday at eleven o'clock and we have got our own training facilities which we *are* very, very *fortunate to have*. The players will *report* at eleven o'clock, they will do a warm up by themselves, then we take them into a ball warm up, so they have two warm up *sessions*. Obviously when you're indoors training in a *gym*, and, the training methods are different from being inside to outside. The area is smaller, you're working on a hard surface, so you've got to be a little bit careful with the players in respect to their ankles and their knees, their *joints*. But we still work very, very hard when we have to and we *incorporate* different tests. One of those tests is the bleep test. The bleep test is an organized test that's been *performed* by top athletes in this country and it's a good method, and a good way of testing the players' fitness all the way through the season.

Last week's game, which was a *top-of-the-table clash* against Chester – Chester were top of the table, we were second – was *called off* because of the snow and the freezing weather that this part of the country had. We were expecting 10,000 people to come to Saturday's game, and to pay obviously and watch the game, and the financial *implications* of 10,000 is very important to us. We were very disappointed that the game was called off and it *upset* the plans obviously of the players and also the financial plans. But we've got to get on with things and we've got a very, very big game coming up against Plymouth and I'm sure we'll get those 10,000 people in then. This season we're actually in the top three. If we finish in the top three we will *gain promotion* to the next league.

I know it's very early in the season and there's still a long way to go but we're very, very optimistic that we can *maintain* the *strides* that have been gained since the beginning of the season and push forward and hopefully maintain the success that we've gained."

The club finished in the bottom three of the third division.	Der Klub beendete die Saison als einer der letzten drei der dritten Liga.
gates	*hier*: Zuschauerzahlen
receiver	*hier*: Gerichtsvollzieher
it was touch and go	es hing an einem Haar, es stand auf des Messers Schneide
chairman	Vorsitzender, Präsident
strides	*hier*: Anstrengungen
push the club on	den Verein voranbringen
strengthen	verstärken
have/has been through the mill	durch eine harte Schule gegangen sein
week in and week out	Woche für Woche

gruelling	strapaziös, aufreibend
commence	beginnen
be fortunate to have	glücklicherweise haben
report	*hier*: sich zum Training melden
session	*hier*: Trainingseinheit
gym	Turn-, Sporthalle
joint	Gelenk
incorporate	*hier*: in das Training einbauen
perform	machen, durchführen
top-of-the-table clash	Spitzenspiel (*im Sport*)
call off	absagen, ausfallen lassen
implication	Folge, Auswirkung
upset	umstoßen, über den Haufen werfen
gain promotion	*hier*: den Aufstieg schaffen
maintain	(aufrecht)erhalten
strides	*hier*: Fortschritte

UNIT 8C

James and Alex and friends have formed a group playing rock. They usually play at home but they hope to *perform* in public soon. Today they have *hired* a van and a hall to practise playing in public.

"We're a four-piece band made up of bass guitar, lead guitar, keyboards and drums. Alex plays keyboards, James, Alex's brother, plays lead guitar and Sally plays bass guitar and I play the drums. We haven't got our own van for transport of our equipment, usually we ask our parents if they can do the transport for us, putting the equipment in their cars but today we had to hire a van to bring all the equipment here and then *unload* it all ourselves and set everything up on the stage, which myself I don't ..., I quite actually enjoy doing that thing, setting up my drum kit. You need to have quite a lot of technical knowledge to be able to set up a lot of the equipment, for example, the guitars, you need to know what you're doing with a guitar to *plug* it *in*, get the right sound that you want and you have to have enthusiasm to actually get it, you know, it's a lot of work, a lot of *effort* to put into setting things up and I enjoy the setting up of my kit or *piecing* it all *together*. I had to cut a *hole* in the *skin* of the drum in order to place a microphone inside it because you get a far better sound by having the microphone nearer the *beater* which is hitting the skin on the other side, so I had to cut a hole in it in order to place the microphone inside.

We all own our own equipment, Alex has a piano in his house and a keyboard – a couple of keyboards – that he uses. I've got my own drum kit which I bought off my cousin a couple of years ago. James plays his own guitar which he bought and he has his own *amp* as well and Sally actually *borrows* James's bass guitar. She doesn't actually have one of her own.

So we originally just played together doing *covers* of Pink Floyd songs and different bands that we liked listening to and from there Alex began to write music and a friend of his wrote *lyrics* for the music that we were going to be then performing, and we started to work that out and from then on we've really been practising and *getting up to performance standard*. At the moment we're *rehearsing* a lot to the intentions of going out and doing concerts and performing to the public. We used to play in Alex's front living-room because they've got all their equipment there, so we used to have to go to his house and I would take my drum kit to their house and set it up there and we would perform, we would rehearse and practise the songs there and play. *Occasionally* we used to do the same thing at my house, if they would just bring their guitars to my house and we would set up there and do the same thing there.

We're actually interested in playing in churches because of the feel that you get in a church, the atmosphere of what the building is, and the feeling we get from that, the amazing sound that you create when performing inside, and that's one of the main things we're interested in when performing there, and the general atmosphere of a church. In the future we intend to get a *recording deal*, hopefully, to then be producing records and albums and to be performing live and to the public our own compositions."

perform	*hier*: auftreten, spielen	amp (= amplifier)	Verstärker
hire	mieten	borrow	sich ausleihen
unload	aus-, entladen	covers	*hier*: Bearbeitungen
plug in	einstecken (in die Steckdose)	lyrics	(Lied-)Texte (*Rock, Pop etc.*)
effort	Mühe, Anstrengung	get up to	sich entwickeln zu
piece together	zusammensetzen	performance	vorführreifes
hole	Loch	standard	Niveau
skin	*hier*: Bespannung	rehearse	proben
beater	*hier*: (Schlagzeug-) Stock	occasionally	gelegentlich
		recording deal	*hier*: Schallplatten-vertrag

UNIT 9C

The *Head* of Eurotunnel's *Public Affairs Department* has worked on the Channel Tunnel project longer than anyone else. At times John Noulton still finds it difficult to believe that the tunnel is a reality. What kind of *engineering problems* did they have during the construction? How did he feel when the project was completed? Does the Channel Tunnel really change the way the British feel about themselves? Listen to John Noulton.

"I was here ten years ago when this was a green field and even today, nearly two years after it opened, I still have to *pinch myself* to believe that it's true. And every time I go through the Tunnel I still *have a sense of wonder* about it. It's been so much part of my life, it is now there, it's now operating successfully and it's now *hugely* popular. In many ways the construction of the Tunnel was the easiest part, that's not to say that there weren't very *severe* engineering difficulties in the way, but they were solved by very competent British and French and other nationalities' engineers.

So there were difficulties, first of all, how do you meet in the middle, for example, which *required* a very, very complicated *feat of navigation*. When you're underground you can't see the stars. Much more difficult than the journey of Christopher Columbus because he could see the sun and the stars, we couldn't. It was a very tough job underground. We, for example, ran into some unexpectedly difficult ground conditions just off the British coast so we had to *pretty well* stop, redesign the machines and carry out extensive *treatment* of the ground in order to get through that *patch*. It was about two kilometres long, but they did that, and in the end one of the British machines set what we think is a world record of *426 meters of fully-lined, large-diameter tunnel* in a week.

There are two *crossover cabins* in the tunnel, people just think of them as tunnels, but there are these two huge cabins, about *equidistant from* each coast. To give you some idea of the size, they are as big as the *nave* of a large cathedral, the Cathedral of Rouen, or Canterbury or Cologne, for example. You could stand three London double deck buses on top of one another in the cabin. Each of these cabins *enables* trains to *switch from* one tunnel *to* the other.

Britain and France aren't the worlds most natural *allies*. I think we've been to war together more times than any other countries and our cultures are totally different even though we're neighbours. To give you one rather *silly* example, the British miners, before they met, worked under coal mining *regulations*, safety regulations. They had to wear on their belts a *respirator*, a *breathing equipment*, they were not allowed to smoke or to drink, and indeed, if they were found in *possession* of tobacco or alcohol, that was a *dismissable offence*. On the French side they did not have to wear respirators, though they were *available in case of need*. Each miner was allowed 25 centilitres of wine with his lunch and smoking appeared to be *compulsory*.

The day of the first undersea breakthrough, that was the first of December, 1990, two years after the machines had set off to meet one another, was one of the longest days I can remember. It was a very emotional day, a very exciting day, a day which I think everybody was touched by. Within Eurotunnel, everybody has to know enough of the other language to be able to do his job without translation. But there are many people, like the train crews, who go backwards and forwards between the two countries, they have to have a good *mastery* of the other language, especially *terms in relation to* safety.

The psychological *impact* of the Tunnel for people in Britain was much greater than for the French. The French have land borders with many, many other countries and to them, they couldn't understand what all the *fuss* was about. But there was quite a lot of excitement and *regret* in this country, that what one *commentator* called our *splendid isolation*, was over. A lot of people were worried that it would somehow *alter* the Britishness of the British people, which of course is clearly nonsense, I mean, people on the continent who have land *boundaries* are no less French than they always were, and no less German than they always were. It is the greatest project of the century, in Europe, if not the world. It's a wonderful piece of missing infrastructure in Europe that will help to join together the future European community."

head	Leiter
public affairs department	Abteilung für Öffentlichkeitsarbeit
engineering problem	technisches Problem
pinch oneself	sich kneifen, zwicken
have a sense of wonder	das Gefühl haben, ein Wunder sei geschehen
hugely	ungemein, ungeheuer
severe	ernsthaft, schwerwiegend
require	erfordern
feat (of)	Großtat, Meisterleistung (an)
navigation	Navigation, Steuerungskunst
pretty well	*hier*: beinahe, fast
treatment	Behandlung
patch	Fleck, *hier*: Stück Boden
426 meters of fully-lined, large-diameter tunnel	ein im vollen Durchmesser ausgebauter Tunnel von 426 Metern Länge
crossover cabin	*Teil des Tunnels, wo die Züge kreuzen können*
equidistant from	gleich weit entfernt, in gleichem Abstand von
nave	Kirchenschiff
enable	ermöglichen
switch	kreuzen, rangieren
from ... to	von ... auf
allies	Verbündete
silly	albern, dumm
regulations	Bestimmungen, Vorschriften
respirator (= breathing equipment)	Atemgerät
possession	Besitz
dismissable offence	Kündigungsgrund
available	verfügbar
in case of need	im Bedarfsfall
compulsory	obligatorisch, Pflicht-
mastery	Beherrschung (*einer Sprache*)
term	Ausdruck, Wendung
in relation to	in Bezug auf
impact	(Ein-)Wirkung, Auswirkung
fuss	Aufregung, Getue, Theater

regret	Bedauern
commentator	Kommentator
splendid isolation	„glorreiche“ Isolierung (*polit. Begriff, der die bewußte Isolierung, d.h. Bündnislosigkeit Englands bezeichnet)*
alter	verändern
boundary	Grenze

UNIT 10C

Lynn Redgrave is the Tourism Development Officer for her local Borough Council. Today she is visiting an unusual bed and breakfast facility, a *floating barge* known as the Captain Webb. What is her connection with bed and breakfast? What does she enjoy about her work? What did she use to do before? Listen to Lynn Redgrave's personal view.

"I have always worked in the leisure and tourism field. I left school at 16 and went to a specialized school in Switzerland to learn foreign languages. After that I stayed abroad and worked in *tour operations*, guiding in various countries, looking after English people visiting foreign countries and from there I came back to Britain and worked in conference organization, *sales marketing* of hotels. One important aspect of my job at the moment is putting together all of the bed and breakfast accommodation to go into the holiday guide for the area. Now that would mean that we write to all the bed and breakfasts in the area and ask them whether they would like to come into the guide. We ask that before they come into the guide they are *registered* with the Regional Tourist Board."

(Owner of the Captain Webb: "This is the *galley*. On a boat of course we call it not a kitchen but a galley.")

"This boat is a *unique* form of bed and breakfast and I think I can safely say that it is the only boat that's offering bed and breakfast in the Heart of Kent area. So it's interesting to look at it, obviously we've got to look at it slightly differently to a house on dry land. We'll be looking at the cabins, not expecting them to be the same size, for example, as they would be in a house."

(Owner of the Captain Webb: "All the cabins are centrally heated and they are nice and cool in summer obviously.")

"We're looking at it from the point of view of the visitor who's looking for an original experience. I would like to see all of the cabins and just chat to the *proprietor* about, for example, where people would leave their cars if they're coming to stay on board, and just generally finding out what sort of welcome they would get. I like meeting people. *Fundamentally* I think you've got to like working with people to be in this business. I also like visiting places myself, and it gives me a wonderful opportunity to combine what I like doing with my work.

When I started in Switzerland I was living in a *ski resort* and very quickly learned to ski and at the age of 17, 18 skiing became very important to me. So I tried after I'd left college in Switzerland to work in ski resorts combining working in travel and tourism with doing what I enjoyed most which was skiing.

The sort of facilities that we're looking at in a bed and breakfast are obviously the bedrooms. We just like to look at the bedrooms and check that they're OK. We then look at the main areas that the bed and breakfast proprietor is using for the visitors: the dining-room, the lounge, if the lounge is available for visitors to sit in, just to get the overall impression that what we have in the brochure is good welcoming accommodation and we find that we have so many different types of accommodation in the bed and breakfast market in our area."

(Talking to another owner of a bed and breakfast: "Hello John, hi." – "Hello." – "Well, this is one of your bikes?" – "Yes.")

"We have in the Maidstone area, just outside of Maidstone, in one of the little villages, a bed and breakfast that offer bicycle hire, and also offer advice to the people staying on *circular routes* that they can do for the day, places to stop at for meal breaks, and they also offer a *back-up service*.

One of the funny frustrations I find in my job is my name. My name is Lynn Redgrave, and the Redgraves are a famous acting family in Britain and I think they're probably quite well known abroad as well. But unfortunately people do always ask me whether I'*m related to* the Redgrave family and in some ways it's quite amusing and it means that people are remembering my name.

Before moving to Maidstone I lived and worked in the Lake District. The Lake District is in the northwest of England and it's quite close to Scotland. It's like Scotland in as much as it is a very mountainous, beautiful countryside but a lot smaller, a lot more compact, and as the word suggests, there are a lot of lakes. I enjoy, in my spare time, visiting restaurants, pubs, tea places, that's probably why I like working in tourism because I like the good things of life.

In the three years that I've lived and worked in Maidstone, I've found that tourism is becoming more and more important to the economy and more and more people are realizing the *benefits* of tourism, both to the area and to *residents* that live in the place. Bed and breakfast, I think, offers visitors a unique opportunity to *sample* the English way of life, and that means that you can stay in a family, in a house, and really get to know the people there."

floating	schwimmend	fundamentally	grundsätzlich
barge	Hausboot, Barke	ski resort	Ski-Gebiet
tour operation	Reiseleitung, Reisebetreuung	circular route	Rundreise, Rundfahrt
		back-up service	*eine Art „Notdienst“*
sales marketing	Verkaufsförderung	be related to	verwandt sein mit
register	eintragen, aufnehmen	benefit	Vorteil
galley	Kombüse (*Küche auf einem Schiff*)	resident	Ortsansässige(r), Einwohner(in)
unique	einzigartig	sample	(aus)probieren, testen
proprietor	Eigentümer, Besitzer		

UNIT 11C

Dr. Richard Suthers is the *rowing coach* at the King's School in Rochester. His son, Simon, is a member of the rowing team. What kind of fitness programme do the rowers follow? Where do they train, and how often? Do they take part in competitions? Find out why these young people have to keep fit.

R. Suthers: "To be a good rower you need four *attributes*. You have to have *stamina*, strength, a good technique in the boats, and a great will to win. I did not row myself when I was younger, I *was* very *keen on mountaineering* and rock climbing. It was only when my oldest son became interested in rowing at the age of twelve, that I myself was introduced to the sport. William was a very good single *sculler* when he was at the school and became the Great Britain Under-18 Junior Single Scull Champion. My younger son, Simon, is still at the school. He is 18 now and together with his friends, they have also had good successes."

S. Suthers: "In rowing I really hope to get into the national *squad* like my brother, and be able to, you know, win the national championships just like him. Although I'm not comparing myself to him, I want to *be* better than him and completely *oblivious to him*, really. I don't want people saying, 'Oh, he's above so and so, and he's just as good as him.' I want people to say, 'He's so and so in his own right.' – not to compare me with anybody."

R. Suthers: "When developing stamina, exercises should be done with a *heart rate* that is only 80% of maximum. When training for fitness and stamina, you must not *destroy* the body, you need to *condition* the body. This takes time and over a period of years the natural heart rate will be reduced.

Before starting any exercises you need to warm up the body, generally, to start with, and then to stretch up the muscles systematically. If you exercise without stretching the muscles, you*'re likely to cause injury*."

S. Suthers: "Aerobic training is basically concentrating on your lung *capacity*. When you race you get out of breath. It builds up your lung capacity so you don't get *acid breath*, and you just *build up* your general fitness on the whole."

R. Suthers: "Simon is now exercising *at a steady rate*. His heart rate should not exceed 160 beats per minute, which is 80% of his maximum of 200. He will exercise at this steady rate for at least 30 minutes and that will condition his body, in particular, his heart and his lungs."

S. Suthers: "*Anaerobic training* is basically training for when you get tired during a race, is trying to keep up the power and the *momentum* you have during a race. So anaerobic is you're actually working once you start getting tired, you're working more and you're trying to build up your *resistance level*."

R. Suthers: "In this work, the athlete goes at maximum rate for a short period of time, in this case 20 seconds and then rests for double that period so that his heart rate and the *lactic acid* will have time to *dissipate* from the muscles. To test the developments of strength, we do tests on various bits of apparatus, including the *bench pull test*, where for 6 minutes the athlete lifts the bar at a steady rate of 30 lifts per minute."

S. Suthers: "I *keep records* for my training because I just want to see what I've done, and how I can improve. I've kept them for quite a while, and now there are other people that are coming up for the boat club, you can actually compare my records with them as well, and we can see how good they actually are, when they are *boasting* that they're good, and I think, 'Oh, you're not as good as me.' And now we've got the records, we can actually see if it's true or not."

R. Suthers: "The boys and girls practise three times a week. They will also be competing on Saturday or Sunday, most weekends *throughout the year*. The job of coach is extremely tiring, especially as one gets older. One needs to *supervise* the training as much as possible to *ensure* that people are following the *set routine*."

S. Suthers: "He pushes the crew very hard. It gets tiring but he's always there, he's always telling us to do more, and we always *end up doing* it."

rowing coach	Rudertrainer
attribute	*hier*: Eigenschaft
stamina	Ausdauer, Durchhalte-, Stehvermögen
be keen on	erpicht, „scharf“ sein auf
mountaineering	Bergsteigen
sculler	Skuller (*Sportruderer*)
squad	Kader, Aufgebot (*Sport*)
be oblivious to sb	jmdn. ignorieren, nicht wahrnehmen
heart rate	Herzfrequenz
destroy	*hier*: ruinieren, zugrunde richten
condition	*hier*: in Form bringen, Kondition aufbauen
be likely to do sth	wahrscheinlich, voraussichtlich etw. tun
injury	Verletzung
capacity	Volumen, Fassungsvermögen
acid breath	übersäuerter Atem *(in der Lunge)*
build up	steigern, festigen
at a steady rate	mit konstantem Tempo, in einem gleichbleibenden Takt
anaerobic training	Ausdauertraining
momentum	Schwung, Antrieb
resistance level	körperliche Widerstandskraft
lactic acid	Milchsäure (*im Blut*)
dissipate	sich auflösen, sich zerstreuen
bench pull test	*Training durch Gewichtheben, wobei der Trainierende in Bauchlage auf einer Bank liegt (= „die Bank drücken“)*
keep records	*hier*: (regelmäßige) Aufzeichnungen machen, Tagebuch führen
boast	sich brüsten, angeben
throughout (the year)	(das ganze Jahr) hindurch, während (des ganzen Jahres)
supervise	überwachen
ensure	sichergehen, sicherstellen
set routine	festgesetzter, festgelegter Ablauf
end up doing sth	am Schluss, schließlich etw. tun

UNIT 12C

Bonnie Lamont is a professional garden designer. She is working on plans to develop the gardens and *woodland* of this beautiful country house. It is the middle of winter now. How will the gardens look in the summertime, and what will the woodland gardens be like in a few years from now? What was this place used for in the old days and what is it going to be? Listen to Bonnie as she talks about the plans.

“I've been working here for the last year and a half, and in that time I've grown to love this place as everybody does. It has such a wonderful atmosphere, and feeling about it, it's hard to describe.

This is the old canal, and during the summer months we will have a boat here, and visitors will be able to take a trip from the *jetty* up to the *Enchanted Forest*. In the Enchanted Forest we have the Gardens of Neptune, the Children's Garden, and the *Serpent's Lair*.

This garden is called the *Spring of Life*, which comes from the idea of there being a spring. It is a *spring-fed* garden. The grotto behind *houses* Neptune who is sitting inside with water *spilling* over his head from the spring.

During the summer months the visitors can come and sit around this garden and enjoy the sound of the water *tinkling* on the stones, and also the *foliage* and flowers that will be *surrounding* this pool. We also have fish in the water, *rainbow trout*. This is one of my favourite gardens of Groombridge, mainly because it's such a peaceful and *tranquil* setting. Many of the visitors, including myself, like to come here and sit, *particularly* on a summer's afternoon, and enjoy the view. At the moment everything looks very *bare apart from* the evergreen *shrubs* that you can see, but at the start of *spring*, all the plants that are sleeping will come to life and give us a wonderful *display* of *bold* foliage plants. The colour theme here is a mixture of *lush* green, purples and whites. We have the *foxglove* tree, Polonia Termintosa, which gives a *marvellous* display of foxglove flowers hidden *underneath* huge *furry* leaves.

This is the area where we're going to build a garden for children based on the book 'The Wind in the *Willows'*. Over where you can see the red *markers* will be Ratty's house, and below on the water's *edge*, a jetty and a boat for Ratty to sail in. Unfortunately because of the risks involved, the children won't be able to climb over the garden, but they will be able to sit and look at it from the *pathway*, and I think that every child knows the story by Kenneth Grahame, 'The Wind in the Willows', and they will be able to *relate to* that and see Ratty and his house.

This is the Serpent's Lair, designed by Ivan Hicks, who specializes in surrealism. The garden, as you can see, is based on the game *'Snakes and Ladders'*. There are two ladies behind me, behind the *spider's web*, guarding the serpent who is at their feet. At the moment you can see very little in the way of planting, but in the summertime, we will have created an atmosphere of mystery. The leaves on the trees will be in full growth, and the ground, which at the moment is bare, will be covered in green foliage, making the whole thing feel very dark and mysterious.

I'm afraid that this area looks rather untidy at the moment as it's under construction. We have the old *dairy* situated behind the *greenhouse*, which is being converted to a restaurant. Here are the plans which show the building which we hope to have finished for the summer, for use this year. The large building situated at the end of what is, at present, the old dairy, is the old barn which we hope to convert into a children's play area though we don't have permission for that yet and it's something to look forward to *in the long term*. When the buildings have been converted we will have a restaurant for formal meals, weddings and private parties, and a tea room for the visitors who come to look at the garden, to enjoy a nice cup of tea and a light snack. We will also sell ice creams. People will be able to sit out here on this lower terrace, and enjoy the flowers that will surround them. *Scent* is the theme here, and it's something that plays a very important part in everybody's life. This is a garden that will *appeal to* the *senses*. We will plant old favourites, such as lavender, *thyme* and *rosemary*, all of which appeal to both touch and scent.

Here we are in the formal gardens and we are looking at the White Garden which is one of my favourites. It's built on the *site* of an old *orchard*, and I designed this garden, and we created it last year. The idea came from an old 17th century garden plan, which we felt would *be in keeping with* this garden, which is also 17th century. In the summertime it is a *riot* of white, the scent is magnificent and some of the plants are out of this world. We have lilies everywhere, and lots of lovely climbing roses, white lavender and other scented white plants, *hence* the name the White Garden.

The thing I find so satisfying about my work here is that I have been able to see things through from the start, from the early stages on the *drawing board* through to the preparation work on the ground, the planting, and then seeing the final garden begin to develop. Obviously it's going to take some time for the gardens to *mature* and I hope that I'll be around to see them."

woodland	Waldung, Waldland
jetty	(Landungs-)Steg
Enchanted Forest	Zauberwald
Serpent's Lair	Schlangengrube
Spring of Life	Quelle des Lebens, Lebensquell
spring-fed	von einer Quelle gespeist
house	beherbergen
spill	sich ergießen
tinkle	*hier*: plätschern
foliage	Laub, Blätter
surround	umgeben
rainbow trout	Regenbogenforelle
tranquil	ruhig, friedlich
particularly	insbesondere, besonders
bare	kahl, nackt, bloß
apart from	abgesehen von
shrub	Strauch, Busch
spring	Frühling
display	*hier*: Schauspiel
bold	*hier*: kühn hervor-tretend
lush	saftig, üppig
foxglove	Fingerhut
marvellous	herrlich, wunderbar
underneath	unter(halb)
furry	pelzig
willow	Weide
marker	Markierung
edge	*hier*: Rand
pathway	Pfad
relate to	in Zusammenhang bringen mit
Snakes and Ladders	*wörtl.*: „Schlangen und Leitern", *ein beliebtes Brettspiel für Kinder*
spider's web	Spinnennetz
dairy	Molkerei
greenhouse	Gewächshaus
in the long term	auf lange Sicht gesehen
scent	Duft, (Wohl-)Geruch
appeal to	wirken auf, reizen
senses	Sinne
thyme	Thymian
rosemary	Rosmarin
site	Gelände, Grundstück
orchard	Obstgarten
be in keeping with sth	mit etw. in Einklang stehen, entsprechen
riot	Aufruhr, *hier*: Rausch
hence	daher, deshalb
drawing board	Zeichenbrett
mature	reifen, *hier*: richtig einwachsen, sich voll entwickeln

UNIT 13C

Sue Johnson has been to Brighton for a day out to meet her friend, Shirley, and see some of the sights. Back home, in the evening, she tells another friend all about her day out. It was one of those days when things didn't go *according to* plan.

Gill: "Now, tell me about your day in Brighton. Did you meet Shirley, and did you enjoy yourselves?"
Sue: "Yes, we had lots of fun."
Gill: "Did everything go all right?"
Sue: "Well, yes and no."
Gill: "How do you mean, yes and no?"
Sue: "Yes, we enjoyed ourselves, and no, everything didn't go all right."
Gill: "Oh dear, tell me about it."
Sue: "It was one of those days, when everything seems to go wrong. Do you know what I mean?"
Gill: "Hmm, I certainly do."

Sue: "Things *started off* badly. First, I was all ready to go and I couldn't find the keys to the car. Well, I looked in the usual place but they just weren't there. So I *set out* late and in a bad mood. Anyway, everything went fine for a bit, but then I took a wrong *turning*. You know how difficult it is to see the signs sometimes if you're driving alone. Well there was nobody to ask, no shops to stop at and ask the way, no pubs, nothing. I *was* completely *lost*. In the end I stopped and looked at the map and got back on the right road. When I got to Brighton the traffic was terrible. I got caught in a traffic jam and I hardly moved for fifteen minutes. I was quite late by that time and I was worried about Shirley. We had arranged to meet at 11 o'clock outside the Pavilion and it was 11.30 when I arrived and of course I couldn't find anywhere to park the car, nowhere at all. I found a car park in the end, but then, of course, guess what? No change for the machine. All I had was a 5-pound note. The next thing was, I *dropped* my handbag. Eventually I found somebody with some change."

Gill: "Oh dear, what a start to a day out."

Sue: "Shirley was still waiting outside the Pavilion so that was all right."

Gill: "Oh good."

Sue: "She was pleased to see me, she *was about to* give up and go home. We did enjoy our visit to the Pavilion, I hadn't been there before. It's well worth a visit. You can just imagine the great *banquets* with the Prince Regent and his *fashionable* friends. It was a *gorgeous* day and we went for a walk by the sea. And then, another *disaster*. I lost an earring. We couldn't find it anywhere."

(Sue: "Oh no, I've lost an earring." – Shirley: "Where were we?" – Sue: "It could be anywhere." – Shirley: "Oh, look here." – Sue: "Brilliant." – Shirley: "Your earring!" – Sue: "Thanks. At last something's gone right." – Shirley: "Oh, well done.")

Sue: "After that we did some *window shopping* and then we had lunch together which was nice. We had a good chat and she told me all her news. She sent you her love, by the way."

Gill: "Oh, that's nice."

Sue: "But after lunch, things started to go wrong again. I tell you, it really was one of those days. We were going to the theatre, to a matinee at 2.30. Well, we got there at 2.15 to pick up the tickets, I'd ordered the tickets in advance. Guess what! No tickets. They had made a mistake, and they had booked tickets for the wrong day. Oh, but they were marvellous and they found us two seats *straight away*, and very good ones. And we enjoyed the play enormously."

Gill: "So, the day finished well, did it?"

Sue: "Yes. Except when I got back to the car, I had a parking ticket. I have to pay a 30-pound fine."

Gill: "Oh no. Next time you'd better take the train!"

according to	nach, gemäß	banquet	Bankett, Festmahl
start off	losgehen	fashionable	vornehm, elegant
set out	sich auf den Weg machen	gorgeous	wunderschön
turning	Abzweigung	disaster	Unglück, Katastrophe
be lost	sich verirrt haben	window shopping	Schaufensterbummel
drop	fallen lassen	straight away	sofort, auf der Stelle
be about to	im Begriff sein zu		

KEY TO EXERCISES

UNIT 1

1A

Text

1. True (lines 4 and 6) – **2.** True (lines 6 and 9) .– **3.** False (lines 5 and 12) – **4.** True (lines 5 and 12) – **5.** to get to know somebody (line 2) – **6.** housework (line 5) – **7.** the best way to learn the language (line 10) – **8.** *Example*: I think it will be Manuela. She has got a good friend, Pam, and Pam will help Manuela to get to know other English people. – **9.** *Example*: I think Jean-Charles will earn the most money. He is a waiter so he will not only get his regular wages. He will also get tips from his guests. – **10.** *Example*: I think Jean-Charles has got the most interesting job. He meets a lot of people and will have time to do some travelling.

Exercises

I. **1.** Our train is coming! – **2.** I'm trying to read. – **3.** It's not raining anymore. – **4.** We're leaving now. – **5.** She's not going home yet. – **6.** They're crossing the road.

II. **1.** Why are you feeling ...? – **2.** Is David staying ...? – **3.** Are the other students enjoying ...? – **4.** Is Stephen looking for ...? – **5.** Why is Karl working ...? – **6.** What are you studying?

III. **1.** This is Manuela. She comes from France. She's staying with her friend Pam. She's working at a house for elderly residents. Today she's shopping at the local market. She's buying some fruit and vegetables. – **2.** This is Erich. He comes from Germany. He's a student. He's living on a university campus. He's staying in England to learn the language. – **3.** I'm Laszlo. I come from Hungary. I'm living in a friend's flat. I'm working as a waiter in a restaurant. At the moment I'm setting up the tables. – **4.** This is Tadziu. He's from Poland. He's staying at a guesthouse near Victoria Station. He's a tourist. Today he's visiting the British Museum. – **5.** This is Sven and Mara. They come from Sweden. They're staying at a campsite in Wales. They're having a two-week holiday in Britain. Today they're travelling to Scotland. – **6.** My name is Guido. I come from Switzerland. I'm riding around Britain on my motorbike for ten days. I'm staying at bed and breakfasts.

IV. Pam and I are having ... We are doing ... I am learning ... I am writing ... I am drinking ... watching ... is shopping ... is buying

V. **1.** helpful (line 8) – **2.** important (line 10) – **3.** accommodation (line 7) – **4.** way (line 10) – **5.** world (line 11) – **6.** international (line 12)

VI. **1.** England – **2.** the French – **3.** Germany – **4.** Portugal – **5.** Scotland – **6.** the Welsh – **7.** the Netherlands (Holland) – **8.** Spain – **9.** the Italians – **10.** Greece

VII. Scotland, Wales, United Kingdom

VIII. *Example*: My name is Adrian. I'm from a small town near Karlsruhe. I live in Baden-Baden. I work for a company which makes cars.

1B

Text

1. b) – **2.** b) – **3.** b) – **4.** c) – **5.** d) – **6.** d) – **7.** b) – **8.** b) – **9.** *Example*: I learnt English at school. – **10.** *Example*: As I'm a technician I sometimes need English when I have to install a new machine. The instructions are mostly in English.

Exercises

I. 1. When does Deborah get up every morning? – **2.** How does she get (go) to the adult education centre? – **3.** How often does she teach English? – **4.** Why does she like teaching? – **5.** Which languages does she speak? – **6.** What does she do in the afternoon?

II. 1. I don't go ... . – **2.** I cannot get up ... . – **3.** I don't have ... . – **4.** The children don't always do ... . – **5.** School isn't easy. – **6.** Deborah doesn't correct ... .

III. 1. What time do you get up in the morning? – **2.** Do you go to work by car? – **3.** When do lessons begin at the centre? – **4.** Do you work in the evening? – **5.** Do you earn enough money? – **6.** Do you like your job?

IV. 1. c) – 2. g) – 3. i) – 4. a) – 5. b) – 6. f)

V. 1. I come from ... . – **2.** Why are you going now? – **3.** She is living ... . – **4.** Where do you live? – **5.** Do you go to school ...? – **6.** We are coming now.

VI. 1. Where do you come (= are you) from? – **2.** How long are you staying in Germany? – **3.** How good is your German? – **4.** What do you do? – **5.** What do you do in your freetime? – **6.** Do you like (it in) Germany?

1C

I. 1. b) (page 218, line 1) – **2.** b) (line 4) – **3.** c) (lines 5–36)

II. 1. Holland (line 4) – **2.** thirteen (line 6) – **3.** two (line 8) – **4.** American English (line 9) – **5.** fall (line 15) – **6.** Holland (line 20) – **7.** two (line 17) – **8.** Pooh (line 24) – **9.** Dutch (line 20) – **10.** builder (line 29)

III. 1. bilingual (line 22) – **2.** pronunciation (line 9) – **3.** difference (line 14) – **4.** Cockney (line 31) – **5.** confusing (line 23) – **6.** enormous (line 8)

1D

I. "Meterman is my name
Reading meters is my game
I know everyone
Everyone knows me
Read your meter and
Have a cup of tea."

II. 1. c) – 2. e) – 3. d) – 4. a) – 5. f) – 6. b)

III. 1. b) – 2. a) – 3. c) – 4. e) – 5. d)

1E

aromatherapy/essential oils – indoor sports/badminton for beginners – photography/black and white portraits – business presentations/preparing colour handouts – car maintenance/checking and changing oil – desk top publishing/keyboarding skills – grammar workshop/English as a foreign language.
(*Note*: course titles come first.)

UNIT 2

2A

Text

1. a) (line 5) – **2.** c) (line 22) – **3.** b) (lines 34-36) – **4.** b) – **5.** b) – **6.** c) – **7.** b) – **8.** *Example*: Yes, I think it is advisable to take travellers' cheques abroad because they are much safer than cash or credit cards. You can only cash travellers' cheques when you can show your passport and give your signature. – **9.** *Example*: The last time I stayed in a hotel was about three years ago when I was on holiday in Spain. – **10.** *Example*: The play 'Amadeus' describes the life and death of the composer Wolfgang Amadeus Mozart.

Exercises

I. 1. d) – 2. a) – 3. e) – 4. c) – 5. b)

II. Meaning 1 = sentence 3, Meaning 2 = sentence 5, Meaning 3 = sentence 4, Meaning 4 = sentence 2, Meaning 5 = sentence 1

III. I'd like to change one hundred German Marks into English pounds, please. – Yes, thanks, but I would like to have ten pounds in one-pound coins, please. – Thank you very much. Goodbye.

IV. I'd like a double room for one week, please. What does it cost? – Yes, all right. A double room with bath for one week, please. – Just a small bag.

V. **2.** meeting – **4.** signature – **5.** saying – **6.** explanation – **8.** help – **9.** change – **10.** reservation – **11.** saying – **12.** help

2B

Text

1. c) (line 4) – **2.** a) (line 9) – **3.** c) (line 11) – **4.** a) (line 13) – **5.** You can get leaflets, brochures and street maps. (lines 4-5) – **6.** They don't take much luggage with them because they like to buy clothes when they are on holiday. (lines 5-6) – **7.** They are called "backpackers" because they take their camping equipment with them in their rucksacks and they carry their rucksacks on their backs. – **8.** It means (that) you don't take much luggage with you when you travel. – **9.** She smiles and says "even in England" because she knows that the weather is rarely as hot and sunny in England as it is in other European countries. – **10.** *Example*: I had a holiday in Austria last winter. – **11.** *Example*: I like to fly or go by train because I don't like sitting in a car for a long time. – **12.** *Example*: I like to buy a map and find out where to go and what to see.

Exercises

I. **1.** The two girls often stay ... . – **2.** They never have enough ... . – **3.** They are always interested in ... . – **4.** They rarely speak ... . – **5.** They sometimes have ... . – **6.** They would never do ... .

II. **1.** Do you usually stay in (= at) expensive hotels? – **2.** Do you sometimes reserve (= book) a room at bed and breakfasts? – **3.** Do you always have (= Have you always got) your mobile (phone) with you? – **4.** Can you often pay with credit cards in hotels? – **5.** Are you never too lazy to eat out? – **6.** Is the weather always so bad in England?

III. **1.** Do you want to know ...? – **2.** She doesn't like ... . – **3.** I don't feel comfortable ... . – **4.** Does she travel abroad ...? – **5.** I don't travel ... . – **6.** I don't really have the time.

IV. **1.** No, her car ... . **2.** Yes, my birthday ... . – **3.** No, it's his mother. – **4.** Is its balcony ...? – **5.** Where is their office? – **6.** Yes, our train leaves ... .

V. **1.** Yes, it's mine. – **2.** No, hers is white. – **3.** This is his. – **4.** And what's yours? – **5.** You should see ours! – **6.** My parents like theirs.

VI. **1.** 'four pounds fifty' – **2.** 'one pound eighty-two' – **3.** 'fifty p' /pi:/ – **4.** 'six pounds five p' – **5.** 'nine pounds ninety-nine' – **6.** 'three pounds thirty-three' – **7.** d) – **8.** a) – **9.** b) – **10.** c)

2C

I. a) (page 219, e.g. lines 5–6) – c) (e.g. lines 21–26) – e) (e.g. lines 21–31)

II. **1.** b) (line 3) – **2.** b) (line 12) – **3.** b) (line 13) – **4.** b) (line 18) – **5.** a) (line 20) – **6.** b) (line 23) – **7.** b) (line 28) – **8.** a) (line 34)

2D

I. Meterman is very happy because today is a very special day. He is going to read the meter in one of the stately homes of England.

He drives up to the back entrance of the historic house. A group of tourists is standing in the drive. Meterman honks his horn at them and almost runs them down. He seems to be angry. "Tourists aren't allowed to go in this way," he says. "They have to go in by the front entrance; buy the guide books; buy the leaflets; buy the tickets; pay the guide. In my job I can go round the back. England by the back door!"

Meterman finds the meter and reads it. He is shocked at the amount of electricity they use. He decides to find out why they use so much. He follows the wiring and comes across the group of tourists again. He carries on following the wiring. He goes down on his hands and knees. People fall over him. A lamp is knocked over. Eventually he is thrown out.

The tourists carry on with their tour. Slowly they climb the oak staircase to the famous bedroom where Queen Elizabeth once slept. The guide opens the door. Someone is on the royal bed! It's Meterman! He is fast asleep! On his chest there is a sign: "Do not touch the furniture."

II. **a.:** sentences 1 and 5. – **b.:** sentences 2 and 4. – **c.:** sentences 3 and 6.

III. 1. b) – 2. a) – 3. e) – 4. d) – 5. c)

2E

1. True – **2.** False – **3.** False – **4.** True – **5.** True

UNIT 3

3A

Text

1. c) (line 4) – **2.** b) and c) (lines 7 – 8) – **3.** Yes, they do. They give them pocket money every month. They also get some extra money if they help in the garden, for example, or do some work on the computer. (lines 4-6 and 8-10) – **4.** Four of her grandchildren don't appear in the module. (line 12) – **5.** She likes working in her garden better than working in her house. (lines 14-15) – **6.** No. He is half English because his father was Welsh. (line 16) – **7.** *Example*: I like doing sport and listening to music. – **8.** *Example*: I don't like getting up early and doing homework.

Exercises

I. **1.** The Joneses have got ... . – **2.** Hugh has got ... . – **3.** Nick and Hugh haven't got ... . – **4.** Gill has got ... . – **5.** Keith has got ... . – **6.** Nick and Gill have got ... .

II. **1.** Hugh has got ... . – **2.** Has Nick got a ...? – **3.** Gill and Keith haven't got ... . – **4.** Gill hasn't got ... . – **5.** Keith and Gill have got ... . – **6.** Grandmother has got ... .

III. **1.** I haven't got ... . – **2.** She's got ... . – **3.** They've got ... . – **4.** Tom's got ... . Mark's got ... . – **5.** You haven't got ... . – **6.** Sarah's got ... .

IV. **1.** Keith is ... . – **2.** Gill is ... . – **3.** Hugh has got ... . – **4.** It is ... . – **5.** Nick is ... . – **6.** Grandmother has got ... .

V. **1.** doing – **2.** to do – **3.** do – **4.** make – **5.** make – **6.** doing – **7.** make – **8.** do

VI. **1.** Would you like to come ...? – **2.** I like driving ... but I don't like cleaning it. Would you like to wash ...? – **3.** Would you like to have ...? – **4.** Would you like to go ...? I don't like getting up ... .

3B

Text

great-grandfather			**1903** (lines 19-21)		great-grandmother
grandfather			**1939** (lines 21-22)		grandmother
Keith (line 23)	–	Gill	Jonathan	–	**Ruth** (lines 7-8)
Hugh (line 7)		Nick	**Timothy** (line 4)		Simon

1. family members – **2.** mother-in-law – **3.** nephew – **4.** grandchild (grandchildren) – **5.** wife – **6.** bridegroom – **7.** bridesmaid – **8.** top hat – **9.** be proud of – **10.** wedding photos – **11.** Have you got a photo of your mother-in-law? – **12.** How many grandchildren has your father got? – **13.** My brother-in-law lives in California. – **14.** Is he proud of his wife? – **15.** Where is the bridegroom? He is talking to the photographer.

Exercises

I.

one syllable	two syllables		three syllables
-er,-est	-er, -est	more, most	more, most
cold, quick, hot, big, tall, small, deep, fast, wide, loud	clever, easy, pretty, simple, dirty	crowded, careful, boring, stupid	wonderful, exciting, difficult, beautiful, dangerous

II. **1.** faster – **2.** hotter – **3.** quicker (more dangerous) – **4.** more difficult (simpler) – **5.** taller – **6.** louder

III. **1.** the fastest – **2.** the most boring – **3.** the most popular – **4.** the friendliest – **5.** the oldest – **6.** the easiest

IV. **1.** higher than – **2.** better ... worse – **3.** finds ... as – **4.** more ... than – **5.** best ... cleverest – **6.** more ... than

V.

be – was, were	do – did	get – got
have – had	want – wanted	train – trained
grow – grew	leave – left	say – said
work – worked	hate – hated	finish – finished

VI. was born – grew up – had – were – worked – did – wanted – left – was – hated – got – trained – said – was – finished

VII. **1.** Where were you born? – **2.** How old were you when you left school? – **3.** Where was your first job? – **4.** Why did you stop working six months later? – **5.** When did you get married? – **6.** How many children have you got? – **7.** Where did you have a parttime job later? – **8.** Why didn't you want any more children?

VIII. *Example*: My parents were born in Hamburg. They got married in 1971. They had three children. My sisters were born in 1972 and 1974 and I was born in 1975.

3C

I. **1.** c) – **2.** b) – **3.** a)

II. 1947 (page 220, line 5) – often (lines 5 and 7) – quite near to (lines 1–2) – sister (line 14) – ponds (line 16) – still (line 20) – 1987 (line 27) – garden (lines 27–28) – weeks (line 30) – wallpaper (line 33) – growing up (line 1)

III. **1.** kitchen – **2.** sitting room – **3.** bedroom – **4.** bathroom – **5.** stairs – **6.** under – **7.** smallest – **8.** hall

3D

I. window – moment – meter – sure – idea – audience – sayings – day

II. 1. d) – 2. a) – **1.** Stellen Sie sich vor, dass jemand das nicht weiß. – **2.** Ich werde sie ein bisschen an der Nase herumführen.

III. The underlined words in sentences 2a/2b and 4a/4b are pronounced in the same way.

UNIT 4

4A

Text

1. b) (line 7) – **2.** c) – **3.** a) – **4.** b) – **5.** a) – **6.** a) – **7.** a) d) and f) – **8.** The old man says this because his car is behind Kevin's. (line 7) – **9.** *Example*: Yes, I do. I use it every day to get to work. – **10.** *Example*: I can do simple things. For example, I can check the spark plugs (*Zündkerzen*), change the oil and tighten the fanbelt (*Keilriemen*).

Exercises

I. **1.** This sign means that you can't turn left. – **2.** ... that you can't ride a bike (= cycle) here. – **3.** ... that you can't drive faster than 40 miles per hour. – **4.** ... that you can't overtake (another car).

II. 1. c) – 2. f) – 3. d) – 4. b) – 5. a) – 6. e)

III. **1.** You'd better sit down. – **2.** We'd better book a table. – **3.** You'd better stay at home. – **4.** I'd better not swim in it. – **5.** You'd better take a taxi. – **6.** I'd better go to the dentist.

IV. **1.** What ...? – **2.** When ...? – **3.** Where ...? – **4.** Whose ...? – **5.** Which ...? – **6.** Who ...? – **7.** Who ...? – **8.** How ...? – **9.** Why ...?

4B

Text

1. c) (lines 8-12) – **2.** b) (lines 16-18) – **3.** a) (lines 26-27) – **4.** The mechanic changed the windscreen wiper and a bulb. (lines 22-23) – **5.** He will have to pay for the service and the MOT certificate. – **6.** a) – **7.** c) – **8.** *Example*: Yes, in Germany there is a similar service. It's called TÜV. There they check whether vehicles are safe to be driven on public roads.

Exercises

I.

be	– was, were	– been	have	– had	– had
break	– broke	– broken	lose	– lost	– lost
do	– did	– done	see	– saw	– seen
find	– found	– found	sell	– sold	– sold
go	– went	– gone			

II. **1.** I have sold it. – **2.** I have lost it. – **3.** I have seen it. – **4.** I have broken it. – **5.** I have (already) had one. – **6.** I've (just) been.

III. R.: Has anything happened? – J.: Yes, I've lost my car keys. – R.: Have you looked in all your pockets? – J.: Yes, I've searched everywhere. – R.: Have you been back to your car? – ... – R.: ... I've often done that. – J.: ... I've found them! They were in my bag all the time!

IV. One big one and five small ones – two brown ones – one black one – one purple one – one blue one and one red one – Which ones are his and which ones are hers?

V. **1.** Would you like one? – **2.** The ones from Ireland ... . – **3.** ... but the ones from Spain ... . – **4.** That one is ... . – **5.** No, use the ones over there. – **6.** The red one. – There are three red ones!

VI. bonnet – engine – service – MOT – ring – certificate – have topped up – low – replaced – Everything – how – cheque

4C

I. **1.** b) (page 222, line 1) – **2.** a) (e.g. lines 19–25) – **3.** c) (lines 33–37) – **4.** b) (lines 40–49) – **5.** b) (lines 41 and 48)

II. **1.** There are three mechanics. (line 16) – **2.** Looking after his customers is more important for Mr Bourne than looking after his Morgans. (line 21) – **3.** It began in 1910. (line 29) – **4.** A Morgan car is made of wood and steel. (line 34) – **5.** Mr Bourne likes to drive his own Morgan on those days when there is a little frost and the sun is shining. (lines 50–52)

4D

I. e – g – d – b – c – a – f

II. **1.** You must be on the road to success. – **2.** They're on the road to ruin. – **3.** Would you say exercise is the right road to beauty? – **4.** You're on the road to nowhere.

III. 1., 2., 3., = **a)**

4E

I. **1.** b) – **2.** c) – **3.** a) – **4.** c) – **5.** a) – **6.** b)

II. British people drive on the left.

UNIT 5

5A

Text

1. c) (lines 3–9) – **2.** b) (lines 18-19) – **3.** a) (lines 30 and 33) – **4.** knife (line 31) – **5.** fork (line 31) – **6.** spoon (line 31) – **7.** glasses (line 32) – **8.** freezer (line 44) – **9.** *Example*: I know bacon and eggs, lamb chops, roast beef and fish and chips. – **10.** *Example*: I cook but I don't like cooking very much. I cook light meals like boiled or scrambled eggs, spaghetti or soup. As I'm single I often eat out. *Example*: Yes, I like cooking very much. It's me who does most of the cooking in our family. I have two children and I want to look after them and feed them properly.

Exercises

I. 1. someone – **2.** any – **3.** anything – **4.** some – **5.** any – **6.** anything – **7.** anywhere – **8.** anybody – **1.** Es ist jemand an der Türe. Kannst du (= Können Sie) nachsehen? – **2.** Jane hat keine Geschwister. – **3.** Wir sagten hallo, aber er antwortete uns nicht. – **4.** Ich mag einige englische Gerichte, aber nicht alle. – **5.** Hast du auf der Party Fotos gemacht? – **6.** Wir hatten ein ausgiebiges Frühstück, deshalb werden wir nichts zu Mittag essen. – **7.** Sie verbrachten die Nacht auf dem Bahnhof, weil sie nirgendwo schlafen (= übernachten) konnten. – **8.** Hat heute morgen schon irgendjemand Daniel gesehen?

II. 1. Would you like anything to drink? – **2.** Has anybody called (= Did anybody call) for me? – **3.** I don't have (= haven't got) any time. – **4.** Is there any tea left? – **5.** Have (= take) some biscuits. – **6.** We haven't brought anything with us.

III. 1. families – **2.** addresses – **3.** secretaries – **4.** sixes – **5.** knives – **6.** names – **7.** oranges – **8.** languages – **9.** potatoes – **10.** bushes – **11.** peas – **12.** lorries

IV. 1. buses ... taxis – **2.** roofs ... houses – **3.** ladies ... gentlemen ... children – **4.** people ... women – **5.** pages ... textbooks – **6.** boxes ... oranges

V. Vegetable: tomato, cucumber, onion, beans, peas, spinach, mushrooms, brussel sprouts.
Fruit: apple, pear, melon, raspberry, apricot, gooseberry, peach, lemon, grapes, cherries.
Ways of cooking: boil, fry, bake, roast, grill.

5B

Text

1. c) (line 3) – **2.** a) (line 3) – **3.** b) /ˈflaʊə/ – **4.** a) /bəʊl/ – /həʊl/ – **5.** b) /ˈʌvn/ – /ˈʌðə/ – **6.** a) /ˈvedʒtəblz/ – **7.** b) – **8.** b) – **9.** a) – **10.** b) – **11.** *Example*: They probably think Yorkshire pudding is something sweet. – **12.** *Example*: I think it is not easy to make. You have to make sure, for example, that you don't leave it in the oven too long. If you do, it will burn very quickly.

Exercises

I. 1. David reads slowly. – **2.** Anna sings brilliantly. – **3.** Maud dances beautifully. – **4.** Daniel works quickly. – **5.** Rachel cycles dangerously. – **6.** Terry swims excellently. – **7.** Peter writes carefully. – **8.** Gabriele speaks English perfectly.

II. 1. electronically – **2.** well – **3.** fast ... aggressively – **4.** wonderful – **5.** brilliant – **6.** happy ... successfully – **7.** loudly ... great

III. 1. They seldom go out ... . – **2.** We sometimes have ... . – **3.** She occasionally has ... . – **4.** I rarely have ... . – **5.** Have you never eaten...? – **6.** Is he normally on ...? – **7.** My diet always varies. – **8.** She frequently has ... .

IV. 1. Would you like some gravy with your meat? – **2.** Could I have a spoon, please? – **3.** I don't eat eggs. – **4.** The cherries are in the large bowl. – **5.** Did you say "flour" or "flower"?

V. f. – c. – e. – h. – j. – b. – d. – a. – g. – i. – k.

5C

I. 1. b) (page 224, lines 4–6) – **2.** a) (line 8) **3.** c) (e.g. lines 12–17) – **4.** b) (line 21)

II. 1. jam (line 1) – **2.** ceiling (line 10) – **3.** decorating (line 13) – **4.** study (line 14) – **5.** pond (line 16) – **6.** flavour (line 8)

III. 1. *Example*: He (She) likes to repair and build things himself (herself). – **2.** *Example*: This means a hectic, noisy way of doing things.

5D

I. **1.** Secondhand clothes (line 3) – **2.** Two cups of tea, please. (lines 7-8) – **3.** She doesn't smoke. (line 12) – **4.** Newspaper? Birthday present? (line 15) – **5.** The job is quite interesting.(line 19)

II. Movement: 1a/b – Change: 2a/b – Receiving: 3a/b

III. **1.** clothes /kləʊ(ð)z/ – close /kləʊz/
2. draft /drɑːft/ – giraffe /dʒəˈrɑːf/
3. chess /tʃes/ – jazz /dʒæz/
4. won't /wəʊnt/ – want /wɒnt/
5. bad /bæd/ – bed /bed/
6. juice /dʒuːs/ – shoes /ʃuːz/

5E

I. **1.** yards – **2.** stone(s) – **3.** Fahrenheit – **4.** miles – **5.** pints – **6.** feet – **7.** feet – **8.** gallon

II. *Example*: I'm six feet (= foot) (and) three (inches tall). I take size ten shoes.

UNIT 6

6A

Text

1. b) – **2.** c) – **3.** c) – **4.** a) (line 27) – **5.** We've been there before. – **6.** Where are you moving to? – **7.** Doesn't time fly! (= How time flies!) – **8.** We're having a chat. – **9.** *Example*: I like having my hair cut at least once a month. – **10.** *Example*: No, I wouldn't like to work in a hairdressing salon. It's a hard job with long hours. You are standing on your feet all day and you have to be friendly to your customers all the time – and even if you don't like them.

Exercises

I. Malcolm: ... I'm going ... . – My parents are coming ... . – ... I'm working ... . – ... I'm baby-sitting ... . – ... Tracy and I are driving ... . – John: Are you coming ...? – Malcolm: ... we are staying ... .

II. **1.** What is Tom doing this summer? He is going camping. Really? When is he coming back? He is coming back on July 31. – **2.** Is Sally going away? Yes, she is. She is flying to Spain. That sounds nice. Is she going away for long? I'm not sure. About a fortnight, I think. – **3.** Are Peter and Sue having a holiday this year? No, they aren't. What are they doing? They are staying at home. – **4.** Are Pam and Rick doing anything this summer? Yes, they're visiting Pam's sister. Really? How long are they staying? Not long. One (= A) week, I think.

III. 1. d) – 2. f) – 3. a) – 4. e) – 5. b) – 6. c)

IV. **1.** What were you listening to when I phoned? – **2.** Who did you write a letter to last week? – **3.** What did he pay for while you were on holiday? – **4.** What is she interested in? – **5.** Which club is he a member of? – **6.** Who did he run away from?
1. Was hörtest du dir gerade an, als ich dich anrief? – **2.** Wem hast du letzte Woche einen Brief geschrieben? – **3.** Wofür bezahlte er, als ihr im Urlaub wart? – **4.** Für was interessiert sie sich? – **5.** Von welchem Club ist er ein Mitglied? – **6.** Vor wem ist er davongelaufen?

V. I'd like to make an appointment ... . – When do you want to come? – Is that (= Would that be) possible? – That sounds fine. – Sorry but I didn't catch your name. – Have we got your phone number? – Tomorrow (afternoon) at 2.30. – Thanks for calling (= your call).

6B

Text

1. b) (lines 4-6) – **2.** b) (see unit 5E, page 85) – **3.** b) – **4.** a) – **5.** a) – **6.** a) – **7.** b) – **8.** It suits me well. – **9.** It looks good. – **10.** I agree (with you). – **11.** *Example*: As a man I prefer a barber's shop as I don't like women to see how I have my hair cut. I think women in clips look funny so I think they also might feel happier in a salon for women only. – **12.** *Example*: If I'm pleased with the service and it's not the owner himself who cuts my hair then I tip the hairdresser, of course. It is expected and a common thing to do in Germany.

Exercises

I. 1. No, they had it painted. – **2.** No, we had them cut down. – **3.** No, he had it repaired. – **4.** No, he had it cut. – **5.** No, I had it taken. – **6.** No, I had it cleaned.

II. 1. We had our house painted. – **2.** I had my jacket repaired. – **3.** I'm having my hair cut next week. – **4.** They had the photos taken. – **5.** We had the tickets posted. – **6.** I have had the programme recorded.

III. 1. Does the United Nations have ...? – **2.** Here is the news ... . – **3.** All the important data is ... . – **4.** The United States is ... . – **5.** Do you know where my new trousers are? – **6.** Our new furniture comes from ... .

IV. 1. Have you got (= Do you have) (any) binoculars? – **2.** I need (some) new glasses. – **3.** The (= These) scissors don't work. – **4.** Are these your clothes in the wardrobe? – **5.** Have you seen these new headphones (= earphones)? – **6.** The news came too late.

6C

I. a), c) and f) (page 225, e.g. lines 1–4)

II. b)

III. d) (lines 34–35)

IV. 1. difference – **2.** to satisfy – **3.** to succeed – **4.** invitation – **5.** to plan – **6.** preference – **7.** conversation – **8.** to treat – **9.** satisfaction, succeed – **10.** invitation – **11.** conversation – **12.** difference

6D

I. I have just looked (= I have just been looking, I just looked) ... . – I have decided ... .- I don't understand ... . – I have always wanted ... . – I will! – I'd like ... . – Do you have (= Have you got) ...? – Would you like ...? – If you don't mind ... . – We don't want ..., do we? – I have (= have got) ... .

II. 1. b) – 2. a) – 3. c) – 4. c) – 5. a)

III. 1. a boy's bike – **2.** women's shoes – **3.** a children's toy – **4.** a man's jumper – **5.** girls' clothes – **6.** a teachers' book

6E

1. d) – 2. c) – 3. b) – 4. a)

UNIT 7

7A

Text

1. b) – **2.** c) – **3.** b) – **4.** b) (see unit 5, page 85) – **5.** c) – **6.** *Example*: I like walking best as you can walk any time of the year. You don't need expensive equipment and you do not need to travel far before you start. – **7.** *Example*: Apart from walking I like skiing and snow boarding. Whenever there is an opportunity I also like to go tobogganing (= sledging) with my children. – **8.** *Example*: I prefer team sports. There's always a nice atmosphere in a team. After a match you can go out for a drink and talk about the game with your friends.

Exercises

I. **1.** doesn't he? – **2.** isn't it? – **3.** aren't we? – **4.** didn't they? – **5.** hasn't she? – **6.** aren't you?

II. **1.** do they? – **2.** would you? – **3.** is it? – **4.** has she? – **5.** did you? – **6.** were we?

III. **1.** isn't he? – **2.** were you? – **3.** can't you? – **4.** have you? – **5.** mightn't she? – **6.** don't you?

IV. **1.** do you? – **2.** aren't I? – **3.** shall we? – **4.** haven't you? – **5.** didn't they? – **6.** do we? (The word "never" makes the statement negative.)

V. **1.** No, he isn't. – **2.** Yes, I can. – **3.** Yes, I would. – **4.** No, she doesn't. – **5.** No, they haven't. – **6.** Yes, I am (= we are). – **7.** Yes, I was. – **8.** Yes, I did (= we did). – **9.** No, she may not. – **10.** No, he won't (= will not).

VI. **1.** teams, game – **2.** game – **3.** Games – **4.** game – **5.** play – **6.** games – **7.** to play

7B

Text

1. No, he coaches them on Saturday mornings. (line 5) – **2.** True. (lines 8-9) – **3.** No, they play tennis in their free time. (e.g. lines 17-18 and 20-22) – **4.** No, they play throughout the year. (line 17) – **5.** True. (e.g. line 46) – **6.** No, they were happy because their team won. (line 58) – **7.** c) served – **8.** a) lost – **9.** d) scored – **10.** b) won – **11.** It was close. – **12.** It's my turn now. – **13.** *Example*: I enjoy playing basketball although I'm not very good at it. I am not very tall and I'm not very fast but I can still score some points. – **14.** *Example*: I like watching football but I never play football myself.

Exercises

I. Between 8.00 and 8.15 she was speaking to the secretary at the tennis club. Between 8.15 and 9.00 she was reading the paper and having breakfast. Between 9.00 and 9.30 she was going shopping. Between 9.30 and 10.00 she was driving to the tennis club. Between 10.00 and 11.30 she was having her tennis lesson. Between 12.00 and 12.30 she was talking to her friends in the club. Between 12.30 and 13.00 she was driving to her sister's house. Between 13.00 and 13.30 she was having lunch with her sister.

II. **1.** Gregory was sitting in his bath (and) reading the paper. – **2.** Kate and her sister were watching an American soap on TV. – **3.** Jonathan was writing a letter to his ex-girlfriend. – **4.** Meterman was repairing his car. – **5.** Jackie and her husband were having an argument. – **6.** Rachel was baking a cake. – **7.** Richard was reading a story to his children (= his children a story). – **8.** Jane was talking to her parents on the phone.

III. We scored ... . – We were playing ... and hit ... . – ... the Blues woke up and scored ... . – We couldn't stop ... . – The score was ... . – ... the Blues scored ... .

IV. How was your game? – Did you beat her? – No, she beat me. But it was very close. She played very well. She served (= was serving) excellently. – I had a lot of problems ... . You won the first three quite easily, didn't you? – But I lost all the rest ... . I just couldn't concentrate, I think. – What was the final score? – I won both sets. By the way, when is your game beginning? (= when does your game begin?) – Have you got (= Do you have) the time? – I'd better go then.

V. **1.** very quickly – **2.** extremely hard – **3.** really seriously – **4.** well – **5.** colourfully dressed – **6.** automatically – **7.** hardly – **8.** easily

VI. **1.** does – **2.** do – **3.** do – **4.** do – **5.** do – **6.** do

7C

I. **1.** Then he left football for two years and decided to open up a pub. (see page 226, lines 6–8) **2.** He sold his house and his villa in the south of France and gave all the money to the club. (lines 13–14) – **3.** Now the matches are on television every week and the Chairman has become a well-known face throughout Britain.

II. 1. b) – 2. h) – 3. g) – 4. i) – 5. d)

III. team – games – clubs – season – promotion – league

7D

I. centre – meters – cricket – instructions – amazing – interesting – trousers – instructor – enjoying – phrases – lesson – racket – floor

II. 1. g) – 2. f) – 3. b) – 4. h) – 5. d) – 6. e) – 7. a) – 8. c)

7E

1. athletics – **2.** horse racing – **3.** golf – **4.** football – **5.** motor racing – **6.** tennis – **7.** cricket – **8.** boxing

UNIT 8

8A

Text

1. c) – **2.** b) (e.g. lines 38 and 46) – **3.** b) – **4.** c) – **5.** b) – **6.** *Example*: Music is extremely important to me. It opens up a whole world of feeling and emotions. – **7.** *Example*: I like different types of music including classical (Bach and Beethoven), jazz (Charlie Parker, Oscar Peterson), rock (Rolling Stones) and more modern music like Rap. – **8.** *Example*: Unfortunately I don't play an instrument myself. If I had the opportunity, I would like to play the piano. It's an instrument you can play individually. Also the repertoire of music written for the piano is enormous, ranging from classical sonatas to jazz and experimental pieces of the avant garde.

Exercises

I. **1.** Do many young people like classical music? – **2.** Did you go to a concert last year? – **3.** Do you have a lot of CDs at home? – **4.** Do you play a musical instrument yourself?

II. **1.**Why do you like music? – **2.** Which (kind of) music do you play? – **3.** Do you listen to music much? – **4.** When do you listen to music? – **5.** Do you play an instrument? – **6.** Is music important to you? – **7.** Which (kind of) music do you enjoy? – **8.** Have you got your own guitar?

III. **1.** Who is playing ...? – **2.** What woke ...? – **3.** Who gave ...? – **4.** What happened ...? – **5.** Who phones ...? – **6.** What fell off ...? – **7.** Who said ...? – **8.** Who plays ...?

IV. 1. John saw her. – **2.** She saw Tom.

V. 1. sad – **2.** embarrassed – **3.** lonely – **4.** disappointed – **5.** angry – **6.** irritated – **7.** bored

8B

Text

1. c) (line 5) – **2.** b) – **3.** a) (line 7) – **4.** a) (line 10) – **5.** b) – **6.** advantage (line 7) – **7.** volume (line 16) – **8.** tracks (line 17) – **9.** explain (line 2) – **10.** operate (line 16) – **11.** *Example*: No, I can't, because I need a safe job and a regular income. I would always be worried about not making enough money from music. **12.** *Example*: No, I wouldn't. The life of a professional musician can be very irregular, which would not be good for my family life.

Exercises

I. 1. The music is composed. – **2.** The lyrics are written. – **3.** Then the songs are rehearsed. – **4.** Later they are recorded in a studio. – **5.** The tracks are mixed. – **6.** A master tape is made. – **7.** At the same time a CD cover is designed. – **8.** The CDs are produced. – **9.** The product is sold to record stores. – **10.** The new release is advertised in the media.

II. 1. Have you ever been asked ...? – **2.** Was the CD given ...? – **3.** Our college was built ... . – **4.** Was music taught ...? – **5.** How many people have been told ...? – **6.** The lesson was cancelled ... .

III. 1. The teachers must be told about the problem. – **2.** The tickets can't be found anywhere. – **3.** Food should not be eaten in the classroom. – **4.** Your car might be stolen if ... . – **5.** The open-air concert could not be held because ... . – **6.** The exams will be written at ... .

IV. 1. e) – 2. c) – 3. b) – 4. f) – 5. a) – 6. d) – **1.** Während (Solange) die Band spielt, ist das Rauchen nicht erlaubt (gestattet). – **2.** Getränke von der Bar werden in Plastikbechern serviert (werden). – **3.** Dem Publikum wurde gesagt, dass es nicht applaudieren solle. – **4.** Einige Karten werden (noch) eine halbe Stunde vor Beginn des Konzerts verkauft. – **5.** Aufzeichnungsgeräte dürfen nicht mit in die Konzerthalle genommen werden. – **6.** Während der Pause können CDs, T-Shirts und Mützen gekauft werden.

V. 1. The opera *Porgy and Bess* was composed by George Gershwin. – **2.** *Jailhouse Rock* was sung by Elvis Presley. – **3.** The song *Help!* was first recorded by the Beatles. – **4.** The *Jupiter Symphony* was written by Mozart. – **5.** *West Side Story* is based on Shakespeare's play *Romeo and Juliet*. – **6.** *Live Aid* was organized by Sir Bob Geldof, the famous Irish singer.

8C

I. 1. False (see page 228, lines 1–2) – **2.** True (lines 21–22) – **3.** True (lines 24–29) – **4.** False (lines 30–33) – **5.** True (line 34)

II. 1. hire(s) (line 6) – **2.** knowledge (line 9) – **3.** hole (line 12) – **4.** lyrics (line 21) – **5.** rehearse, public (lines 23–24) – **6.** deal (line 33)

III. Sentence b) (line 19)

8D

I. Sentence b) summarizes the story best.

II. 1. hang – **2.** got – **3.** think – **4.** understand

III. Sentence a)

8E

1. Radio One – **2.** Radio Four – **3.** Classical – **4.** Radio Four – **5.** Radio Four – **6.** Radio Five

UNIT 9

9A

Text

1. b) – **2.** d) – **3.** a) – **4.** seasick (line 15) – **5.** claustrophobia (line 23) – **6.** trust (line 16) – **7.** view (line 7) – **8.** abroad (line 11) – **9.** *Example*: I would prefer the train as I haven't been through the Tunnel yet. It would be a new experience for me. Going long distances by train is also very relaxing. – **10.** *Example*: I go to Italy or France if I want a short break. I usually take the car and stay in bed and breakfast places or cheap hotels.

Exercises

I. **1.** They enjoy looking at the sea. – **2.** We are considering driving to England. – **3.** She dislikes flying. – **4.** Yes, I do. I don't mind feeling a bit seasick. – **5.** We suggest booking early. – **6.** Not if you can avoid going during the day.

II. **1.** Do you like getting up early? – **2.** Does he enjoy learning a foreign language? – **3.** Do they suggest making a reservation? – **4.** Do you admit saying (= having said) that to them? – **5.** Do you mind travelling alone? – **6.** Does she avoid talking to him?

III. European countries: **2.** the Portuguese – **3.** Greece – **4.** the Turks – **5.** Norway – **6.** the Belgians – **7.** Holland (= the Netherlands) – **8.** the Austrians – **9.** *Example*: ... hospitality and their holiday resorts. **10.** *Example*: ... is Greece because of the weather, food and the way of life there. – **11.** *Example*: ... to Austria ... because I like skiing. – **12.** *Example*: The Turks ... nice ... .They know how to make guests feel welcome and they love children.

IV. **1.** frustrating – **2.** inspiring – **3.** depressing – **4.** exciting – **5.** worrying – **6.** confusing

V. *Examples*: **3.** sea – **4.** sale – **5.** wore – **6.** court – **7.** peace – **8.** through

VI. Lettuce /ˈletəs/ = *Kopfsalat*

9B

Text

1. False (lines 11-12) – **2.** True (line 18) – **3.** False (lines 25-29) – **4.** c) – **5.** c) – **6.** a) (lines 14-15) – **7.** c) = 1, d) = 2, f) = 3, a) = 4, e) = 5, b) = 6, g) = 7 – **8.** wallet (line 18) – **9.** exits (line 26) – **10.** departure (line 37) – **11.** *Example*: A tunnel for cars would have been much more dangerous because accidents might block one side of the tunnel. You would also need a special ventilation system to remove the car exhausts and this would have been very expensive. **12.** *Example*: Yes, I think it will. A link between England and France will mean that more and more English people will travel to France and other European countries. It will become just as easy as travelling anywhere else in Great Britain.

Exercises

I. **1.** we have to pass ... . – **2.** We have to take ... . – **3.** I must buy ... . – **4.** You have to show ... . – **5.** The woman has to ask ... . – **6.** We have to go ... .

II. **1.** Do we have to book ...? – **2.** Does he have to give ...? – **3.** Must you say ...? – **4.** Did they have to book ... ? **5.** Must they charge ...? – **6.** Do I have to tell ...?

III. **1.** You don't have to ... . – **2.** You mustn't ... . – **3.** You mustn't ... . – **4.** You don't have to ... . – **5.** You don't have to ... . – **6.** You mustn't ... .

IV. **1.** ... easier ... than ... . – **2.** ... more helpful ... more understanding than ... . – **3.** ... as ... as ... . – **4.** ... quickest ...? – **5.** ... earlier ... surer ... . – **6.** ... longer ... . – **7.** ... more convenient ... than ... . – **8.** ... more thorough ... than ... .

V. **1.** don't you? – **2.** do you? – **3.** wouldn't you? – **4.** could you? – **5.** do you? – **6.** am I? – **7.** will you? – **8.** won't we?

VI. **1.** take – **2.** bring – **3.** bring – **4.** take

VII. **1.** some – **2.** any – **3.** some – **4.** –

9C

I. a) (see page 229, lines 10–19) – c) (lines 25–32) – d) (lines 47–48) – e) (lines 33–35)

II. **1.** meet (line 12) – **2.** switch (line 24) – **3.** regulations (line 28) – **4.** wine (line 31) – **5.** undersea (line 33) – **6.** isolation (line 43)

III. greatest (line 46) – century (line 46) – Europe (line 46) – wonderful (line 47) – infrastructure (line 47) – join together (lines 47–48) – community (line 48)

9D

I. history – opened – animals – Britain – years! – battles – lose? – hero – danger – comment – defence – noticeboard – invade

II. Look, why ... . – Let me see, I've ... . – Well, near ... . – Anyway, thanks ... .

9E

The cock symbolizes France, the lion England. The cock is coming out of the Channel Tunnel. It looks as if it is coming out of the muzzle (*Mündung*) of a cannon and driving the lion away. The picture shows the power and influence of France over England.

UNIT 10

10A

Text

1. a) c) g) f) d) e) b) – **2.** When they arrive at the Wateringbury Hotel, the French couple is surprised because they find out that something has gone wrong. A room has not been reserved for them as they had expected. – **3.** The English woman speaks to the French woman first because she hears that she is worried about something. – **4.** The couple obviously have different ideas about where to stay. In the end he decides where they should stay. She accepts his decision. – **5.** I'm afraid not. (line 6) – **6.** Can you suggest anything? (line 10) – **7.** Don't worry. (line 16) – **8.** I'd prefer to go there./ I'd rather go there. (lines 23 and 32) – **9.** *Example*: Many tourists like B&B because it is cheaper and you get to know English people more easily. – **10.** *Example*: If I were on holiday in England, I would choose B&B because I want to practise my English. People who offer B&B in their homes are usually prepared to give some advice about places of interest to visit and other things to do in the area.

Exercises

I. **1.** Have you ever seen ...? – **2.** Have you ever been ...? – **3.** Have you ever met ...? – **4.** Have you ever broken ...? – **5.** Have you ever had ...? – **6.** Have you ever worked ...? – **7.** Have you ever stayed ...? – **8.** Have you ever been involved ...?

II. **1.** I've not (= I haven't) seen it yet. – **2.** He's not (= He hasn't) spoken to him yet. – **3.** We've not (= We haven't) asked them yet. – **4.** He's not (= He hasn't) received an answer yet. – **5.** We've not (= We haven't) been to that many places yet. – **6.** The post hasn't arrived yet. – **7.** I've not (= I haven't) tasted it yet. – **8.** He's not (= He hasn't) told them yet.

III. **1.** eben (= gerade), gerecht, nur – **2.** just = fair, just = only

IV. **1.** never – **2.** twice – **3.** once – **4.** yet

V. **1.** Have you ever been to Great Britain? – **2.** We've always wanted to go to Ireland. – **3.** My brother has been to Scotland twice. – **4.** I've never been to an English-speaking country.

VI. **1.** Have you tried leaving them at the railway station for a day? Why not try leaving them ...? – **2.** Have you tried looking around the National Gallery? Why not try looking around ...? – **3.** Have you tried going sightseeing by bus? Why not try going ...? – **4.** Have you tried having fish and chips? Why not try having ...? – **5.** Have you tried paying by credit card? Why not try paying ...? – **6.** Have you tried getting into conversation in a pub? Why not try getting into ...?

VII. **1.** I'd rather stay at a hotel. – **2.** I'd prefer to go on a boat trip. – **3.** I'd rather have Indian food. – **4.** I'd prefer to sit on the beach. – **5.** I'd rather play cards. – **6.** I'd prefer to go to the theatre.

10B

Text

1. True (line 10) – **2.** False (lines 13-14) – **3.** False (line 12) – **4.** False (lines 13-14) – **5.** True (line 14) – **6.** They are both interested in gardening. (lines 26-27) – **7.** John says that he has retired. (line 28) – **8.** unless – **9.** How long have you lived there? – **10.** Do you look after it yourself (yourselves)? – **11.** *Example*: I think people have a B&B because they like having contact with tourists and getting to know people from other countries. Also they can earn some extra money. – **12.** "Small talk" is talking about general subjects like the weather, holidays, food and drink. "Small talk" is talking about subjects which everybody can say something about and which nobody can be offended (*beleidigt*) by.

Exercises

I. **1.** c) He's been working all night. – **2.** f) He's been repairing his motorbike. – **3.** a) She's been shopping all afternoon. – **4.** d) It's been raining of course! – **5.** b) I've been running. – **6.** e) We've been watching a very sad film.

II. **1a.** He has written ... . **1b.** She has been writing letters ... . – **2a.** Have your ever cycled ...? **2b.** ... I have been cycling. – **3a.** ... I have been talking ... . **3b.** We have talked ... . – **4a.** He has repaired ... . **4b.** He has been repairing ... . – **5a.** She has learnt ... . **5b.** She has been learning ... .

III. **1.** for – **2.** for – **3.** since – **4.** since – **5.** since – **6.** for – **7.** since – **8.** for

IV. He has been living there since he was ... . – He has been working as a teacher of English for the last ... . – He has been a member of the local cricket club for ... . – "I have been mad about cricket since I was ... ."

V. **1.** ... How long have you had it? For about two years. How much did it cost? – **2.** ... How long have you lived (= have you been living) there? Since 1992. And where did you live before that? Oh, we had a small house in Oxford before. – **3.** Have you worked (= been working) in a post office long? Since I was 22. ... And what did you do before that? I worked in a travel agency. Did you like the work? ... That's why I left.

VI. **1.** He used to go ... . – **2.** She used to play ... . – **3.** They used to go ... . – **4.** She used to smoke ... . – **5.** We used to go ... . – **6.** They used to travel ... . – **7.** He used to eat ... . – **8.** She used to bite ... .

VII. **1.** John and Jean leben (wohnen) ... – **2.** direkt, unmittelbar – **3.** Ich lebte früher ... – **4.** Ich habe ... benutzt (verwendet) – **5.** es gerne mögen (lieben): Sie leben gerne ... – **6.** (nicht) wie – **7.** ... dauert die Vorstellung – **8.** letzten – **9.** schön – **10.** Strafzettel

10C

I. 1 = b), 2 = d), 3 = e), 4 = c), 5 = a) (see page 231, lines 5–12)

II. c) (e.g. lines 8–10 and 15–24)

III. c) (line 15 and lines 39–41)

IV. b) (lines 42–45)

V. b) (lines 51–53)

VI. northwest – close – mountainous – compact – spare – good (lines 46–50)

10D

I. b)

II. **1.** away, all – **2.** holiday – **3.** farmhouse – **4.** fishing – **5.** fishing – **6.** work

III. mushrooms, home-made jam, honey

UNIT 11

11A

Text

1. b) (line 16) – **2.** c) (lines 17-18) – **3.** b) (line 21) – **4.** How are you getting on? – **5.** That's what I found. – **6.** Well done! – **7.** twice a week. – **8.** every other day. – **9.** *Example*: I would never go to a fitness studio and waste my money on something you can get anywhere and at any time. Jogging near your own home is easy and costs nothing. – **10.** *Example*: Yes, I think it can be a good way of getting fit if you go regularly and follow a programme.

Exercises

I. been – are – were – be – be – are – are – is – be

II. **1.** a) I speak English. b) I don't speak English. c) Do you speak English? d) My sister speaks English. e) My brother doesn't speak English. f) Does your brother speak English? g) We didn't speak English yesterday. h) Did you speak English yesterday? – **2.** a) I work in a computer company. b) I don't work in a computer company. c) Do you work in a computer company? d) My sister works in a computer company. e) My brother doesn't work in a computer company. f) Does your brother work in a computer company? g) We didn't work in a computer company last year. h) Did you work in a computer company last year?

III. **1.** Full – **2.** Helping – **3.** Helping – **4.** Full – **5.** Helping – **6.** Helping

IV. **1.** because – **2.** so – **3.** so – **4.** Because – **5.** so – **6.** Because

V. **1.** to – **2.** so that – **3.** to – **4.** so as not to – **5.** to – **6.** so that

11B

Text

1. a) – **2.** a) – **3.** a) – **4.** a) – **5.** blood pressure (line 3) – **6.** scales (line 5) – **7.** breathe deeply (line 19) – **8.** There you are. (line 27) – **9.** Certainly. (line 27) – **10.** Not at all. (line 30) – **11.** *Example*: No, I couldn't. Even if the money was all right doing the job of a trainer would be too boring for me. Once you know how the machines work the job is very monotonous I suppose. It is true that there are many different people to talk to in a studio but I think the conversations are probably quite superficial (*oberflächlich*). – **12.** *Example*: I personally welcome the use of machines at work. I think many people suffered a lot many years ago when they had to do boring, repetitive jobs or hard physical work. Their health was bad and later in life some of them had permanent injuries because of the work they did. Today the danger is that people get too little exercise. Like many things, the right balance is important. If you sit in front of a computer all day, for example, it is helpful to get regular exercise. If, on the other hand, you are on your feet all day, it is important to sit down and relax occasionally. In my opinion you don't have to go into a fitness studio if you want to get fit. There are many other ways of getting exercise which are just as effective.

Exercises

I. 1. She's going to crash into the tree. **2.** He's going to fall off that chair.

II. 1. d) – 2. c) – 3. a) – 4. b) – 5. f) – 6. e)

III. 1. I'm going to start ... . – **2.** ... he's going to take me. – **3.** I'm going to get ... . – **4.** What are we going to have ...? – **5.** No, we are going to take ... . – **6.** You are going to spill ... .

IV. 1. them – **2.** their – **3.** their – **4.** them – **5.** them – **6.** they

V. 1. they – **2.** them – **3.** their – **4.** their – **5.** they – **6.** They

11C

I. 1. b) (see page 232, line 1) – **2.** a) (lines 7–11) – **3.** b) (lines 12–13)

II. 1. d) (line 23) – **2.** a) (lines 29–32)

III. 1. (lines 47–48)

IV. training – see – improve – while – times – weekends – tiring – older

11D

I. hill – song – army – discipline – smart – elbow – building – honour – best – area – report – touch – mistake – job – showers – uniform – fitness – hurry – important – nothing

II. 1. e) – 2. a) – 3. b) – 4. d) – 5. c)

11E

1. e) – 2. c) – 3. f) – 4. g) – 5. d) – 6. a) – 7. b)

UNIT 12

12A

Text

1. a) (line 2) – **2.** c) (lines 5-6) – **3.** c) (lines 10-11) – **4.** a) (line 15) – **5.** The first woman is worried about getting a job as an actress. The second woman, who wants to become a stylist, is worried about her exams. (lines 4 and 9-10). – **6.** After he has finished his course he wants to get a good job so that he can afford a flat in London. (lines 6-8) – **7.** She wants to have children of her own one day. (line 16) – **8.** I'm taking (= doing) my exams soon. (line 10) – **9.** I'll train for three years. (line 15) – **10.** I'm finishing (= I'll be finishing) my course in June. (line 6) – **11.** *Example*: I want to qualify as an engineer and gain some experience abroad. Later I would like to try and get a good position in a large company in this country. – **12.** *Example*: I will have to get a diploma at a technical college and gain some years of experience with different firms, preferably abroad.

Exercises

I. 1. Working – **2.** staying – **3.** Cycling ... driving – **4.** watching – **5.** to do – **6.** Being

II. 1. He hates getting up ... . – **2.** We're thinking of going ... . – **3.** Why do you insist on talking ...? – **4.** He objects to sitting ... . – **5.** She's talking about leaving ... . – **6.** Please stop shouting, ...!

III. 1. We're looking forward to going to their party. – **2.** He often dreams about living in Paris. – **3.** I apologize for not ringing you yesterday. – **4.** She insisted on paying for the coffee. – **5.** Thank you for coming. – **6.** She succeeded in passing the exams.

IV. 1. and c) – d) and 2. – e) and 3. – 4. and a) – 5. and b)

V. 1. wants ... will have to – **2.** will be ... goes – **3.** don't mind ... will sit – **4.** are ... will go – **5.** will take ... doesn't rain – **6.** don't hurry ... will miss

VI. 1. is ... will spend – **2.** will need ... turns – **3.** fails ... will have to – **4.** gets ... will be – **5.** will buy ... passes

VII.

German	English
schließlich, endlich	eventually
werden	to become
nicht dürfen	must not
Bedeutung	meaning
Koch, Küchenchef	chef
nicht werden	will not

German	English
eventuell	perhaps, probably
bekommen	get, receive
muss nicht	need not
Meinung	opinion
Chef	boss, principal
will nicht	don't/doesn't want to

12B

Text

1. b) (lines 2-4) – **2.** b) (lines 5-8) – **3.** **"exactly"** is to be replaced by **"approximately"**; **"every other day"** is to be replaced by **"a day"**; **"climbing"** is to be replaced by **"walking"**; **"and white linen gloves"** is to be replaced by nothing; **"bruised wrists"** is to be replaced by**"sprained ankles"**; **"fields"** is to be replaced by **"terrain"**; **"along whips"** is to be replaced by **"some money"**; **"to beat"** is to be replaced by **"to tip"**; **"sherpas"** is to be replaced by **"porters"**. – **4.** border point (line 6) – **5.** climb (line 10) – **6.** waterproof clothing (line 18) – **7.** sprained ankles (line 21) – **8.** however (line 22) – **9.** *Example*: I think these people want to find out more about Africa. They want to get to know the African people and their culture. They want to see the exotic wildlife and plant life there. I also think that some of them want to discover a certain type of adventure that can only be found in a country – and under conditions – that are very different from the ones they are used to at home. – **10.** *Example*: I would like to go to New Zealand, especially South Island. I would like to see the exotic vegetation, the rivers and waterfalls and I would like to experience the Maori.

Exercises

I. We will meet – we will be driving – we will complete – We will be spending – we will travel

II. We won't meet – we won't be driving – we won't complete – We won't be spending – we won't travel

III. 1. Where will we fly (= will we be flying) to? – **2.** When will we meet (= will we be meeting)? – **3.** What will we do (= will we be doing) after that? – **4.** Will we be going (= Will we go) by bus? – **5.** Will we stop (= Will we be stopping) at the border? – **6.** Where will we be spending (= will we spend) the first night? – **7.** Where will we start (= will we be starting) the climb? – **8.** Will we be travelling (= Will we travel) in groups? – **9.** Will we cook (= Will we be cooking) our own food? – **10.** Will we be carrying (= Will we carry) our own luggage?

IV. **1.** want – **2.** won't – **3.** won't – **4.** want. – **1.** Wohin möchtest du (= möchten Sie) gehen? – **2.** Er wird noch nicht hier sein, oder? – **3.** Wir werden morgen Vormittag nicht abreisen (aufbrechen). – **4.** Sie möchte nicht mit uns kommen.

V. 1. d) – 2. f) – 3. a) – 4. c) – 5. g) – 6. b) – 7. h) – 8. e)

12C

I. **1.** a) (see page 234, e.g. lines 9–35) – **2.** a) (line 11) – **3.** c) (lines 24–27) – **4.** b) (lines 30–35) – **5.** c) (e.g. lines 36–38) – **6.** b) (line 49) – **7.** b) (lines 54–56)

II. **1.** trout (line 16) – **2.** evergreen (line 19) – **3.** thyme (line 46) – **4.** foliage (line 15) – **5.** dairy (line 37) – **6.** barn (line 39) – **7.** orchard (line 49) – **8.** rosemary (line 46) – **9.** lavender (line 46) – **10.** scent (line 44)

12D

I. strange – colourful – young – tall – dear – Amazing – wonderful – blonde – useless – plastic

II. These sentences are the same when you read them forwards and backwards (a palindrome).

12E 1. c) – 2. e) – 3. a) – 4. d) – 5. b)

UNIT 13

13A

Text

I. **1.** c) (lines 16-17) – **2.** c) – **3.** c) – **4.** relaxing (line 8) – **5.** (traffic) jam (line 10) – **6.** parking ticket (line 14) – **7.** environment (line 18) – **8.** public transport (line 19) – **9.** unless (line 9) – **10.** fortune (line 16) – **11.** *Example*: Many people still go to town by car because public transport is still rather expensive. Additionally, in the suburbs of towns or in the country trains and buses often don't go frequently enough. – **12.** *Example*: I'm not sure. One reason in favour of banning cars from inner cities is that it would be better for the environment. In this way a lot of people would get used to going by underground, bus or train even for journeys outside the cities. On the other hand there are many people who rely on cars in the cities: old people, ill people, parents with small children and so on. I don't think we can ban cars in inner cities but we can make public transport more attractive.

Exercises

I. **1.** Sie sollten (Du solltest) den Zug nehmen. – **2.** Sie sollten (Du solltest) das Auto am Bahnhof stehen lassen. – **3.** More people should take (= use) public transport. – **4.** You should think of the environment.

II. **1.** You should ring the police. – **2.** You should take it back to the shop. – **3.** You shouldn't smoke all day. – **4.** You shouldn't eat so much. – **5.** He should have a holiday. – **6.** You shouldn't moan so much.

III. **2.** ferry, boat – **3.** train – **4.** road – **5.** bike, motorbike – **6.** flight ... ferry (boat) – **7.** train ... bike – **8.** journey ... car – **9.** car ... bike

IV. **1.** You should use public transport unless you want to get a parking ticket. – **2.** You should leave your car at home unless you'd like to have it clamped. – **3.** You shouldn't go by car unless you are prepared to spend half a day in a traffic jam. – **4.** You should take the train unless you'd prefer to get there even later.

V. **1.** fit – **2.** remember – **3.** remind – **4.** bring – **5.** borrow – **6.** suit – **7.** take – **8.** lend – **1.** Diese Hose passt mir nicht. Sie ist zu klein. – **2.** Erinnerst du dich, als wir im Urlaub vor vier Jahren nach Griechenland fuhren? – **3.** Erinnert dich die Frau dort drüben nicht an meine Mutter? – **4.** Können Sie (Kannst du) mir die Zeitung bitte bringen? Sie liegt dort drüben auf dem Tisch. – **5.** Kann ich mir Ihr (dein) Auto bis morgen Vormittag ausleihen? – **6.** Dieser Pullover steht mir überhaupt nicht. Er hat die falsche Farbe. – **7.** Können Sie (Kannst du) uns am Sonntag zum Bahnhof bringen (fahren)? – **8.** Können Sie (Kannst du) mir Ihren (deinen) Laptop für ein Wochenende leihen?

13 B

Text

I. **1.** True (lines 2-4) – **2.** True (line 9) – **3.** False (lines 12-14) – **4.** False (lines 27-28) – **5.** False (lines 31-32) – **6.** b) – **7.** b) – **8.** platform (line 9) – **9.** to ask the way (line 18) – **10.** Go straight along. (line 20) – **11.** headache (line 24) – **12.** passer-by (line 24) – **13.** *Example*: I would go to the Cathedral and the Castle and then I would do some shopping. Later it would be nice to go to an old traditional pub. – **14.** The Canterbury Tales were written by Geoffrey Chaucer. They are a collection of stories or tales, each told by a pilgrim on the way to and back from the shrine of Thomas Becket in Canterbury.

Exercises

I. **1.** The bus leaves ... and arrives ... . – **2.** When does the plane leave ...? Does it get to ...? – **3.** The football match starts ... and finishes ... . When does the film begin? – **4.** The new exhibition ... opens ... . when it ends?

II. **1.** We are having ... Are you coming? – **2.** ... you are getting ...? – **3.** ... the next Eurostar for Brussels leaves? – **4.** Does the concert really start ...?

III. tell – Walk – right – left – straight along – museum – before – West Gate – half a – You're welcome.

IV. I'd like ... . – When are you leaving (will you be leaving)? – We're taking (= We will be taking) ... . – Single or return? – First or second class? – Here (= There) you are. – And £4.35 change. – Have a good journey.

V. *Example*: **1.** art museum, toy museum, wax museum – **2.** city centre, shopping centre, job centre – **3.** youth club, book club, country club – **4.** travel agency, advertising agency, model agency.

VI. *Example*: I'd like to tell you something about the centre of Munich. Munich itself has about 1.3 million inhabitants and is the capital of Bavaria, one of 16 "Laender" or states in Germany. If we start at "Marienplatz" (St. Mary's Square) we can see the "Neues Rathaus" or New City Hall. It is built in the Flemish Gothic style and was completed in the first decade of the nineteenth century. At 11 o'clock each morning the "Glockenspiel" in the clock tower begins to play. Figures move in two scenes. The first commemorates the wedding of a famous prince. The second shows the "Schäfflertanz" (Coopers' Dance) celebrating the end of the Great Plague in 1683. At the centre of St. Mary's Square you will see the "Mariensäule" (St. Mary's Column). This is the heart of Munich and the centre of Bavaria. Behind you stands the Old City Hall. This is a fine example of Bavarian Gothic-style architecture. It was built in 1474 according to the plans of Jörg von Halsbach. He also designed the "Frauendom" (Cathedral Church of our Lady) with its twin spires and "Italian caps". We will pass this magnificent cathedral as we walk along the Kaufingerstraße, the main shopping street in Munich.

13C

I. d) e) i) (see pages 236–237; a) = line 14, b) = line 16, c) = lines 19–20, f) = line 23, g) = line 31, h) = lines 40–41, j) = line 44)

II. **1.** mood (line 15) – **2.** change (line 23) – **3.** gorgeous (line 30) – **4.** window shopping (line 35) – **5.** chat (line 36) – **6.** advance (line 40)

III. **1.** by the way (line 36) – **2.** straight away (lines 41–42) – **3.** according to plan (line 3) – **4.** hardly (line 20) – **5.** to arrange (line 21) – **6.** Guess what! (line 40)

13D

I. a) and 2. – b) and 4. – c) and 3. – d) and 5. – e) and 1. – **6.** *Example*: It's all very quiet after the cowboys have gone back to the saloon.

II. **1.** undertaker (*Leichenbestatter*) – **2.** entrepreneur (*Unternehmer*) – **3.** sensible (*vernünftig*) – **4.** sensitive (*empfindlich*) – **5.** interrupt (*unterbrechen*) – **6.** interfere (*sich einmischen*) – **7.** people (*Menschen*) – **8.** persons (*Personen*) – **9.** pubs (*Kneipen*) – **10.** locals (*Einheimische*)

III. 1. c) – 2. b) . **1.** Unter uns (= Im Vertrauen) gesagt. – **2.** Ich halte mich bedeckt.

ENGLISH SOUNDS

In der Lautschrift wird jeder Laut durch ein bestimmtes Zeichen dargestellt. Da es mehr Laute gibt als Buchstaben, hat man eine Reihe von zusätzlichen Lautschriftzeichen erfunden.

Vokale (vowels)

ɪ	it, is, him, six
e	yes, red, many, ten
æ	black, at, stamp, hat
ɒ	not, shop, what, song
ʌ	but, number, London, one
ʊ	good, look, put, woman
ə	letter, father, another, sister
i:	he, she, teacher, three
ɑ:	class, ask, past, car
ɔ:	sport, door, wall, four
u:	you, school, blue, two
ɜ:	girl, church, word, first
eɪ	great, name, today, eight
aɪ	my, nice, nine, five
əʊ	no, so, hello, envelope
aʊ	how, now, house, out
ɔɪ	boy, coin, toy, Lloyd's
ɪə	here, dear, beer, near
eə	where, there, chair, pair
ʊə	tour, poor, sure, your

Konsonanten (consonants)

p	pet, stamp, top, up
b	boy, black, bye, Bob
t	ten, water, want, eight
d	day, and, bad, good
k	car, king, ask, desk
g	good, big, great, English
f	four, fifteen, floor, left
v	five, seven, eleven, twelve
s	six, seven, it's, what's
z	is, boys, girls, classes
ʃ	she, English, sure, sugar
ʒ	television, pleasure
tʃ	chair, church, teacher, "h"
dʒ	German, garage, geography
θ	three, thank you, thirteen
ð	they, with, without, weather
w	well, window, where, whether
l	well, wall, hall, also
r	right, wrong, three, true
ŋ	sing, song, English, single

WORDLIST

The numbers refer to the Modules in which the word or expression occur for the first time. The words and expressions in Module C are listed after the corresponding tapescript (see pages 218).

A

abroad əˈbrɔ:d 2B
accommodation əˈkɒmədeɪʃən 1A
according to əˈkɔ:dɪŋ 13C
achieve əˈtʃi:v 4C
acid breath ˈæsɪd breθ 11C
actually ˈæktjʊelɪ 9A
adapt əˈdæpt 4C
adult education centre ˈædʌlt 1B
advanced booking ədˈvɑ:nst 9B
agent ˈeɪdʒənt 4C
alleyway ˈælɪweɪ 6C
allies ˈælaɪz 9C
almond ˈɑ:mənd 5D
alter ˈɔ:ltə 9C
although ɔ:lˈðəʊ 5A
amount (of) əˈmaʊnt 2D
amp (= amplifier) æmp 8C
anaerobic ænɪˈrəʊbɪk 11C
anagram ˈænəgræm 12D
angle ˈæŋgl 4C
ankle ˈæŋkl 12B
apart from əˈpɑ:t 12C
appeal to əˈpi:l 12C
apple crumble ˈæpl ˈkrʌmbl 5A
apply to əˈplaɪ 4C

approach əˈprəʊtʃ 4D
approximately əˈprɒksɪmɪtlɪ 9B
arrow ˈærəʊ 9D
as if əzˈɪf 9A
as soon as əzˈsu:nəz 13B
ask about ˈɑ:sk 1B
ask for 1B
ask the way 13B
at least ət ˈli:st 3C
attribute ˈætrɪbju:t 11C
aunt ɑ:nt 3B
autumn ˈɔ:təm 1C
available əˈveɪləbl 9C
average ˈævrɪdʒ 11B
avoid əˈvɔɪd 12B

B
back-up service ˈbæk ʌp ˈsɜ:vɪs 10C
backhand ˈbækhænd 7A
backpacker ˈbækpækə 2B
bailey ˈbeɪlɪ 2C
baked potatoes ˈbeɪkt pəˈteɪtəʊz 5A
baking tin ˈbeɪkɪŋ ˈtɪn 5B
bamboo shoot bæmˈbu: ˈʃu:t 5D
banquet ˈbæŋkwɪt 13C
bar bɑ: 11B
barber('s) shop ˈbɑ:bə[z] ˈʃɒp 6B
bare beə 12C
barge bɑ:dʒ 10C
barn bɑ:n 10A
barrier ˈbærɪə 9B
bat bæt 3B
bath bɑ:θ 10D
BC (= before Christ) ˈbi:ˈsi: 9D
be about to (was, been) ˈbi: əˈbaʊt tə [wɒz, bi:n] 13C
be after ˈɑ:ftə 6C
be amazed at əˈmeɪzd 2C
be based in beɪst 4C
be born bɔ:n 3B
be covered in ˈkʌvəd 3C
be determined to do sth dɪˈtɜ:mɪnd 13D
be due for ˈdju: 4B
be due to return ˈdju: tə rɪˈtɜ:n 2C
be fortunate to have ˈfɔ:tʃnət tə ˈhæv 7C
be hand crafted ˈhænd ˈkrɑ:ftɪd 4C
be highly trained ˈhaɪlɪ ˈtreɪnd 6C
be in keeping with sth ɪn ˈki:pɪŋ wɪð 12C
be keen on ki:n ɒn 11C
be likely to do sth ˈlaɪklɪ 11C
be lost lɒst 13C
be oblivious to sb ˈəˈblɪvɪəs 11C
be off ɒf 7D
be out aʊt 3B
be pleased pli:zd 13B
be prepared to do sth prɪˈpeəd 2C
be related to rɪˈleɪtɪd 10C
be worried about ˈwʌrɪd 12A
beam bi:m 5C
beard bɪəd 6B
beater ˈbi:tə 8C
bench bentʃ 3B
bench pull test ˈbentʃ pʊl ˈtest 11C
benefit ˈbenɪfɪt 10C
bilingual baɪˈlɪŋgwl 1C
binoculars bɪˈnɑ:kjʊləz 7A
blister blɪstə 13B
blood pressure ˈblʌd ˈpreʃə 11B
blow dry (blew, blown) ˈbləʊ draɪ [blu:, bləʊn] 6D
blow out bləʊ aʊt 3C
board bɔ:rd 9B
boast bəʊst 11C
body frame ˈbɒdɪ ˈfreɪm 4C
boil bɔɪl 5A
bold bəʊld 12C
bonnet ˈbɒnɪt 4A
book in advance ˈbʊk ɪn ədˈvɑ:ns 2B
booklet ˈbʊklɪt 10A
boot bu:t 4B
border point ˈbɔ:də ˈpɔɪnt 12B
borrow ˈbɒrəʊ 8C
both bəʊθ 6B
bother ˈbɒðə 4D
boundary ˈbaʊndrɪ 9C
bowl bəʊl 3B/5B/10D
brakes breɪks 4B
break down (broke, broken) breɪk daʊn [brəʊk, ˈbrəʊkən] 4A
breakdown service ˈbreɪkdaʊn ˈsɜ:vɪs 4A
breathe bri:ð 11B
breathing equipment ˈbri:ðɪŋ ɪˈkwɪpmənt 9C
bride braɪd 3B
bridegroom ˈbraɪdgrʊm 3B
bridesmaid ˈbraɪdzmeɪd 3B

bring up (brought, brought) brɪŋ ʌp [brɔːt] 3C
brochure ˈbrəʊʃə 2B
brownstone wall ˈbraʊnstəʊn ˈwɒl 3C
brush brʌʃ 6B
bucket ˈbʌkɪt 3A
build up (built, built) bɪld ʌp [bɪlt] 11C
builder bɪldə 1C
building inspector ˈbɪldɪŋ ɪnˈspektə 1C
bullet ˈbʊlɪt 13D
bump into bʌmp 12D
button ˈbʌtən 8B

C

call off kɔːl ɒf 7C
campsite ˈkæmpsaɪt 2B
cane keɪn 11D
Canterbury Tales House ˈkæntəbrɪ ˈteɪlz ˈhaʊs 13B
capacity kəˈpæsɪtɪ 11C
career kəˈrɪə 12A
carry out ˈkærɪ aʊt 4B/4C
casserole ˈkæsərəʊl 5A
cave man ˈkeɪvmæn 9D
ceiling ˈsiːlɪŋ 5C
cereal ˈsɪərɪəl 5A
certificate səˈtɪfɪkət 4B
chairman ˈtʃeəmən 7C
change money ˈtʃeɪndʒ ˈmʌnɪ 2A
channel ˈtʃænl 8B
chaps tʃæps 11D
character ˈkærəktə 1C
chassis ˈtʃæsɪz 4C
chat tʃæt 6A
Chaucer, Geoffrey ˈtʃɔːsə ˈdʒəfrɪ 13B
chemist('s) ˈkemɪst[s] 13B
chest tʃest 2D
child care ˈtʃaɪld ˈkeə 12A
children's nurse ˈtʃɪldrənz ˈnɜːs 12A
china ˈtʃaɪnə 5B
chopstick ˈtʃɒpstɪk 5D
circular route ˈsɜːkjʊlə ˈruːt 10C
clamp klæmp 13A
claustrophobia klɔːstrəˈfəʊbjə 9A
clerk klɑːk 2A
client ˈklaɪənt 6B
climb klaɪm 12B
clip klɪp 6B
clipper ˈklɪpə 6B
close kləʊs 7B
clothes kləʊz 2B
Cockney ˈkɒknɪ 1C
coffin ˈkɒfɪn 13D
coins kɔɪnz 2A
colourful ˈkʌləfəl 7B
comb kəʊm 6B
come (came, come) kʌm [keɪm, kʌm] 4C
commence kəˈmens 7C
commentator ˈkɒmenteɪtə 9C
competition kɒmpɪˈtɪʃən 4C
complain kəmˈpleɪn 13B
complete kəmˈpliːt 12B
compulsory kəmˈpʌlsərɪ 9C
condition kənˈdɪʃən 11C
cones kəʊnz 4C
confirm kənˈfɜːm 9B
consist of kənˈsɪst 4C
consume kənˈsjuːm 13D
contented kənˈtentɪd 3C
convert kənˈvɜːt 5C/10A
cooking stove ˈkʊkɪŋ ˈstəʊv 2B
cotton clothing ˈkɒtən ˈkləʊðɪŋ 12B
countryside ˈkʌntrɪsaɪd 3C/10A
couple ˈkʌpəl 10A
cover ˈkʌvə 4C
covers ˈkʌvəz 8C
craftsman ˈkrɑːftsmən 4C
crop krɒp 3C
cross krɒs 10D
cross country running ˈkrɒs ˈkʌntrɪ ˈrʌnɪŋ 11D
crossover cabin ˈkrɒsəʊvə ˈkæbɪn 9C
cubicle ˈkjuːbɪkl 6C
cup of tea ˈkʌp əv ˈtiː 7D
customer ˈkʌstəmə 6B
customs ˈkʌstəmz 9B
cut costs (cut, cut) kʌt kɒsts 6C
cut off 3C
cycling ˈsaɪklɪŋ 2C

D

dairy ˈdeərɪ 12C
damage ˈdæmɪdʒ 3C
dash dæʃ 4C
dashboard ˈdæʃbɔːd 4C
a day out deɪ 13A

day return ticket ˈdeɪ rɪˈtɜːn ˈtɪkɪt 13B
decorate ˈdekəreɪt 5C
definitely ˈdefɪnɪtlɪ 13A
delight dɪˈlaɪt 3C
den den 12D
depending on dɪˈpendɪŋ 8A
destroy dɪˈstrɔɪ 11C
die daɪ 3B
dig (dug, dug) dɪg [dʌg] 3C
disaster dɪˈzɑːstə 13C
discover dɪˈskʌvə 10A
dismissable offence dɪsˈmɪsəbl əˈfens 9C
display dɪˈspleɪ 12C
dissipate ˈdɪsɪpeɪt 11C
dormer window ˈdɔːmə ˈwɪndəʊ 3C
drainage ˈdreɪnɪdʒ 1C
draw (drew, drawn) drɔː [druː, drɔːn] 3A
draw into 5B
drawing board ˈdrɔːɪŋ ˈbɔːd 12C
drive (drove, driven) draɪv [drəʊv, ˈdrɪvn] 2D/6C
drop drɒp 13C
drop in 1D
drum drʌm 8A
drum kit ˈdrʌm ˈkɪt 8A
dry draɪ 5C
dryer ˈdraɪə 6B
duster ˈdʌstə 11D
duvet ˈdjuːveɪ 10D

E

eager ˈiːgə 2C
eating habits ˈiːtɪŋ ˈhæbɪts 5A
edge edʒ 12C
effeminate ɪˈfemɪnɪt 6C
efficiency ɪˈfɪʃənsɪ 11D
effort ˈefət 8C
enable ɪˈneɪbl 9C
Enchanted Forest ɪnˈtʃɑːntɪd ˈfɒrɪst 12C
end up end ʌp 8D/11C
engine ˈendʒɪn 4B
engineering problem endʒɪˈnɪərɪŋ ˈprɒbləm 9C
enquire about ɪnˈkwaɪə 2C
ensure ɪnˈʃʊə 11C
entrance fee ˈentrəns fiː 2C
environment ɪnˈvaɪərnmənt 13A
equidistant from iːkwɪˈdɪstənt 9C
even ˈiːvən 7B
event ɪˈvent 8B
eventually ɪˈventʃʊəlɪ 12A
every other day ˈevrɪ ˈʌðə ˈdeɪ 11A
exceed ɪkˈsiːd 4D
exercise machines ˈeksəsaɪz məˈʃiːnz 11B
exhibition ɪksɪˈbɪʃən 13B
expensive ɪkˈspensɪv 2A
expression ɪkˈspreʃən 1B
extend ɪkˈstend 3C

F

facilities fəˈsɪlətɪz 7D/10B
fader ˈfeɪdə 8B
fail on feɪl 4B
fail/pass (an exam) 12A
fall back on (fell, fallen) fɔːl [fel, fɔːlən] 8A
fall fɔːl 1C
familiar fəˈmɪljə 3C
fan fæn 4C
fare feə 9B
farmhouse ˈfɑːmhaʊs 10A
fashionable ˈfæʃnəbl 13C
fattening ˈfætnɪŋ 5A
feat (of) fiːt 9C
feel secure (felt, felt) ˈfiːl sɪˈkjʊə [felt] 4C
ferocious fəˈrəʊʃəs 9D
ferry ˈferɪ 9A
field fiːld 3B
fight sb (fought, fought) faɪt [fɔːt] 9D
final score ˈfaɪnl ˈskɔː 7B
final total ˈfaɪnl ˈtəʊtl 7B
fine faɪn 13A
finish off ˈfɪnɪʃ ˈɒf 6B
firearms ˈfaɪəɑːmz 9B
first aid kit ˈfɜːst ˈeɪd ˈkɪt 2B
fishing rod ˈfɪʃɪŋ ˈrɒd 10D
fit sth (fit, fit) fɪt 4C
fix fɪks 1D
flat flæt 12A
flat packed ˈflæt ˈpækt 6C
flavour ˈfleɪvə 5C
floating ˈfləʊtɪŋ 10C
fly (flew, flown) flaɪ [fluː, fləʊn] 6A
fog light bulb ˈfɒg laɪt ˈbʌlb 4B
foliage ˈfəʊlɪɪdʒ 12C
football coaching ˈfʊtbɔːl ˈkəʊtʃɪŋ 7B
footwear ˈfʊtweə 12B

foresee (foresaw, foreseen) fɔːˈsiː [ˈsɔː, ˈsiːn] 12D
foretell (foretold, foretold) fɔːˈtel [ˈtəʊld] 12D
formative ˈfɔːmətɪv 4C
fortune ˈfɔːtʃuːn 13A
fortune teller ˈfɔːtʃuːn ˈtelə 12D
foxglove ˈfɒksglʌv 12C
France frɑːns 1A
freezer ˈfriːzə 5A
French frentʃ 1A
frightening ˈfraɪtnɪŋ 9A
fringe frɪndʒ 6B
fundamentally fʌndəˈmentəlɪ 10C
furniture ˈfɜːnɪtʃə 6C
furry ˈfɜːrɪ 12C
further ˈfɜːðə 3C
fuss fʌs 9C

G
gain promotion ˈgeɪn prəˈməʊʃən 7C
galley ˈgælɪ 10C
game geɪm 3C/7A
gap gæp 6C
garlic ˈgɑːlɪk 5D
gas gæs 9B
gates geɪts 7C
gather ˈgæðə 1D/3E
gauge geɪdʒ 4C
get into shape (got, got) ˈget ɪntə ˈʃeɪp [gɒt] 3C
get married ˈget ˈmærɪd 3B
get off to a good start ˈɒf tə ə ˈgʊd ˈstɑːt 9A
get to know ˈget tə ˈnəʊ 11B
get up to ˈget ˈʌp tə 8C
give (gave, given) ˈgɪv [geɪv, ˈgɪvən] 6B
give sb a ring gɪv ˈsʌmbədɪ ə rɪŋ 4B
give up 11A
gloves glʌvz 3B
go gəʊ 7A
go on to do sth (went, gone) ˈgəʊ ˈɔːn tə ˈduː ˈsʌmθɪŋ [went, gʌn] 9D
go under 6B
go with sth 10D
goal gəʊl 7B
gorgeous ˈgɔːdʒəs 13C
government testing ˈgʌvənmənt ˈtestɪŋ 4C
grade greɪd 6B
granny ˈgrænɪ 3B
gravy ˈgreɪvɪ 5B
greenhouse ˈgriːnhaʊs 12C
grip grɪp 12D
grit one's teeth ˈgrɪt wənz ˈtiːθ 13D
ground floor ˈgraʊnd ˈflɔː 3C
grow up (grew, grown) ˈgrəʊ ˈʌp [gruː, grəʊn] 3A
gruelling ˈgrʊəlɪŋ 7C
guest house ˈgest ˈhaʊs 2C
guide book ˈgaɪd ˈbʊk 2B
gym dʒɪm 7C

H
habitat ˈhæbɪtæt 3C
hairdresser ˈheədresə 6A
handles ˈhændlz 11B
handy ˈhændɪ 5C
hanging tile ˈhæŋɪŋ ˈtaɪl 3C
harvest ˈhɑːvest 5C
have a break (had, had) ˈhæv ə ˈbreɪk [hæd] 7A
have a shower ˈʃaʊə 10B
hazard lights ˈhæzəd ˈlaɪts 4A
head hed 9C
headache ˈhedeɪk 13B
heart rate ˈhɑːt ˈreɪt 11C
hence hens 12C
hi haɪ 3A
hide (hid, hidden) haɪd [hɪd, ˈhidən] 6C
hint hɪnt 10D
hire haɪə 6C/8C
hole həʊl 8C
hollow ˈhɒləʊ 5B
honk hɒŋk 2D
hoot huːt 4D
hops hɒps 5C
house haʊz 12C
housework ˈhaʊswɜːk 3A
hugely ˈhjuːdʒlɪ 9C
hum hʌm 8D
hustle and bustle ˈhʌsel ən ˈbʌsel 5C

I
impact ˈɪmpækt 9C
implication ɪmplɪˈkeɪʃən 7C
in case of need ɪn ˈkeɪs əv ˈniːd 9C
in front of ɪn ˈfrʌnt əv 3B

in no time at all ɪn ˈnəʊ ˈtaɪm ət ˈɒl 1D
in relation to rɪˈleɪʃən 9C
in the long term ɪn ðə ˈlɒŋ ˈtɜːm 12C
inch ɪntʃ 6B
include ɪnˈkluːd 2A
incorporate ɪnˈkɔːpəreɪt 7C
indefinite ɪnˈdefɪnət 1C
ingredients ɪnˈgriːdjənts 5B
injector ɪnˈdʒektə 4B
injury ˈɪndʒərɪ 11C
instruction ɪnˈstrʌkʃən 5B
interfere with sth ɪntəˈfɪə 13D
interview ˈɪntəvjuː 12A
invader ɪnˈveɪdə 9D
iron ˈaɪən 3A

J
jetty ˈdʒetɪ 12C
join dʒɔɪn 1B/7B
joint dʒɔɪnt 7C

K
Keep going! (kept, kept) kiːp [kept] 11A
Keep it up! 11A
keep records ˈkiːp ˈrekɔːdz 11C
keep sb busy ˈbɪzɪ 10B
keep wicket kiːp wɪkət 3B
keyboard ˈkiːbɔːd 3A
keyboard instrument ˈkiːbɔːd ˈɪnstrʊmənt 8A

L
lactic acid ˈlæktɪk ˈæsɪd 11C
lamb chops ˈlæm ˈtʃɒps 5A
land a part in ˈlænd ə ˈpɑːt 12A
lay the table (laid, laid) ˈleɪ ðə ˈteɪbəl [leɪd] 5A
leaflet ˈliːflɪt 2B
lean forward ˈliːn ˈfɔːwəd 11B
leather ˈleðə 12B
leave at (left, left) liːv [left] 13A
leave school skuːl 6A
leg press ˈleg ˈpres 11B
length lengθ 8B
lid lɪd 13D
lift lɪft 11A
lighthouse ˈlaɪthaʊs 9D
line out with laɪn 1C
linguist ˈlɪŋgwɪst 10B
link in with lɪnk 6C
live in lɪv 3B
load ləʊd 9B
local community ˈləʊkəl kəˈmjuːnətɪ 4C
locals ˈləʊkəlz 13D
look after lʊk 10B
look for 2C
look forward to doing sth 12A
lose weight (lost, lost) ˈluːz ˈweɪt [lɒst] 11A
lot lɒt 9D
lounge laʊndʒ 5C
low ləʊ 4B
lush lʌʃ 12C
lyrics ˈlɪrɪks 8C

M
magnificent mægˈnɪfɪsənt 12B
maintain meɪnˈteɪn 7C
major service ˈmeɪdʒə ˈsɜːvɪs 4B
make do with sth (made, made) ˈmeɪk ˈduː [meɪd] 10D
make oneself at home ˈmeɪk wənˈself ət ˈhəʊm 10B
make sb do sth 13D
make sure ˈmeɪk ˈʃʊə 11B
manage to do sth ˈmænɪdʒ 13B
manufacturer mænjʊˈfæktʃərə 4C
marker ˈmɑːkə 12C
marque mɑːk 4C
marvellous ˈmɑːvəles 1C/12C
Masterboard ˈmɑːstəbɔːd 1C
mastery ˈmɑːstərɪ 9C
match mætʃ 7B
mature məˈtʃʊə 12C
may meɪ 13A
maybe ˈmeɪbiː 4A
meanwhile ˈmiːnwaɪl 5B
measuring jug ˈmeʒərɪŋ ˈdʒʌg 5B
medieval medɪˈiːvl 2C
mention ˈmenʃən 10B
mill mɪl 7C
mind maɪnd 1B
mixing desk ˈmɪksɪŋ ˈdesk 8B
mobile phone ˈməʊbaɪl ˈfəʊn 2B
module ˈmɒdjuːl 1A
momentum məʊˈmentəm 11C
MOT ˈem ˈəʊ ˈtiː 4B

motorway ˈməʊtəweɪ 9B
motte mɒt 2C
mountaineering maʊntɪˈnɪərɪŋ 11C
move mu:v 3C
move house 6A
muscle ˈmʌsəl 11B
mutter ˈmʌtə 9D

N

naughty ˈnɔ:tɪ 3B
nave neɪv 9C
navigation nævɪˈgeɪʃən 9C
need ni:d 12B
nephew ˈnevju: 3B
none of that nʌn 3C
not ... either ˈnɒt ... ˈaɪðə 9A
not at all ˈnɒtəˈtɔ:l 11B
nut tree ˈnʌt ˈtri: 3C

O

oak əʊk 2D
oast house ˈəʊst ˈhaʊs 5C
occasion əˈkeɪʒən 5A
occasionally əˈkeɪʒənəlɪ 8C
occupy ˈɒkjʊpaɪ 3C
okay sth ˈəʊˈkeɪ 1C
on site ˈɒn ˈsaɪt 4C
once a month ˈwʌns ə ˈmʌnθ 6B
operate ˈɒpəreɪt 8B
opportunity ɒpəˈtju:nɪtɪ 1B
orchard ˈɔ:tʃəd 12C
ought to ˈɔ:tə 13A
out of bounds ˈəʊt əv ˈbaʊndz 11D
oven ˈʌvən 5B
overtake (overtook, overtaken) əʊvəˈteɪk [ˈtʊk, ˈteɪkən] 4D
owe əʊ 12D
owner ˈəʊnə 6B
ownership ˈəʊnəʃɪp 2C

P

page peɪdʒ 3B
paid-for course ˈpeɪdˈfɔ: ˈkɔ:s 6C
paraphernalia pærəfəˈneɪlɪə 3C
parent ˈpeərənt 7B
parking ticket ˈpɑ:kɪŋ ˈtɪkɪt 13A
particularly pəˈtɪkjʊləlɪ 12C
passer-by pɑ:sə ˈbaɪ 13B
passes for duty-free 9B
patch pætʃ 9C
pathway ˈpɑ:θweɪ 12C
pea pi: 5A
peace and quiet ˈpi:s ən ˈkwaɪət 5C
peer pɪə 4D
percussion pəˈkʌʃən 8A
perform pəˈfɔ:m 7C/8C
performance standard pəˈfɔ:məns ˈstændəd 8C
performing arts pəˈfɔ:rmɪŋ ˈɑ:ts 12A
photo shoot ˈfəʊtəʊ ˈʃu:t 6C
pick up on sth pɪk 6C
piece of advice ˈpi:s əv ədˈvaɪs 4B
piece together ˈpi:s təˈgeðə 8C
pinch oneself pɪntʃ 9C
pinnacle ˈpɪnəkl 11D
pit pɪt 11D
pitch pɪtʃ 7B/8B
pitch a tent 2B
pitch bend 8B
plain flour ˈpleɪn ˈflaʊə 5B
platform ˈplætfɔ:m 13B
play pleɪ 8A
play sb 7B
play sth in 8B
playground ˈpleɪgraʊnd 7B
plough plaʊ 1A
plug in plʌg 8C
point out sth pɔɪnt 13D
point to 10A
pond pɒnd 3C
popular ˈpɒpjʊlə 10A
porter pɔ:tə 12B
possession pəˈzeʃən 9C
post a letter pəʊst 10A
pour pɔ: 4C/5B
preserve fruit prɪˈzɜ:v ˈfru:t 5C
press-up ˈpresʌp 11D
pretend to be prɪˈtend tə ˈbi: 9D
pretty well ˈprɪtɪ ˈwel 9C
probably ˈprɒbəblɪ 10A
production run prəˈdʌkʃən ˈrʌn 4C
pronounce prəˈnaʊns 1C
proprietor prəˈpraɪətə 10C
provide prəˈvaɪd 2C
public affairs department ˈpʌblɪk əˈfeəz dɪˈpɑ:tmənt 9C

public transport ˈpʌblɪk ˈtrɑːnspɔːt 13A
pukka ˈpʌkə 11D
pull back ˈpʊl ˈbæk 11B
puppy ˈpʌpɪ 1C
purple ˈpɜːpəl 4B
push on pʊʃ 7C

R
racing circuit ˈreɪsɪŋ ˈsɜːkɪt 4C
rainbow trout ˈreɪnbəʊ ˈtraʊt 12C
raise reɪz 9B
rate reɪt 11C
receiver rɪˈsiːvə 7C
receptionist rɪˈsepʃənɪst 2A
record rɪˈkɔːd 8B
recording deal rɪˈkɔːdɪŋ ˈdiːl 8C
register ˈredʒɪstə 10C
regret rɪˈgret 9C
regulations regjʊˈleɪʃənz 9C
rehearse rɪˈhɜːs 8C
relate to rɪˈleɪt 12C
reliable rɪˈlaɪəbl 4B
rent rent 6C
replace rɪˈpleɪs 4B
report rɪˈpɔːt 7C
require rɪˈkwaɪə 9C/11B
resident ˈresɪdənt 10C
resistance level rɪˈzɪstəns ˈlevəl 11C
respirator ˈrespɪreɪtə 9C
restore rɪˈstɔː 4C
retail products ˈriːteɪl ˈprɒdʌkts 6C
retail stand stænd 6C
retire rɪˈtaɪə 4C/10B
ridiculous rɪˈdɪkjʊləs 5D
ring (rang, rung) rɪŋ [raŋ, rʌŋ] 4D
rink rɪŋk 7B
riot ˈraɪət 12C
rise (rose, risen) raɪz [rəʊz, ˈrɪzən] 5B
rosemary ˈrəʊzmərɪ 12C
rot away rɒt 3C
roundel ˈraʊndəl 5C
row rəʊ 2A
rowing coach ˈrəʊɪŋ ˈkəʊtʃ 11C
rowing machine məˈʃiːn 11B
rule ruːl 10B
run (ran, run) rʌn [ræn, rʌn] 4C/11D
run down 2D
run out of sth 4A

S
sales marketing ˈseɪlz ˈmɑːketɪŋ 10C
sample ˈsɑːmpəl 10C
savage ˈsævɪdʒ 9D
save a shot seɪv 7B
scales skeɪlz 11B
scarf, *pl*: **scarves** *or* **scarfs** skɑːf, skɑːvz, skɑːfs 12D
scenery ˈsiːnərɪ 12B
scent sent 12C
scissors ˈsɪzəz 6B
sculler ˈskʌlə 11C
seasick ˈsiːsɪk 9A
seatbelt ˈsiːtbelt 4B
secure sɪˈkjʊə 11D
see you later ˈsiːjʊˈleɪtə 7B
self-catering (accommodation) ˈself ˈkeɪtərɪŋ 2C
senses ˈsensɪs 12C
Serpent's Lair ˈsɜːpənts ˈleə 12C
serve sɜːv 7B
service ˈsɜːvɪs 4B/4C
services ˈsɜːvɪsɪz 9B
serving spoon ˈsɜːvɪŋ ˈspuːn 5A
session ˈseʃən 7C
set (set, set) set [set] 6D/7B/11A
set out 13C
set routine ruːˈtiːn 11C
severe sɪˈvɪə 9C
shawl ʃɔːl 12D
shepherd's pie ˈʃepədsˈpaɪ 5A
shift ʃɪft 8B
shoot (shot, shot) ʃuːt [ʃɒt] 6C
show off (showed, shown) ˈʃəʊ ˈɒf [ʃəʊd, ʃəʊn] 4C
shower ˈʃaʊə 10D
shrub ʃrʌb 12C
shuttlecock ˈʃʌtəlkɒk 7D
sift sɪft 5B
sign saɪn 2A
silly ˈsɪlɪ 9C
site saɪt 12C
sizzle ˈsɪzəl 5B
ski resort ˈskɪ rɪˈzɔːt 10C
skill skɪl 4C
skin skɪn 8C
Snakes and Ladders ˈsneɪks ənd ˈlædəz 12C

soft sɒft 8B
son-in-law ˈsʌnɪnlɔː 3B
spear spɪə 9D
spend (spent, spent) spend [spent] 12B
spider's web ˈspaɪdəz ˈweb 12C
spill spɪl 12C
splendid isolation ˈsplendɪd aɪsəˈleɪʃən 9C
spot spɒt 4D
sprain spreɪn 12B
spring sprɪŋ 12C
Spring of Life ˈsprɪŋ əv ˈlaɪf 12C
spring onions ˈsprɪŋ ˈʌnjənz 5D
spring-fed ˈsprɪŋ ˈfed 12C
squad skwɒd 11C
stack stæk 11B
staff stɑːf 2C
stage steɪdʒ 6C
stamina ˈstæmɪnə 11C
start off stɑːt 13C
starter ˈstɑːtə 4A
stately home ˈsteɪtlɪ ˈhəʊm 2C
station car park ˈsteɪʃən ˈkɑː pɑːk 13B
stew stjuː 5A
stick (stuck, stuck) stɪk [stʌk] 13A
still stɪl 3B
stomach ˈstʌmək 11B
store stɔː 3C
straight ahead ˈstreɪt əˈhed 9B/13B
straight along əˈlɒŋ 13B
straight away əˈweɪ 13C
strange streɪndʒ 1B
stream striːm 3C
street map ˈstriːt ˈmæp 2B
strengthen ˈstreŋθən 7C
strides straɪdz 7C
struggle ˈstrʌgəl 9D
study ˈstʌdɪ 5C
suffer from ˈsʌfə 9A
suit sb suːt 6B
suntan lotion ˈsʌntæn ˈləʊʃən 2B
supervise suːpəˈvaɪz 11C
supply səˈplaɪ 4C
support səˈpɔːt 7B
supporter səˈpɔːtə 7B
surgeon ˈsɜːdʒən 6E
surprise səˈpraɪz 1B
surround səˈraʊnd 12C
sweetcorn ˈswiːt ˈkɔːn 5A
swing swɪŋ 3C
switch swɪtʃ 4C
switch from ... to 9C

T

take a driving test (took, taken) ˈteɪk ə ˈdraɪvɪŋ ˈtest [tʊk, ˈteɪkən] 6A
take a photo ˈfəʊtəʊ 3B
takeaway ˈteɪkəweɪ 5D
talcum powder ˈtælkəm ˈpaʊdə 10D
tape teɪp 8B
taxi ride ˈtæksɪ ˈraɪd 13B
tend to do sth tend 1C
tent tent 2B
term tɜːm 9C
There you are! 5B
throughout θruːˈaʊt 11C
thyme taɪm 12C
tidy-up ˈtaɪdɪ ʌp 6B
tight taɪt 7D
tighten ˈtaɪtən 4C
time after time taɪm 4C
tinkle ˈtɪŋkəl 12C
tip tɪp 12B
tip sb 6B
to start with 6C
tool tuːl 6B
the tools of the trade ˈtuːlz əv ðə ˈtreɪd 5D
top tɒp 2A
top hat ˈtɒp ˈhæt 3B
top up 4B
top-of-the-table clash 7C
topic ˈtɒpɪk 2C
it was touch and go ˈtʌtʃ ən ˈgəʊ 7C
tour operation ˈtʊə ɒpəˈreɪʃən 10C
tourist information office ˈtʊərɪst ɪnfəˈmeɪʃən ˈɒfɪs 2B
tow (back) təʊ 4B
towel ˈtaʊəl 10D
traffic jam ˈtræfɪk ˈdʒæm 13A
train treɪn 12A
training ˈtreɪnɪŋ 1C
tranquil ˈtræŋkwɪl 12C
travel agency ˈtrævl ˈeɪdʒənsɪ 9B
travel agent's eɪdʒənts 2B
travel light laɪt 2B
travellers' cheques ˈtrævələz ˈtʃeks 2A
treat triːt 6C

treatment ˈtriːtmənt 9C
trim trɪm 6B
turn a blind eye to sth ˈtɜːn ə ˈblaɪnd ˈaɪ 9D
turn back 9D
turn down 8D
turn up 6B/7D/9B
it's my turn now 7B
turning ˈtɜːnɪŋ 13B/13C
twice a month ˈtwaɪs ə ˈmʌnθ 6B
twin room ˈtwɪn ˈruːm 10B
tyre taɪə 4B

U
underground air raid shelter ˈʌndəgraʊnd ˈeə ˈreɪd ˈʃeltə 9D
underneath ʌndəˈniːθ 12C
unique juːˈniːk 10C
unless ʌnˈles 10B
unload ʌnˈləʊd 8C
unpack ʌnˈpæk 4B
until ʌnˈtɪl 5B
upset ʌpˈset 7C
upstairs ʌpˈsteəz 10B
used to ˈjuːstə 10B

V
value ˈvæljuː 7B
van væn 1D
VAT (value added tax) ˈviː ˈeɪ ˈtiː 2A
vegetables ˈvedʒtəblz 5A
vineyard ˈvɪnjəd 2C
virtually ˈvɜːtʃʊəlɪ 4C
volume ˈvɒljuːm 8B

W
waiter ˈweɪtə 1A
Wales weɪlz 3A
walk off the street wɔːk 6C
walk the dog 3A
walking ˈwɔːkɪŋ 7A
walking boots buːts 2B/12B
walks wɔːks 2C
wallet ˈwɒlɪt 9B
wallpaper ˈwɔːlpeɪpə 3C
wardrobe ˈwɔːdrəʊb 10B
warning triangle ˈwɑːnɪŋ ˈtraɪæŋgəl 4A
wartime ˈwɔːtaɪm 9D
wastepaper basket ˈweɪstpeɪpə ˈbɑːskɪt 1D
wear (wore, worn) weə [wɔː, wɔːn] 3B
weather ˈweðə 5A
wedding ˈwedɪŋ 3B
week in and week out 7C
weigh weɪ 11B
weight stack ˈweɪt ˈstæk 11B
Well done! ˈwel ˈdʌn 11A
Welsh welʃ 3A
What's up? ˈwɒts ˈʌp 4A
wig wɪg 6E
willow ˈwɪləʊ 12C
window display ˈwɪndəʊ dɪˈspleɪ 6E
window shopping ˈʃɒpɪŋ 13C
windscreen washer ˈwɪndskriːn ˈwɑːʃə 4B
windscreen wiper ˈwaɪpə 4B
wiring ˈwaɪrɪŋ 2D
wooden spoon ˈwʊdən 5B
woodland ˈwʊdlənd 3C/12C
work wɜːk 1D
work out 6C/8A
worry (worried, worried) ˈwʌrɪ [ˈwʌrɪd] 12B
I wouldn't mind doing sth ˈaɪ ˈwʊdnt ˈmaɪnd 8A
I'd (I would) prefer (to do) ˈaɪd prɪˈfɜː 10A
I'd (I would) rather (do) ˈaɪd ˈrɑːðə 10A

Y
youth hostel ˈjuːθ ˈhɒstəl 2B

LIST OF IRREGULAR VERBS

arise, arose, arisen aufsteigen, sich erheben
awake, awoke, awoken wecken, aufwachen
be, was, been sein
bear, bore, borne tragen, ertragen
beat, beat, beaten schlagen
become, became, become werden
begin, began, begun anfangen, beginnen
bet, bet, bet wetten
bite, bit, bitten beißen
bleed, bled, bled bluten
blow, blew, blown blasen, wehen
break, broke, broken brechen
bring, brought, brought bringen
build, built, built bauen
burn, burnt, burnt (ver)brennen
buy, bought, bought kaufen
catch, caught, caught fangen, erwischen
choose, chose, chosen (aus)wählen
come, came, come kommen
cost, cost, cost kosten
cut, cut, cut schneiden
deal, dealt, dealt handeln
do, did, done tun, machen
draw, drew, drawn zeichnen
drink, drank, drunk trinken
drive, drove, driven fahren
eat, ate, eaten essen
fall, fell, fallen fallen
feed, fed, fed füttern
fight, fought, fought kämpfen
find, found, found finden
flee, fled, fled fliehen
fly, flew, flown fliegen
forbid, forbade, forbidden verbieten
forget, forgot, forgotten vergessen
forgive, forgave, forgiven vergeben, verzeihen
get, got, got bekommen; werden
give, gave, given geben
go, went, gone gehen
grow, grew, grown wachsen
hang, hung, hung (auf)hängen
have, had, had haben; besitzen
hear, heard, heard hören
hit, hit, hit schlagen
hold, held, held halten
hurt, hurt, hurt verletzen
keep, kept, kept behalten, aufbewahren
know, knew, known wissen, kennen
lead, led, led führen, leiten
learn, learnt, learnt (auch: learned) lernen; erfahren

leave, left, left verlassen; überlassen
lend, lent, lent (ver)leihen
let, let, let lassen
lie, lay, lain liegen
lose, lost, lost verlieren
make, made, made machen, veranlassen
mean, meant, meant meinen, bedeuten
meet, met, met treffen, begegnen
pay, paid, paid (be)zahlen
put, put, put setzen, stellen, legen
read, read, read lesen
ride, rode, ridden fahren, reiten
ring, rang, rung läuten
rise, rose, risen steigen, sich erheben
run, ran, run rennen, laufen
say, said, said sagen
see, saw, seen sehen
send, sent, sent senden, schicken
set, set, set setzen, festsetzen
shake, shook, shaken schütteln, zittern
shine, shone, shone scheinen, glänzen
shoot, shot, shot (er)schießen
show, showed, shown zeigen
shut, shut, shut (zu)schließen
sing, sang, sung singen
sit, sat, sat sitzen
sleep, slept, slept schlafen
smell, smelt, smelt riechen
speak, spoke, spoken sprechen
spell, spelt, spelt buchstabieren; schreiben
spend, spent, spent verbringen, ausgeben
split, split, split spalten
spoil, spoilt, spoilt verderben
spread, spread, spread (sich) ausbreiten
spring, sprang, sprung springen
stand, stood, stood stehen
steal, stole, stolen stehlen
strike, struck, struck schlagen, stoßen
sweep, swept, swept kehren, fegen
swim, swam, swum schwimmen
take, took, taken nehmen
teach, taught, taught lehren, unterrichten
tear, tore, torn (zer)reißen
tell, told, told erzählen, sagen
think, thought, thought denken
throw, threw, thrown werfen
understand, understood, understood verstehen; begreifen
wake, woke, woken (auch: waked) aufwecken, aufwachen
wear, wore, worn tragen (Kleider)
win, won, won gewinnen
write, wrote, written schreiben